DATE DUE

OCT 0 5 1995	
OCT 1 9 1995	
NOV 0 2 1995	
NOV 1 6 1995	
NOV 2 9 1995	
DEC - 9 1996	
JUN - 3 1997	
J 17	
July 2	
JUL 1 6 1997	
J 30	
A 13	
NOV 23 1998	

BRODART   Cat. No. 23-221

DANGEROUS PASSAGE

DANGEROUS PASSAGE

THE SANTA FE TRAIL
AND THE MEXICAN WAR

By

William Y. Chalfant

Foreword by Marc Simmons

Illustrations by Mont David Williams

University of Oklahoma Press : Norman and London

By William Y. Chalfant

Cheyennes and Horse Soldiers: The 1857 Expedition and the Battle of Solomon's Fork (Norman, 1989)
Without Quarter: The Wichita Expedition and the Fight on Crooked Creek (Norman, 1991)
Dangerous Passage: The Santa Fe Trail and the Mexican War (Norman, 1994)

This book is published with the generous assistance of The Kerr Foundation, Inc.

Library of Congress Cataloging-in-Publication Data

Chalfant, William Y. (William Young), 1928–
    Dangerous passage : the Santa Fe Trail and the Mexican War / by William Y. Chalfant.
      p. cm.
    Includes bibliographical references and index.
    ISBN 0–8061–2613–2 (alk. paper)
    1. Santa Fe Trail—History. 2. Mexican War, 1846–1848—Santa Fe Trail. 3. Comanche Indians—Wars. I. Title.
F786.C42   1994
978—dc20   93–38605
                                              CIP

The paper in this book meets the guidelines for permanence and durability of the Committee on Production Guidelines for Book Longevity of the Council on Library Resources, Inc. ∞

1 2 3 4 5 6 7 8 9 10

For my dear wife
Martha Anne Chalfant

Contents

Illustrations

Sketches

Photographs

Maps

Foreword

by Marc Simmons

The Santa Fe Trail, after years of historical neglect, is suddenly in fashion again. It is part of a phenomenon that has witnessed a recent expansion of interest in western trails generally and a new public fascination with the Indian and Hispanic cultures that survive to this day at trail's end, in New Mexico's historic capital of Santa Fe. The subject is benefiting, also, from a flurry of activity on the part of researchers and writers, who are busy opening windows and casting light on previously obscure chapters in the Santa Fe Trail story. Their revelations remind us just how pivotal and dramatic was this particular episode in the development of America's far western frontier.

William Y. Chalfant, already well-known for his books on the Indian wars of the southern plains, now turns his attention to the crucial years, 1846 to 1848, on the Santa Fe Trail, that is, the period of the Mexican War when the United States, among other objectives, fought for control of the southwestern territories. In the early stages of that international conflict, General Stephen W. Kearny's Army of the West marched over the trail to Santa Fe and managed to bring New Mexico securely under the American flag. That event Chalfant covers vividly and with insight in the first chapters of this book.

But the main focus of his narrative is directed toward the troubled and often violent Indian-White relations that plagued the trail during the war years. Digging deeply, the author has

uncovered some almost-forgotten incidents of border tragedy
and here retells them with a twentieth-century perspective.
They include, for instance, the odd circumstances surrounding the death of a Comanche war chief, Red Sleeve, during an
attack on a wagon train; the defeat of Lt. John Love and his
dragoons in the summer of 1847; and details of the Battle of
Coon Creek. Related, as well, is the brief history of the
Indian Battalion, a roving troop that attempted in this bloody
era to bring some measure of protection to traffic on the Santa
Fe Trail.

The war years treated by Chalfant represented a transition
period in the trail saga. As a consequence of the Kearny
conquest of New Mexico, and the subsequent relinquishment
of that territory by Mexico in the treaty of peace (1848), the
Santa Fe Trail lost its international character, since now both
ends of the route were in American hands. That circum-
stance, as the author notes, set the stage for a rapid increase
in military freighting, to supply a string of newly built forts at
trailside, and for a rush of gold seekers on their way to the
California diggings, who elected to follow the southern route
by way of New Mexico.

That the expanding traffic on the Santa Fe Trail contributed significantly to the bitter guerrilla warfare launched by
the Plains Indians in the 1850s and 1860s cannot be doubted.
In *Dangerous Passage*, Chalfant effectively demonstrates that
those hostilities had their antecedents in the turbulent years
of the latter 1840s. For those tribes along the trail, he
observes, the rising tide of alien travel clearly foretold the end
of their world and their way of life.

The authoritative handling in this book of all these hap-
penings adds materially to our knowledge of the middle
period in Santa Fe Trail history. Moreover, the narrative
provides engaging reading, for not only has Chalfant done his
research well, he has told a stirring and finely crafted tale.
All aficionados of the trail will applaud his efforts.

Prologue

In the history of the United States, the Santa Fe Trail has assumed a place so closely identified with romance and high adventure that even in a cynical age, well over a hundred years after the last traders followed its dusty ruts in search of their fortune, the name still evokes a thirst for knowledge of what once occurred along its winding length. Some say the trail was no more than an ancient road—distance and a series of ruts etched into the soil, scarring the country it crossed as it made its way to a remote promised land. Others say it was far more—an era, a way of life, a bridge between cultures, a place of drama. But on one thing all agree: along its course occurred some of the most fascinating of the events that shaped our country. The trail's nearly sixty years of existence as a road of commerce and adventure was a time of growth and change, filled with danger and excitement. This brief period marked an era of glory symbolized by expansion of the nation and a time of shame for what that expansion cost the original inhabitants. In many respects the history of the trail is the saga of the circle of life, of good and evil, of triumph and tragedy, of the yesteryears that washed across it, and of the lives that formed the fabric of its existence.

Although many historians and writers say the trail began in the early nineteenth century as a route of commerce, in truth it is far older. Along its vast length across diverse and remote territories the Santa Fe road often, even usually,

followed the trace of old trails first established by native
Indian peoples hundreds of years before. Nor were whites
strangers to all of these trails before use by the first traders
began. Beginning with Francisco Vásquez de Coronado, a
number of white explorers and adventurers followed significant parts of what later became the Santa Fe Trail in finding
their way across the trackless ocean of grass we call the Great
Plains. Early trappers and traders—French, American, and
Hispanic—used much of the length of the Arkansas River in
going to and from the mountains. And Indian traders doing
business with the Plains tribes did the same. So when Mexico
revolted against Spain in 1821 and the Spanish prohibition
against trade with the Anglo-Americans was repealed, many
living near the western border of the "states," and particularly in Missouri, were already familiar with a route that
would get them to the Mexican province of New Mexico and its
capital of Santa Fe.

Most historians consider a man named William Becknell
to be the "father" of the Santa Fe Trail. His life was previously
unremarkable, but in 1821 he earned lasting fame by leading
the first party of traders to reach Santa Fe after the Mexican
War for Independence. The initial trip, made with a packtrain
loaded with trade goods, followed the Arkansas River into
present-day Colorado, probably crossing the Raton Mountains
over Trinchera Pass or one of the passes adjacent to it. When
Becknell returned to Missouri he traveled the old Indian trails
across the plains, in general tracing the Cimarron Route,
which quickly became established as the Santa Fe Trail. He
used another version of this route in 1822 while taking the
first train of wagons to Santa Fe. Those who followed used
other variations, and in 1825 the government surveyed and
marked what the survey commissioners deemed the best of
these. Increased usage and federal recognition resulted in
the trail becoming the first national highway in the American
West.

William Becknell began his first trip to Santa Fe from his
home outside the little village of Franklin, Missouri, at the
end of the Boonslick Road from St. Charles, Missouri. He

moved westward on an existing trail known as the Osage
Trace, leading to Fort Osage near the western boundary of
Missouri and the edge of the Indian Territory. It was from this
post that the subsequent 1825 survey of the Santa Fe Trail
began. Fort Osage was both a military post and a government-
operated trading post doing business with the tribes living
along the Missouri River, notably the Iowas, Missouris,
Otoes, Kansas, and Osages. From there Becknell followed a
series of intersecting Indian trails leading southwest across
the Osage Plains and Flint Hills to the McPherson lowlands
and high plains, striking the Arkansas River at its Great
Bend of the North. The routes used by Becknell and those who
followed, and that surveyed by the government, continued
along the river to a point of crossing where they plunged into
the desolation of the Cimarron desert, known as "La Jornada"
or the "Water Scrape," a waterless stretch of territory extending from fifty to sixty miles between the Arkansas and
Cimarron rivers, depending on the crossing used. During
trail times there were three principal crossings of the Arkansas: the Lower, the Middle (Cimarron),* and the Upper
crossings. The Upper Crossing was the one recognized by the
1825 federal survey, but the Middle Crossing was the most
popular with travelers over the years. From the Cimarron
River, the trail continued southwesterly to the mountains,

---

*There were several variations in the Middle Crossing. The first in use was
three miles southwest of the lower Point of Rocks, the first landmark by that
name for westbound travelers, which was itself a short distance northwest of the
Caches. This crossing was used until sometime in the 1830s, after which it was
shifted west to the west end of Nine-Mile Ridge, probably the result of changes
in the riverbed. Fort Mann was built in 1847 about a half mile below the
Caches. The measurements made by Randolph B. Marcy in 1849, using an
odometer, placed the Middle Crossing at a point 25.34 miles west of Fort
Mann. This would be about four miles west of present Ingalls, Kansas. It was
this version that was in use during the Mexican War. After 1852, at the
instigation of the military at Fort Atkinson, the Middle Crossing was shifted to
the east end of Nine-Mile Ridge, and several different sites were tried. By
1853 one of these, located about a half mile west of present Cimarron, Kansas,
had become the new main crossing. It was this crossing that eventually (during
the 1860s) became popularly known as the "Cimarron Crossing." See Louise
Barry, "The Ranch at Cimarron Crossing," *KHQ* 39:345–66.

crossed the Sangre de Cristo range by way of Glorieta Pass, then wound its way through Apache Canyon to Santa Fe.

From the time it entered the Indian Territory until it reached the mountains, the trail crossed a great rolling plain resembling an endless sea of grass. Here and there the seemingly unbounded flatland was broken by a range of low hills, by canyons or dry arroyos, or by one of the small streams that flowed silently through the vast emptiness. Except in sparse stands along a few streams, trees were almost totally absent. This remote region was the homeland of the warlike, nomadic Plains Indians, with Cheyennes and Arapahoes living and hunting north of the Arkansas and Comanches, Kiowas, and Plains Apaches to the south. In the mountains to the west were the Utes, and beyond them to the southwest were the Pueblo villages. Along the eastern stretches of the trail the Siouxan Osage Indians, a large and powerful tribe, lived south of the Kansas River; to the north were the Kansa and Otoe tribes, also Siouxans. Early contact with whites and intertribal warfare had weakened the Kansas and Otoes and neutralized the Osages. In 1825 the Osages and Kansas signed treaties with the United States allowing the trail to cross the country claimed by them near its eastern end. But out on the plains, other Indians proved less malleable. The advent of commerce and travel along the road to Santa Fe had greatly angered the horse Indians. Their fear and hatred increased rapidly as they witnessed the destruction of the great herds of buffalo and other forms of wildlife they depended on for survival and as they suffered the effects of European diseases for which they had no natural immunity. They reacted to the entry of whites into their country in the only manner they could — by raiding and making war. And so, from its earliest days, the Santa Fe Trail was the scene of sporadic conflict as the Plains Indians fought to resist and expel the intruders.

The hostilities that flared across the plains soon resulted in calls by the Santa Fe traders for government protection of the commerce of the trail. In 1829 President Andrew Jackson ordered the first armed escort for the annual trading caravan.

It consisted of four companies of the Sixth Infantry under command of Maj. Bennet Riley and was ordered to accompany the traders as far as the Upper Crossing of the Arkansas near Chouteau's Island. There the caravan crossed into Mexican territory for the remainder of the trip to Santa Fe. Subsequent escorts were ordered in 1833, 1834, 1843, and 1845, the latter three by units of the First Dragoons. In all of these, the object was to defend trading caravans from attack by the Indians or other marauders and not to patrol the trail itself. Although the occasional presence of American troops north of the Arkansas, and of troops from New Mexico south of the river, did deter attacks on organized caravans, smaller unprotected parties crossing the plains were at great hazard. Despite the danger, traffic along the road continued to grow, with Anglo-American traders heading west from Missouri and with Mexican merchants moving eastward from Santa Fe. By the 1840s the Mexicans had become dominant in this two-way trade.

The commercial opportunities and the apparent wealth of upper California and New Mexico eventually caused Americans to take notice of the western territories. A swelling population and growing demand for more land and natural resources began to convince many that the United States was meant to expand from coast to coast and that there was a divinely approved plan to this end. "Manifest Destiny" became a byword among these people, and with the annexation of Texas in 1845, the cause gained greater momentum. In 1844 this cause found a champion when James K. Polk was elected as the new American president. To resolve the dispute between Mexico and the United States concerning the correct boundary line between Texas and Mexico, in 1845, after he had assumed office, Polk devised a plan to pay for the disputed territory and purchase the northern Mexican provinces as well. He dispatched an emissary named John Slidell to Mexico City to make an offer. It seemed an eminently sensible solution to Polk, but he failed to take into account either the nationalism of the Mexican people or the anti-American feeling engendered by the annexation of Texas. The

Mexican president, José Herrera, knew he could not consider the American offer. Instead he ordered his most capable general, Mariano Paredes y Arrillaga, to raise an army and reconquer the rebellious province of Texas. But Paredes, who hated Americans, turned the army against Herrera, deposed the president, installed himself as the new president, and then promptly turned down Polk's offer. President Polk interpreted this reaction as an intention to make war, and he ordered Maj. Gen. Zachary Taylor to march to the Rio Grande to defend the disputed lands. Paredes moved his army to the border, and the two countries teetered on the brink of open conflict.

The winds of war that blew along the Rio Grande were stirring well to the south of the Santa Fe Trail, but the effects were to be felt along its length as well. An army would now march across it to accomplish the conquest of New Mexico and California, and the Plains Indians would intensify their raids to resist increased travel through their lands. And so the first great road in the West, a highway of trade and adventure born of the desire for commerce, now became a road to war.

WILLIAM Y. CHALFANT

Hutchinson, Kansas

DANGEROUS PASSAGE

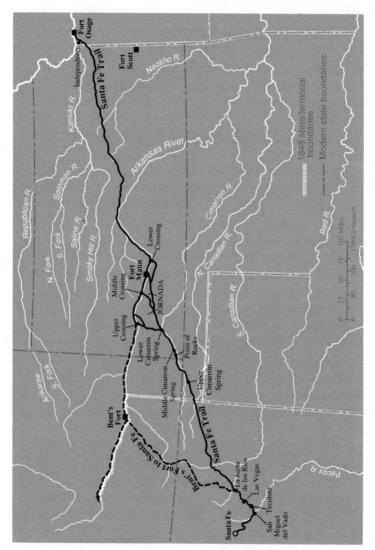

Route of the Santa Fe Trail in 1846–48

1

The Army of the West

Saturday, April 25, 1846: Capt. Seth B. Thornton, Second Dragoons, mounted his huge roan horse and, with a wave of his arm and a sharp command, led a cavalry patrol of sixty-five men westward along the Rio Grande del Norte. They had been ordered to investigate a report that Mexican lancers had crossed the stream into the state of Texas.* Thornton and his men rode into an ambush, which resulted in eleven dead, five wounded, and all survivors captured. Maj. Gen. Zachary Taylor, on receiving the news, promptly sent a dispatch to President James K. Polk advising that hostilities had commenced and American blood had been spilled. The message reached Washington on May 9, and on May 13 the president signed a law providing for prosecution of the "existing war" initiated by Mexico. It authorized raising troops and procuring supplies, and it appropriated money to bring the hostilities to a "speedy and successful termination." The Mexican War had begun.[1]

The outbreak of the conflict provided the opportunity to accomplish an objective dear to the heart of President Polk — expansion of the United States through acquisition of New Mexico and California. The same day the president issued his proclamation of war, the War Department took the first steps

*The territory into which the lancers crossed was disputed, claimed by both Mexico and Texas.

to raise a volunteer force to send to Santa Fe. The secretary of war dispatched a copy of the proclamation to Col. Stephen W. Kearny, commanding officer of the First Dragoons headquartered at Fort Leavenworth, and concurrently requested the governor of Missouri to organize eight companies of mounted volunteers and two of artillery. At the same time the adjutant general, Brig. Gen. Roger Jones, advised Kearny that a force of fifteen hundred volunteers was to be raised to seize New Mexico. Two companies of artillery and two companies of the First Dragoons would serve with the expedition, probably under the command of Kearny. He was in fact appointed commander the following day. So was born the "Army of the West."[2]

Speed was of extreme importance in organizing, equipping, and dispatching the Army of the West. There was considerable concern lest Mexico organize a sizable military force to defend its northern provinces if conquest was not accomplished rapidly. Moreover, movement of so many men and animals had to be undertaken while the season of growth continued and adequate grazing was available. The War Department, Colonel Kearny, and Governor John Edwards of Missouri all reacted with remarkable swiftness, and the first steps toward putting troops in the field were taken as soon as intentions were known and orders received. On May 24 the adjutant general of Missouri issued a call for volunteers from St. Louis and the counties along the Missouri River. During late May and early June so many eager recruits joined that the quota for the regiment was quickly filled. They organized themselves, elected officers, and marched off to Fort Leavenworth, the headquarters of the expedition, to be mustered into the service of the United States. Three companies of the volunteers arrived at the fort on June 6, and the remainder reached the post by June 27. There were eight cavalry companies constituting the First Regiment of Missouri Mounted Volunteers under Col. Alexander W. Doniphan, Lt. Col. Charles F. Ruff, and Maj. William Gilpin. Supplementing these were two companies of volunteer light artillery from St. Louis and two companies of volunteer infantry requested by

Kearny, each marching as a separate battalion. The St. Louis volunteer cavalry, known as the Laclede Rangers, was attached to the First Dragoons. These and a small detachment of topographical engineers constituted the Army of the West, a total of 1,658 men and sixteen pieces of artillery.[3]

While the volunteers were getting organized, equipped, and receiving rudimentary training, Colonel Kearny was busy with other preparations. He asked and received permission to add two additional dragoon companies to the expedition, those of his two best captains, Edwin Vose Sumner and Philip St. George Cooke. More significant, he took the necessary steps to provide for the logistical needs of his troops. Records of the quartermaster general show that during the fiscal year 1846–47, the Army of the West was provided with not less than 1,556 wagons, 14,904 oxen, 3,658 mules, 459 horses, and 516 pack saddles. Kearny had asked for supplies sufficient to maintain his expedition for twelve months, an impossible objective in such a short period of time. But his experience in previous operations across the plains, combined with his common sense, made him realize there would be no military success without adequate logistical support. The quartermaster and commissary officers were therefore kept busy procuring the equipment, weapons, ammunition, foodstuffs, and other supplies necessary to keep the army in the field, and soon huge piles of stores had been accumulated on the banks of the Missouri River at Fort Leavenworth. As wagons arrived aboard the riverboats from St. Louis, they were quickly loaded and prepared for departure for Santa Fe. During the early part of June, Kearny began sending small supply trains, with twenty-five to thirty wagons each, out on the trail so that sufficient provisions would be available for the troops when they marched. By June 20, before the last of the expedition's units left Fort Leavenworth, enough provisions for 1,300 men for three months were said to be carried by wagons already headed across the plains.[4]

The first of the companies to march from Fort Leavenworth left on June 5. The route they were to take led down the Santa Fe Trail to the Upper Crossing, then followed the trappers and

traders trail (sometimes known as the "Bent's Fort Trail"),
which continued along the north bank of the Arkansas River
to the mountains. The troops of Kearny's army were going only
as far as the famous trading post. From there they were to
follow the trail used by the Bent's trading parties, which
paralleled the line of the Purgatoire River and crossed the
Raton Mountains via Raton Pass. The pass had previously
been used primarily by packtrains, was extremely rocky and
difficult, and was considered by many to be impassable for
large wagons. But the route held certain advantages for the
Army of the West. It bypassed the dreaded Jornada, was less
exposed to the danger of travel through the lands of the
Kiowas and Comanches, and had ample water for livestock.
Further, it had the advantage of a relatively secure place
where supplies could be stockpiled—Bent's Fort. It also
avoided much of the Mexican portion of the Santa Fe Trail,
where an invading army might be expected and where patrols
were most likely. Lastly, the mountain trail was deemed so
difficult and time-consuming to travel with wagons that it
would not be an anticipated route, thus providing an element
of surprise.[5]

Constituting the nucleus of the Army of the West were the
companies of the First Dragoons assigned to it, the only well-
trained, disciplined, and reliable units in the command.
Unfortunately, before the Missouri Volunteers could be organized, equipped, and given a modicum of training, it was
necessary to send elements of the dragoons out on special
missions. First went a small detachment of seven men as
escort for George T. Howard, an experienced Santa Fe trader,
en route from Washington, D.C., on a War Department
mission to New Mexico. They left on May 28. On June 3
Howard sent back a dispatch advising Colonel Kearny that two
wagon trains several days ahead on the trail, belonging to
Manuel Armijo (New Mexico's governor) and his partner,
Albert Speyer, were carrying arms and ammunition. Kearny
promptly sent back orders for Howard to catch up with and
halt the two trains until a force of dragoons could reach them.
On June 5 Kearny ordered Capt. Benjamin D. Moore to take

Companies C and G, First Dragoons, and with the famous
mountain man Thomas Fitzpatrick as guide, overtake and
detain the Armijo and Speyer trains and all other traders on
the trail. By forced marches over an exceptionally dry and
dusty road, Moore and his men reached the Middle Crossing
of the Arkansas in only eleven and a half days after leaving
Fort Leavenworth. There they found that Speyer's train had
crossed on June 10 and was about six to eight days ahead, too
far in advance to be overtaken. Having lost the race, and with
inadequate grazing available near the crossing, Moore took
his force back to the Pawnee Fork and went into camp. There
he had sufficient grass to support the cavalry horses and the
livestock of the trains he would detain pending arrival of the
rest of the army. On June 12 another detachment of fifty men of
Company I, under command of 2d Lt. Patrick Noble, was sent
to reinforce Moore's command. They were joined at the
Pawnee Fork on July 8 by Companies A and D of the First
Regiment of Missouri Mounted Volunteers, and on July 11 the
five units broke camp and marched for Bent's Fort, followed by
the trading caravans Moore had halted. They arrived there on
July 21 and 22.[6]

While the lead companies were encamped on the Pawnee
Fork, those still at Fort Leavenworth were just beginning their
long march to Bent's Fort, the appointed rendezvous. Companies A and D, First Regiment of Missouri Mounted Volunteers,
with about two hundred men, departed on June 22, joining
with Captain Moore's command on July 8. On June 26,
Companies B, C, and F started down the trail, and on June 27
they were followed by Company G. They joined together on
Stranger Creek on June 29. There they organized themselves
as a battalion for the remainder of the march, all under the
command of Lt. Col. Charles F. Ruff. Also leaving Fort
Leavenworth on June 27 was the detachment of topographical
engineers. Their mission was to collect data on the mete-
orological, geographical, and natural history of the country
through which they passed. On June 29 Companies E and H
of the Mounted Volunteers, commanded by Maj. William
Gilpin and accompanied by Col. Alexander W. Doniphan, the

Laclede Rangers, and the two companies of Missouri volunteer infantry began their march. They were followed on June
30 by the two companies of Missouri volunteer light artillery
and by Col. Stephen W. Kearny, commander of the Army of the
West, with his escort of dragoons. Last to leave Fort Leavenworth were Companies B and K, First Dragoons, commanded
by Captains Edwin Vose Sumner and Philip St. George
Cooke, which started their march on July 6.[7]

Except for the dragoons, few of the men serving in the
Army of the West had ever crossed the plains or even been
west of their Missouri homes. For them, it would be a time of
new and strange experiences—and a time of suffering. As
they marched away from Fort Leavenworth they entered a
world devoid of trees, except along a few of the shallow
streams that infrequently intruded on the landscape. From
the Missouri River west to the Council Grove, the land was
typified by rolling limestone hills covered by big and little
bluestem grasses that often reached as high as the shoulders
of the horses. When the ever-present south winds swept across
the hills, the grass bent and swayed, creating swells that
seemed to roll from one horizon to the next. Beyond the Grove,
the last hard timber they would see before reaching the
mountains, they came to the high plains and began a steady
but imperceptible ascent to the Rockies. Though interrupted
from time to time by small ranges of hills, sand dunes along
the Arkansas, and frequent draws and dry arroyos, the plains
now spread out before them in a seemingly limitless expanse
of shortgrasses, somehow surviving in a dry and harsh environment that appeared without end. And the road they
followed pursued a horizon that retreated as they advanced,
as if to lead them nowhere. They were engulfed by an
enormous sea of grass. Only occasionally, when they sighted
some rocky prominence that served as a marker for travelers,
were they reassured theirs was a trail with a destination.

The men of the Missouri Volunteers were a hardy lot of
frontiersmen and were used to working in the sun. But now
they found themselves in a place without shade, with rock-
hard ground covered by brown sun-scalded grasses, and with

only occasional water, too often the putrid contents of a fouled buffalo wallow. As they marched beneath the searing heat of an unrelenting sun, their skin burned, their lips cracked, and their eyes dried. Yet they struggled on, punished by both the sun and the fierce, dry south wind. From time to time the monotony was broken by the appearance of huge herds of buffalo or pronghorn antelope, and a few men tried to hunt. They marched on, somehow managing to make the twenty-five to thirty miles a day demanded by Colonel Kearny. Beyond the Little Arkansas, Indian signs were seen with greater frequency, and by the time the strung-out companies passed the Plum Buttes, they knew they were being watched by unseen observers. And so it would be almost until they reached the Big Timbers and, some twenty-five miles beyond, Bent's Fort.

Once on the plains, misery took new and diverse forms. Swarms of buffalo gnats rose from the grass to harass both men and their animals; and when they reached the Arkansas, great clouds of mosquitoes attacked with a ferocity few men had previously experienced. Hour after hour they stumbled through the unchanging monotony, beset by the stings and bites of insects, whipped by the ceaseless wind, numbed by a burning sun, and choked by the great columns of dust that marked the passage of those in the lead and settled on those who followed. Large numbers of rattlesnakes, sunning themselves on the bare tracks of the Santa Fe road, challenged men and animals alike, defying their presence. And so they marched, day after day.

Most days featured empty skies and a scalding sun, but from time to time clouds scudded across the horizon from the south and west, building themselves suddenly into towering anvils, as if preparing to receive the blows of Thor's hammer. Soon the sun was gone, and a violent, wind-whipped rain poured upon them in torrents, sometimes accompanied by thunder and lightning and large biting hailstones, frightening the animals and meting out misery for all. The raindrops struck the earth and bounced on its rock-like surface, then quickly formed streams of water that sought out the bone-dry gullies and arroyos. Normally empty stream beds became

raging torrents in a matter of moments, and the small creeks
feeding the Arkansas, swelling with the flood tide, emptied
their burden into the larger stream. There the water sank
quickly beneath the sands that shielded the river's flow from
the relentless sun. Usually the storms ended almost as rapidly
as they began, and the sun reappeared. Except during rare
periods of protracted rains, the evidence of each deluge
disappeared as quickly as the storms that brought them.
Water that did not run off through the natural drainage
courses sank beneath the surface, and in a short time the sun
burned away all evidence of moisture. The marching columns
generally halted for such occurrences, then resumed the
march when the storms passed.

If nature conspired to sap the strength of the adventurous
rabble constituting the Army of the West, bureaucratic bungling and poor planning by both the army and the civil
government joined to compound the problems. Kearny had the
foresight to have his supply columns in the field in advance of
the troops, intending that supplies be there for them as the
march exhausted their original provisions. But a farsighted
plan went awry. The wagons provided to Kearny by the
quartermaster came from distant points; many of them were
old and in poor condition, sold to the army by anyone with an
extra to sell at a premium price. There were few experienced
teamsters available to fill the sudden need. As a result many
young men who had rushed to the frontier with the object of
joining the Army of the West, finding enlistments closed,
signed on as teamsters. Most had neither the experience nor
the necessary skills for the job. Thus the supplies for Kearny's
troops were entrusted to unqualified men for transport in
unreliable wagons across a vast distance through the lands of
Indian tribes, themselves in a near starving condition, who
were hostile to the presence of whites in even limited numbers. Compounding the problem, no military escort was
provided the wagon trains, and only limited quantities of arms
and ammunition were given them for self-defense, some
receiving as little as two rounds per train.[8]

Once on the road, inexperience showed itself in many

ways. The men were not familiar with the needs of their animals, nor with how to handle several yoke of oxen or mule trains in the summer heat on a desolate plain. Grass and water were short, and both animals and wagons were abused, inevitably leading to the death of large numbers of oxen and mules and the breakdown or abandonment of many wagons. Few men were trained as either wheelwrights or blacksmiths, and most could do nothing to replace or repair broken or worn wheels or tires or the shoes on the animals. Fires—some set by Indians, some by lightning, but most by careless whites reduced the sparse grazing even further. The bitter penalty imposed by the lack of competent teamsters or suitable wagons was felt most keenly by Kearny's men for whom the supplies were intended. It was reported that the trail from Fort Leavenworth to Santa Fe was strewn with "about $5,000,000.00 worth of U. S. government supplies, the bones of cattle, and in many places the drivers, lie side by side—a melancholy result, brought about alone by inexperience."9

Not all the problems of the supply trains were the fault of teamsters. The loading of wagons by volunteer troops at Fort Leavenworth, supervised by inexperienced officers and wagonmasters, resulted in overloading and poorly balanced loads. The crossing of streams or difficult terrain often caused overloaded wagons to become mired or to break wheels or axles. The speed demanded by Kearny was more than could be accomplished by teams drawing such heavy wagons, and even company wagons carrying tents and camp equipment soon fell behind. Poor planning resulted in the provision trains moving well ahead or behind the marching columns, rather than being distributed through them. Many of the companies had only minimal amounts of provisions with them, and this led to their men being on short rations for most of the long march to Bent's Fort.10

Notwithstanding their many problems, supply trains dispatched in advance of the march of troops somehow managed to gain a near insurmountable lead over those who followed later. So bad was the situation that on July 8 or 9, only a week

and a half after departing Fort Leavenworth, Colonel Doniphan sent a dispatch to Lieutenant Colonel Ruff's battalion,
requesting provisions because the approximately 220 men
with his column were on the verge of starvation. Ruff's own
men were then on reduced rations, but he nonetheless left two
barrels of flour, two of pork, and one of salt at the side of the
road where they would be found by Doniphan's advancing
troops. At the same time he dispatched a rider ahead to halt
enough wagons bearing provisions to feed nearly the entire
Army of the West. Doniphan's column reached Cow Creek
Crossing on July 11 and there joined with Ruff and his men. To
his dismay, Doniphan found that between them they had
provisions for no more than four or five days. To make matters
worse, Kearny and those marching with him were a short day's
march to their rear, trying to catch up and share in the meager
food supply. This problem of inadequate or unavailable
provisions was to haunt the Army of the West all the way to
Bent's Fort, and beyond to Santa Fe.[11]

The road most of the troops followed southwest to the main
Santa Fe Trail was a new one, first blazed by Colonel Kearny
and some 280 dragoons on their return march from South Pass
in August 1845. A fatigue party had been dispatched in mid-
June 1846 to clearly mark this road for the troops who would
follow, but had apparently performed its task in a rather
indifferent manner, because the trail was described as "faint
and indistinct." This caused several detachments to go astray
both north and south of the crossing of the Kansas River. The
trail itself led from Fort Leavenworth south down the Fort
Scott Military Road to Nine Mile Creek, then turned southwest for eight or nine miles to Stranger Creek, and continued
beyond another eight or ten miles to a flatboat ferry operated
by a French-Shawnee half-blood named Paschal Fish. After
crossing the Kansas River on Fish's ferry and another operated by a Delaware, the troops continued along and parallel to
the right (south) bank of the Wakarusa River to Blue Mound,
then moved west either on or parallel to the Oregon Trail. They
crossed that trail a mile or two west of Blue Mound and
marched southwest to an intersection with the main Santa Fe

Trail at the west end of "The Narrows," a mile or so east of
Willow Springs.[12]

Except for the difficulties encountered in following the
poorly marked trail from Fort Leavenworth to the main Santa
Fe Trail, none of the marching units experienced any serious
problems before reaching Walnut Creek, if the discomfort of
sun, heat, rain, insects, dust, sandstorms, rattlesnakes,
blistered or bloodied feet, and other similar afflictions are
overlooked. On July 4, wherever each of the companies were,
they stopped to celebrate the national day with a drink of
whiskey, singing, and loud hurrahs. Unfortunately, by the
time they reached the Walnut, there were from seventy-five to
ninety men on the sick list of the combined command (Companies E and H under Major Gilpin, and accompanied by
Colonel Doniphan, had joined Ruff's battalion at Cow Creek
on July 11), and many of their animals had either died or
become lame or crippled, and were left for the wolves. They
continued on, and by the time they reached Pawnee Rock they
were all greeted with the sight of an enormous herd of bison,
stretching to the west and north as far as the eye could see.
Hunters killed many, and the larder of the famished troops
was considerably supplemented with their meat, to the relief
of all.[13]

On July 13 Pvt. Nehemiah Carson, a member of G Company from Glasgow, Howard County, Missouri, died, apparently
the first such loss for the Army of the West during the march to
Santa Fe. His comrades excavated a grave on the top of
Pawnee Rock, and he was buried there on the fourteenth. Ruff
and Gilpin's combined command reached the Pawnee Fork the
same day (July 13) and went into camp, the stream being at
flood stage and unfordable. Pvt. Arthur E. Hughes, a member of the Laclede Rangers (then a day's march behind),
arrived on "express" duty and drowned while attempting to
cross the Pawnee. He was with two other rangers dispatched
to halt one of the commissary trains in advance of the column.
The swift and violent current swept him downstream, away
from his friends. His body was later recovered from the
Arkansas, and he was buried on July 15 on the left (north)

bank of the Pawnee at the foot of the bluff about two hundred yards above the usual crossing of the Santa Fe Trail. It was a "prairie burial" without ceremony. The dead man was wrapped in his clothing and blanket, laid in the grave, and then the grave was filled and covered with rocks to prevent wolves from digging up the body. From that point on, more graves would mark the lonely road the troops were following to Santa Fe.[14]

During late afternoon on July 15 Colonel Kearny and his escort, along with the remaining companies of Doniphan's command, arrived at the Pawnee Fork and went into camp. Except for Companies A and D and the dragoons under Captain Moore, ahead of them on the trail, and Sumner and Cooke's two dragoon companies, about sixty miles behind, all troops of the Army of the West, more than twelve hundred men, were now in camp on the banks of the Pawnee. Because the normally placid stream remained at flood stage, they were forced to wait for the water to drop. The brief pause on the Pawnee must have been a welcome relief to all, for the rapid pace, lack of food, want of grazing for animals, and harsh conditions were having a debilitating effect, especially on the livestock. 2d Lt. George R. Gibson painted a graphic picture when he stated, "The whole country from the Little Arkansas is like a slaughter pen, covered with bones, skulls, and carcasses of animals in every state of decay." But Kearny was not one to endure delay, man-made or otherwise, and on the sixteenth he ordered that a crossing be forced. Trees were felled to permit the men to cross on the trunks. Wagons were emptied of cargo, which was then carried over in like manner. The livestock were forced to swim, while the wagons were floated and drawn across with ropes. The balance of the troops crossed on the morning of the seventeenth, and the march resumed.[15]

The march of the Army of the West beyond the Pawnee Fork followed the Arkansas, using the so-called Wet Route. Heat was the most dangerous problem faced by the soldiers, but broken-down animals were an increasing concern, as was the appearance of dysentery, measles, and several other diseases. The country became increasingly dry and desolate, with dried, brown buffalo grass covering the uplands, sprinkled with sagebrush, yucca, and cacti as far as the eye could see. On the nineteenth the column passed Jackson's Grove near the south bend of the Arkansas.* The following morning Colonel Kearny took ill and had to go into camp after moving only eight miles upstream. The rest of the troops marched to beyond the Caches.† But on Tuesday, July 21, Kearny was much improved, and he and his escort moved ahead twenty-three miles. A few Indians were seen on the south side of the river, probably Comanches, and a number of horses were reported missing, possibly stolen by the same Indians. Somewhere in this vicinity the command came upon a small grove of trees, one of which had what appeared to be a huge nest high up in its branches. Investigation revealed it to be the burial platform of an Indian chief or very important warrior, laid out in state with his finest clothing, weapons, and pipes. The following day they passed the "Pawnee Forts," the remains of a crude stockade erected in a grove of trees on an island in the Arkansas River during pretrail times by a party

*Jackson's Grove was a large stand of cottonwoods on an island and along the south side of the Arkansas about sixty-four miles from the crossing of the Pawnee Fork by way of the Wet Route. It was there, in 1843, that Capt. Philip St. George Cooke, in command of four companies of the First Dragoons, had surrounded and disarmed Jacob Snively and his Invincibles, freebooters commissioned by Texas to harass and raid Mexican traffic along the Santa Fe Trail through Texas territory. At the time, the northern boundary of Texas followed the Arkansas west of the one-hundredth meridian. Snively and his men thought they were west of the meridian and hence in Texas. Cooke calculated they were east of the line and thus in U.S. territory. He was correct. See Otis E. Young, *The West of Philip St. George Cooke*, 109–25; see also "Notes of Lieutenant J. W. Abert," House Ex Doc. No. 41, 30th Cong., 1st Sess., 403.

†The "Caches" were two or three large, open pits approximately one hundred yards north of the trail, about three miles west of present Dodge City, Kansas. They were originally jug-shaped holes dug in 1822–23 by the trading party of James Baird and Samuel Chambers as a place to store their trade goods after a blizzard had killed most of their pack animals. When they returned to pick up their goods in 1823, they dug out the pits and left them open. As long as the trail remained in use, these pits were a trail marker in a land of few natural features. See Gregory M. Franzwa, *The Santa Fe Trail Revisited*, 120.

of Pawnees, apparently as an unsuccessful defense against the unforgiving enemy that had discovered their presence, reputedly the Cheyennes. Company A of the Missouri Volunteer Infantry, under the command of Capt. W. Z. Angney, was forced to delay its march to bury one of its men, Sgt. Augustus Leslie, who had died during the night. He was interred in a grave on a high point of the plains four miles west of the Pawnee Forts. After a brief religious exercise, three volleys were fired over his grave, the body was covered with staves from a flour barrel, heavy timbers were placed over these, and the grave was filled with dirt to protect the body from wolves or Indians. A headboard was placed over the grave, and the company resumed its march.[16]

On Friday, July 24, Kearny's party and accompanying troops, including Captain Woldemar Fischer's battery, passed the Upper Crossing and Chouteau's Island during the morning. It was there that the surveyed route of the original Santa Fe Trail turned south, passed through the sand hills by way of Bear Creek (an intermittent stream bed), and headed for the Lower Cimarron Spring and beyond. The column was continuing west along the Arkansas on what was then known as the "Bent's Fort Trail," later to be known as the Mountain Branch of the Santa Fe Trail. While at Chouteau's Island, the men of the artillery took a brief respite to explore. Two of them found the body of a dead Indian and proceeded to play one of those tasteless and insensitive practical jokes that sometimes are perpetrated by young men under stress, with their lives at risk. They propped the body up by means of sticks and in this manner made it appear to walk about the island, surprising and terrifying many of their comrades.[17]

The march beyond Chouteau's Island to their rendezvous was uneventful. They camped at Pretty Encampment on July 25, Big Salt Bottom on July 26, and the Big Timbers on July 27. By the twenty-eighth they were within eighteen miles of Bent's Fort, and the following day went into camp along the Arkansas in an area extending from about seven to twelve miles below it. Remarkably, the first to arrive were the two companies of infantry. Except for the two dragoon companies

of Sumner and Cooke, most of the Army of the West was finally
united, with Doniphan's regiment of mounted volunteers in
camp on the south (right) bank of the river and the balance of
the command on the north. In addition to Kearny's men, the
area was crowded with the trains of all the traders detained by
Captain Moore.[18]

Arrival at Bent's Fort provided the weary troops with an
opportunity for rest, or at least a break in the constant
marching. However, there was much to be done before continuing: making repairs to wagons, shoeing horses and mules,
replenishing supplies, and grazing livestock. Kearny was
busy with plans for the remainder of the march to Santa Fe.
When he reached Bent's Fort and made contact with Captain
Moore, he found that Moore had three Mexicans in custody
who had been sent by Governor Armijo as spies to observe the
size, composition, and movement of the American force
marching against him. The Army of the West was by now
close enough to the crossing of the Raton Mountains, that it
was unlikely sizable enemy units could arrive in time to
contest its passage. Kearny thus had no hesitancy in re-
leasing these men so that they might return and report to
Armijo the strength of his advancing army. This, he hoped,
would so demoralize the New Mexicans that they would
conclude resistance was useless. With these men, Kearny
also sent a proclamation addressed to the citizens of New
Mexico, announcing his intention to take over the province
and make it a part of the United States, thereby "ameliorating
the condition of the inhabitants." Those who continued in
their usual civil pursuits were to be respected and left in
peace, but any who took up arms against the invading army
were to be deemed enemies and "treated accordingly."[19]

When the army reached its Bent's Fort campground,
Kearny took stock of the logistical needs, and what he found
was appalling. The food supplies were so dangerously low it
was necessary to immediately put the troops on half rations.
Worse, the colonel now discovered what must have been the
height of the bureaucratic bungling that was plaguing what
should have been a farsighted logistical plan for the operation.

Once all of the supply trains had reached Bent's Fort and necessary repairs were made, it was expected they would follow the Army of the West to Santa Fe. But many of the teamsters now declared that their agreement with the quartermaster was to take their cargo only to Bent's Fort, not Santa Fe. In the confusion surrounding the hasty organization and departure of Kearny's force, someone had blundered and billed the cargo through only to the trading post, the point of departure for the march into Mexican territory. So few wagons stayed with Colonel Kearny and his men that from August 1 until the end of September, they had no sugar or coffee and only one-half the usual ration of flour. Before the troops reached Santa Fe, their food had been reduced to one-third that specified, and the night before they entered the city they had nothing at all. Eventually soldiers were dispatched back to Bent's Fort to assist in moving the supplies, and by the latter part of October some thirty wagons a week were reaching Santa Fe. The lack of adequate provisions and other supplies proved to be the greatest danger faced by the Army of the West during the conquest of New Mexico.[20]

Kearny and his men remained at Bent's Fort for only two to three days. The dragoon companies of Captains Sumner and Cooke had arrived on July 31, and in the interim the most pressing of repairs had been made, provisions replenished so far as was possible, and replacement horses and mules acquired, some from William Bent and others from a band of Arapahoes camped nearby. Anxious to be about the task before him, Colonel Kearny put his men back on the road as soon as he could, some starting their march on August 1, with the balance leaving the following day. The few supply trains continuing with them followed in their rear and once again quickly fell behind. On August 2, Captain Cooke and a small detachment of dragoons were sent ahead under a flag of truce as escort for James Magoffin, bearing secret instructions from President Polk. Magoffin was to meet with Governor Armijo, his wife's cousin, in an effort to persuade the governor to surrender the province without a fight.[21]

The crossing of Raton Pass proved as difficult as predicted. There was no cleared or graded road, only a path passable by the more surefooted horses and mules. Several wagons were lost in the course of the laborious operation, but by August 8 the Army of the West had emerged from the mountains and was back on a plain. On August 15, only two weeks after leaving Bent's Fort, Kearny and his men occupied Las Vegas, the first of the Mexican towns in their line of march. There the colonel addressed the inhabitants, proclaiming the province a part of the United States, absolving its citizens from their allegiance to Mexico, and administering the oath of allegiance to the American constitution. Leaving local government in the hands of the alcalde, Kearny moved on. The troops passed through Tecolote the same day and San Miguel del Vado on August 16, at each town stopping to repeat the same ceremony conducted at Las Vegas. The defense of Santa Fe dissolved when Governor Armijo, having assembled a ragtag army of regular dragoons, militia, and Pueblo Indians to fortify and hold Apache Canyon, ordered them home on August 16 on the grounds they had neither the means nor the experience to successfully oppose the Americans. Armijo fled south to Chihuahua and Durango with his dragoons. The Army of the West, sabers drawn and banners flying, entered Santa Fe on the evening of August 18, hoisting the American flag over the Palace of Governors and again repeating the citizenship ceremony first administered at Las Vegas. New Mexico had been taken without firing a shot. [22]

The Army of the West remained in Santa Fe only long enough to establish a civil government, headed by Charles Bent as the first American governor. On September 25, Kearny left the city at the head of the four companies of the First Dragoons, bound for California to assist in the conquest of that state. Colonel Doniphan and the First Regiment of Missouri Mounted Volunteers had meanwhile been ordered south to join the forces of Gen. J. E. Wool, commander of the American army of Chihuahua, Mexico. Doniphan and his men fought their way south, defeating a well-armed Mexican army at the Battle of Sacramento and finally moving on to join

up with Gen. Zachary Taylor's army at Monterrey. Kearny and
his dragoons* fought the California Lancers in a bloody battle
at San Pasqual in December, then joined with the forces
under Commodore Robert F. Stockton to defeat the Mexican
army at Los Angeles in January 1847. The march of the Army
of the West was successful beyond the wildest imaginings of
all but its own members. [23]

*Only two companies of dragoons continued to California with Kearny, the
other two having been sent back to Santa Fe under Captain Sumner. See K.
Jack Bauer, *The Mexican War, 1846–1848*, 137.

2

Soldiers and Traders:
The Trail in 1846

The road followed by the Army of the West during its march to
Bent's Fort ran directly through the lands of the five most
powerful tribes of Indians inhabiting the southern plains:
the Cheyennes, Arapahoes, Kiowas, Comanches, and Plains
Apaches. Southern bands of Cheyennes and Arapahoes occupied the territory north from the Arkansas to the South Platte
and Platte and from the foothills of the Rocky Mountains on
the west to the crossing of the Little Arkansas on the east,
about the line of the ninety-eighth meridian. Kiowas, Comanches, and Plains Apaches roamed over the country south
of the Arkansas. The Kiowas, close friends and allies of the
Comanches, lived in the area between the Red River and the
Arkansas, from Bent's Fort on the west to the Cross Timbers
on the east, approximately the ninety-seventh meridian. The
Plains Apache homeland was much the same as that of the
Kiowas, though they tended to stay farther to the west. The
Comanches were the largest and most powerful of these three
tribes, and they claimed a loosely defined territory the
Spanish called Comancharía. It extended from the Arkansas
south nearly to the confluence of the Pecos and the Rio
Grande and from the Pecos on the west to the Cross Timbers
on the east, encompassing within its northern reaches most of
the country of the other two tribes. Within this vast domain
roamed a number of Comanche bands, each large enough to
operate essentially as an independent tribe. During the first

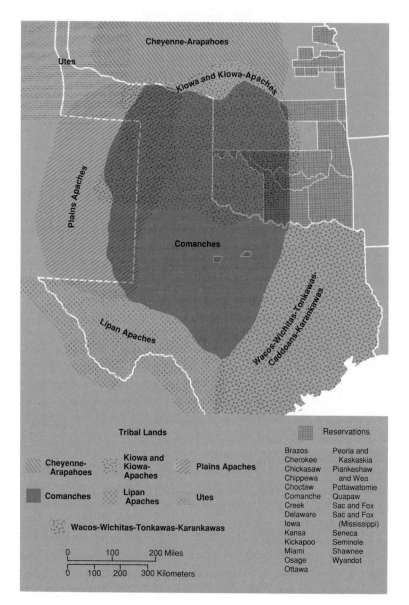

Tribal territories on the southern Great Plains

half of the nineteenth century there were seven principal bands, of which the Yamparikas, Kotsotekas, Nokonis, and Kwahadis regularly camped in separately defined and preferred territory of their own north of the Red River. The Santa Fe Trail either passed through the lands of these four "northern" bands or came so close as to be a tempting target for raiding.

The Indians of the plains were by necessity territorial, requiring more or less exclusive use of an area sufficiently large to support the bison and other wildlife on which they depended for survival. They tolerated friends and allies in their lands from time to time, so long as there was adequate food for all, but there were understandings between tribes as to the usual boundaries to be observed. When large numbers of American traders traveling the Santa Fe Trail began to penetrate the Plains Indian country during the late 1820s, they immediately started killing great quantities of game, particularly bison. The latter were frequently killed for nothing more than the tongue, considered a great delicacy, and were too often killed only for sport. The great beasts began to decline in numbers and move away from the river, where they were most easily hunted, and this caused hardship and starvation in Indian camps. The tribes reacted accordingly, making war to resist the intrusions into their country and halt the traffic. In so doing, they discovered a practical value in the form of captured trade goods. Thereafter, raids on trading caravans were motivated nearly as much by economic factors as by a desire to expel the whites.

Also players in the drama then unfolding on the plains were the Pawnees, a seminomadic Caddoan-speaking people who lived in earth-lodge villages along the Platte and Loup Fork rivers in what is now east-central Nebraska. The Pawnees' habit of stealing livestock from travelers along the Oregon-California Trail had made their name so familiar to whites entering the western plains that they were commonly attributed with many raids they had not committed and with far more than they reasonably could have. There were four principal bands of Pawnees: the Grand Pawnees (Chauis), the

Kitkehahkis, the Pitahauerats, and the Skidis. In earlier
times the first three bands regularly hunted down into the
country drained by the Arkansas, sometimes raiding deep
into Texas, while the Skidis traditionally hunted west along
the Platte. By the nineteenth century their Caddoan relatives—the Wichitas, Anadarkos, Wacos, Tawakonis, and
Caddos—were living in central Texas and what is now central
Oklahoma. These southern Caddoan tribes were often called
Pawnees, Black Pawnees, White Pawnees, or Pawnee Picts by
whites entering their country, which frequently led to mis-
identification of the tribes guilty of raids by persons not
sufficiently knowledgeable of the differences between them,
compounding the problem for the Pawnees.[1]

The Pawnees themselves had been pushed from the buffalo
plains south of the Platte by the southern bands of Cheyennes
and Arapahoes during the second and third decades of the
nineteenth century and north of the Platte by the northern
bands of those two tribes along with the Oglalla, Brulé, and
Miniconjou Sioux. The Pawnees had been greatly reduced by
constant wars with their many enemies and wasted by the
ravages of smallpox, cholera, and other European diseases.
On October 9, 1833, they had signed a treaty with the U.S.
government surrendering their right to hunt in the lands south
of the Platte. Moreover, between 1842 and 1846 their villages
on the Loup Fork had been subjected to devastating raids by
the Sioux, and they had been forced to move to new villages
farther east and south of the Platte. In January 1846 the Sioux
attacked a Skidi and Pitahauerat hunting camp near the forks
of the Platte, killing thirty-two. These Sioux attacks continued during 1847 and, in combination with their many other
problems, make it doubtful that the Pawnees could have been
guilty of most charges of raiding made against them by
travelers crossing the Santa Fe Trail during the war with
Mexico. Investigation often showed that raids on trail traffic
during this period were in fact made by Kiowas, Comanches,
and Arapahoes. Thus, although there were certainly some
Pawnee raiders along the Arkansas from time to time during
this period, and although the Skidis raided the Wichita

villages on the Red River, in general the Pawnees were improperly and unfairly blamed for many of the attacks made by others.[2]

In 1846, as war with Mexico was about to break out along the Rio Grande, relations with the Plains Indians were tenuous. Northward from the Santa Fe Trail, the Cheyennes and Arapahoes were nominally at peace, largely due to the efforts of William Bent, who had married into the Cheyenne tribe. But neither tribe had signed a treaty authorizing travel across their lands, and both raided trading caravans from time to time. Southward the Comanches, Kiowas, and Plains Apaches were all involved in attacks on the commerce of the trail. As a result of efforts by the 1834 dragoon expedition, some of the northern bands of Comanches had signed a treaty of friendship with the United States on the Canadian River in August 1835. Although it called for the Comanches to cease attacks on traffic along the Santa Fe Trail, permit whites to travel to and from New Mexico unmolested, and make peace with their Indian neighbors, only a small part of the tribe was represented and bound by it. Worse, it required little of the U.S. government and provided no annuities. As a result, the treaty was ignored. On May 15, 1846, just two days after war with Mexico was declared, government commissioners signed a treaty of peace and friendship with the Penateka Co-manches, the largest and most important of the southern bands, but both parties failed to abide by its provisions, and it too was soon ignored. Comanche raids on Santa Fe traffic continued unabated. The Kiowas, who had signed a peace treaty with the United States in 1837, observed it for a time, if one does not count raids into Texas both before and after annexation, since during their free period none of the Plains Indians ever equated Texans with the United States. As was common with all Plains Indians, the people, leaders, and bands who had not signed the treaty felt no obligation to abide by it, something few Americans ever understood. Raids by Kiowas who had not signed (and some who had) continued along the road to Santa Fe.[3]

Most traffic on the Santa Fe Trail moved during the period

from late April and early May through October, the season of
growth when livestock would have sufficient grazing. But
during the years of greatest traffic there were always a few
hardy souls who would cross the plains during late fall and
winter. Some were in a hurry to return to their wives, families,
and business. Others probably thought they would be safer
from Indian attack, with all tribes and bands in winter camp
and their horses in marginal condition for use by a war or
raiding party. The greater danger during this time was the
possibility of a blizzard. The southern plains were, and still
are, a land of extremes. Seldom is there snow on the ground for
extended periods during winter, and cold weather comes and
goes. But when it comes, temperatures plummet, and blind-
ing snow, driven by a relentless wind that sweeps unopposed
across the treeless expanse, may come suddenly and unexpectedly, obliterating any trace of a road or trail. After a few
days the temperature usually moderates, and the snow disap-
pears. During trail times if the cold and snow lasted for long
periods, domestic livestock might die from lack of food or
water, and without them, the trade goods, the wagons and
equipment, and the very lives of the traders might well be
lost. Thus, parties undertaking a trip to or from Santa Fe or
Independence, Missouri, during wintertime had to be well
prepared and hope for good weather, lest springtime find the
bones of their animals and men moldering along the road.

The first traffic along the trail in 1846 was a caravan of
traders that left Santa Fe on December 21, 1845, and reached
St. Louis, Missouri, during the latter part of January. They
encountered exceedingly severe weather on the plains, crossed
the Arkansas on ice, and saw immense numbers of buffalo in
the bottoms along the river, driven there by the cold. On
February 3, the trading party of Houck and Beck of Boonville,
Missouri, and a Mr. Hicks of Boone County reached Independence after a thirty-four-day journey from Santa Fe. They had
left Chihuahua the preceding December 1 and departed
Santa Fe on January 1. The party encountered only one
snowstorm and few Indians during their trip, suggesting the
coldest weather had come early, then moderated. Troubles

with Indians redeveloped when, on March 7, the trading party of Messrs. Armijo and Co., traveling with the trader Norris Colburn and his wagons, was struck by raiders, allegedly Pawnees, at the Cow Creek crossing. They had left Santa Fe on February 16, the Armijo train heading for St. Louis to purchase a supply of trade goods and Colburn making his return trip to Missouri. The Indians captured seventeen mules from Colburn, while the Armijo caravan lost two horses and twenty-seven mules. The Armijo party was left with few animals and had to walk the remaining two hundred miles to Independence, where they arrived on March 17. Colburn took charge of their baggage and money but was delayed and arrived a few days later than they did.[4]

During late March, Dr. Eugene Leitensdorfer and his family, with three wagons and one hundred mules, reached Independence, Missouri, possibly in the company of Norris Colburn. They had left Santa Fe on February 10 and en route had suffered an Indian raid, losing a part of their provisions. Leitensdorfer's wife, Soledad, was the daughter of Santiago Abreu, a former governor of New Mexico, and certainly one of the earliest women to have crossed the trail. From April 27 to 29 several more traders, totaling about forty-five men with seventeen wagons, arrived at Independence. Principals of the party were Lewis Jones, of Independence, and Samuel Wethered and Thomas J. Caldwell, both of Baltimore, Maryland. They left Chihuahua on March 3 and Santa Fe on March 30. Fortune attended them, and they made a rapid trip unimpeded by either bad weather or Indians. Between May 8 and May 14 additional trading parties reached Independence, all having commenced their trip in Chihuahua. In the lead were the parties of Francisco Elguea and Henry Skillman, who made the trip in just forty-six days. They were followed by the traders Peo Semirane, Jose Gonzales, and Louis Yaulwager. Last to arrive was the train of James W. Magoffin, with thirty wagons. In combination, these traders were said to have brought with them nearly $350,000 in specie and mule herds totaling approximately one thousand animals. They were among the last traders to reach the "states" from Chihuahua before the outbreak of war.[5]

From May 8 to May 16 the first westbound trading caravans
of the year began to move down the Santa Fe Trail, headed for
New Mexico and Chihuahua. None, of course, were aware that
hostilities had begun and even then war was being declared.
There were about forty wagons with the first parties to leave,
and more were preparing for departure. Most wagons were
drawn by ox teams, a slow mode of travel but reliable and
economical. Included in the first of the trains to leave were
the wagons of George Doan and James J. Webb (five wagons),
W. S. McKnight, Norris Colburn (beginning a new trip), Juan
Armijo, and J. B. Turley, all of whom left on May 9. The
Armijo wagons, including those of a train that apparently left
on May 8, were the property of Manuel Armijo, the governor of
New Mexico. Accompanying them was Francis X. Aubry,
embarking on his first trading trip to Santa Fe. By the
fifteenth and sixteenth, several other experienced traders
departed, including Benjamin Pruett, George H. Peacock,
"Weick," "Mayer," Charles Blummer, Samuel Ralston, Adam
Hill, and Henry and Edwin Norris. With them, as a co-
traveler, was the artist Alfred S. Waugh. They crossed the
Arkansas at the Middle Crossing, reached the vicinity of the
Middle Cimarron Spring by the middle of June, and arrived at
Santa Fe by the end of the month. It was while traveling along
the Cimarron that they first received confirmation of the
declaration of war, although they had heard of the fight on the
Texas border when about one hundred miles beyond Indepen-
dence.[6]

On May 22 Albert Speyer, a German-Jewish trader and
business partner of Governor Armijo, departed Big Blue
Camp* bound for Santa Fe and beyond to Chihuahua. His
train consisted of twenty-two large wagons, each drawn by ten
mules, several smaller wagons, and thirty-five men. Two of
his wagons carried munitions purchased in England to fill an

---

*Big Blue Camp was adjacent to the Fort Leavenworth–Fort Towson (La.)
military road near the western boundary of Missouri, about twenty miles
northwest of Independence.

order made by the governor of Chihuahua the previous year. Speyer was considered to be thoroughly anti-American. Accompanying his caravan was Dr. Frederick A. Wislizenus of St. Louis, with a servant and a "small wagon on springs" to carry his baggage and instruments. Wislizenus was making a private expedition to collect scientific data. By May 24 the caravan had passed the junction with the Oregon Trail and on June 3 arrived at the crossing of the Little Arkansas. There they met a twenty-two-wagon train belonging to Bent, St. Vrain, and Co., which had left Bent's Fort in mid-May. The men from the Bent train warned of Indian troubles ahead, reporting that one of their men had been killed and scalped by Comanches a few miles southwest of the Pawnee Fork crossing around May 28. Speyer and his men pushed on and by June 5 were beyond Walnut Creek, where they encountered an enormous herd of bison estimated at thirty thousand head. Later the same day they reached Pawnee Rock,* and the following day the Speyer party crossed the Pawnee Fork and passed the grave of the Bent employee killed by the Comanches. On June 8 the caravan camped by the Caches and on June 9 reached the Middle Crossing of the Arkansas River. Here they found a corral of wagons formed on the south bank by some of the smaller caravans that had left Missouri a week or so earlier. The Speyer train reached this point in only nineteen days, averaging nearly eighteen and a half miles per day, an exceptional speed for wagon trains even when pulled by mules.[7]

On June 1, when Speyer and his men were probably reaching and camping at Cottonwood Crossing, George T. Howard left the Fort Leavenworth Agency with 2d Lt. Julian May of the U.S. Mounted Riflemen, an escort of seven dragoons from the fort, and about as many Shawnee and

---

*Pawnee Rock is a large sandstone projection that was a famous trail marker. It apparently received its name when a party of Pawnees raiding southward was discovered and chased there by a war party from one of the southern Plains tribes. All of the Pawnees were killed, but their enemy so admired their brave defense that Plains Indians thereafter referred to the projection as "Pawnee Rock." Early traditions differ as to the tribe that caught them, some saying it was the Cheyennes, others the Comanches. Both tribes were mortal enemies of the Pawnees.

Delaware Indians. Howard was on a War Department mission to New Mexico but intended to overtake the trading caravans in advance of him and warn them of hostilities. Two days later, and about fifty miles beyond Fort Leavenworth, Howard sent a dispatch to Colonel Kearny informing him that the Speyer and Armijo trains, then several days ahead of him, were said to be carrying a quantity of arms and ammunition to New Mexico and were to be met at the Middle Crossing by an escort of two companies of Mexican cavalry. It was this message that prompted Kearny to send Capt. Benjamin D. Moore with companies C and G on their unsuccessful mission to overtake and detain the two trains. When it was clear they could not catch the Speyer or Armijo trains, Moore took his men back to the Pawnee fork, where there was better grass, to await arrival of other elements of the Army of the West.[8]

Speyer crossed the Arkansas on June 10 and immediately hurried on. Word had reached him that he was being pursued by dragoons. Along the Cimarron River he overtook most of the trains that had left Independence before him. He informed them of the declaration of war and of his pursuit by dragoons to prevent his entry into Mexican territory, then quickly moved on. Knowledge of war and the probability of inflated wartime prices for scarce merchandise also spurred on the others, and though using oxen instead of mules, they kept hard on the heels of the Speyer wagons. Speyer and his men reached Santa Fe on June 30, with the others only half a day behind him.[9]

Although Captain Moore had failed to overtake Speyer and the others ahead of him, he had better luck with those who followed. Manuel X. Harmony, a native Spaniard, had left Independence on May 27 with a train of fourteen heavily laden wagons, each drawn by twelve oxen. He had trading goods worth nearly thirty-nine thousand dollars. His train was overtaken by Moore and his men on June 17 near the Pawnee Fork and was detained there for some twenty days. Eventually he followed Moore to Bent's Fort, which he reached on July 26, then entered Santa Fe a month later behind the Army of the West. Several other traders, including Christopher C. Branham, James P. Hickman, Cornelius Davy, Alexander C. Ferguson, and Edward

The onset of the Mexican War and the vast increase in traffic along the Santa Fe Trail soon aroused the animosity of the Plains Indians. Whites destroyed the occasional small stands of trees along the Arkansas for firewood and wantonly slaughtered bison and other game animals. This generated increased hostility from the tribes, and white travelers moving without escort or in small numbers were at great hazard from roving war parties.

J. Glasgow (the latter accompanied by his brother-in-law, George R. H. Clark, who was traveling for health and pleasure), all started their journey in early June and were all halted by Moore and his men at the Pawnee Fork.[10]

Other traders left Independence during the second week in June, reaching 110-Mile Creek about June 15 and the Council Grove on the nineteenth and twentieth. These included Samuel Magoffin (with his young wife, Susan), Samuel C. Owens and James Aull, Dr. Eugene Leitensdorfer (with his wife, Soledad), Frank McManus, Gabriel Valdez, and a member of the Armijo family. Traveling with them were Dr. Philippe Masure and the artist John Mix Stanley,* the latter with the Owens-Aull party, which initially also included Josiah Gregg. The Magoffin train consisted of fourteen large ox-drawn wagons filled with trader goods, a baggage wagon, a dearborn and a carriage, both drawn by mules. With the train were eighteen men under the leadership of Samuel Magoffin and "Mr. Hall," the wagonmaster, as well as Susan Magoffin and her maid, some two hundred oxen, nine mules, two riding horses, and the Magoffin's greyhound, "Ring." In all there were forty-five wagons. They left Council Grove on June 21 as a combined caravan and reached the Pawnee Fork early in July, at which point they were detained by Captain Moore and his troops. By July 8 approximately 150 traders' wagons were being held by Moore, and grazing for their livestock was being rapidly depleted. On July 9 Captain Moore gave permission for all of the traders to move on along the Arkansas and camp at either of the principal trail crossings or to continue to Bent's Fort but to go no farther. By July 11 most had left, and by July 26 they were in camp at Bent's Fort. They followed in the wake of the Army of the West for the remainder of the journey to Santa Fe.[11]

On July 7 a large train of commissary wagons left Fort Leavenworth under a Mr. King as wagonmaster. When King

*Stanley, a noted artist of the day, gained fame by painting both Indians and western landscapes. When the Owens-Aull train reached Santa Fe, Stanley was engaged as an artist for the scientific staff under Lt. W. H. Emory. He continued on to California with Kearny's dragoons. *KHQ* 20:6.

reached Santa Fe on September 24, he reported that all fifty of the teamsters hired to drive the wagons had turned back after discharging their loads at Bent's Fort. Leaving Fort Leavenworth at about the same time as King was Maj. Thomas Swords, the chief quartermaster of the Army of the West, bearing mail, orders, and Colonel Kearny's commission as a brigadier general, dated June 30, 1846, and the large trading party of Messrs. Hoffman from Baltimore. Swords caught up with Kearny on August 15 at Las Vegas. The Hoffman train reached the Great Bend of the Arkansas on July 11 and the following day camped by the Walnut Creek crossing. Unfortunately, Lt. Col. Charles F. Ruff and his command also arrived at Walnut Creek on the twelfth, leading to one of those incidents between the military and civilian traders that sometimes resulted in friction. A Jewish trader named Goldstein, accompanying the Hoffman train, began selling whiskey to Ruff's troops at exorbitant prices. A pint of whiskey normally costing eighteen cents in the States he sold for one dollar, and for one drink he charged fifty cents. Ruff became so infuriated by this profiteering at the expense of his worn, impoverished, and hungry men that he sent a sergeant with a small detachment to close down the Goldstein operation and confiscate his goods. By July 14 the train and the troops had reached the Pawnee Fork where, because the stream was then at flood stage, they were all forced to make camp.[12]

Except for the occasional hard winters, July and August were probably the most difficult months for large caravans to travel the Santa Fe Trail. The intense heat of the summer lay heavily across the plains, and the near-constant south wind hurled itself at man and beast, leaving them dry and parched. There was no shade to protect them except the night, and only the increasingly infrequent thunderstorms to cool them. The shortgrasses of the plains curled, turned a bleached brown, and grazing became poor. All suffered from exposure to this harsh environment, but the experienced private traders tended to fare better than the green teamsters accompanying the government supply wagons. The traders knew the best camping grounds, the surest water supplies, the most advantageous time and place to hunt game, and how best to protect themselves from attacks by the angry Indians whose country they encroached on and whose game they killed.

There was, unfortunately, no protection for any of the travelers from the losses that might be incurred when wagons broke down because of worn and broken iron tires, broken spokes, and the like. To remedy this problem, at least in part, on July 18, 1846, the quartermaster at Fort Leavenworth, Capt. Robert E. Clary, sent two men, a blacksmith-wheelwright and an assistant, to establish a government smithy at Council Grove. They were to set up their shop and then perform such repairs and other services as the passing troops and wagons might require. The little installation was apparently located under the protective canopy of a huge oak tree near the west end of the grove and was in operation by the end of the month. West of Fort Leavenworth it provided the only possibility of crucial repairs for those embarked on the long, hazardous journey to Santa Fe. But it was a mere 140 miles beyond the fort and only at the edge of the great flat desolation of the high plains. A breakdown beyond this point could spell disaster.[13]

Even as the Army of the West neared the last phase of its long march to Santa Fe and great caravans of traders and government supply trains plodded slowly across the dangerous middle stretches of the trail, additional steps were taken by the Polk administration to ensure there would be a sufficient force to accomplish their goal. A new body of volunteers was recruited from the eastern counties of Missouri to reinforce the advancing army. Ten companies of cavalry were organized as the Second Regiment of Missouri Mounted Volunteers, commanded by Col. Sterling Price, Lt. Col. David D. Mitchell, and Maj. Benjamin B. Edmondson. Four more companies were organized as an "extra" or separate battalion under the command of Lt. Col. David Willock, and placed under the overall command of Colonel Price. Price, a congressman from Missouri, had resigned his seat to accept command of the new "army." These troops were supplemented with several pieces of heavy artillery and a large number of

supply wagons. Similar to what Kearny had done for the Army
of the West, Price organized his wagons into trains of thirty or
more and put them on the trail in advance of the march of
troops to ensure availability of provisions and other supplies
as needed. The teamsters, unfortunately, were little better
than those assigned to Kearny.[14]

Colonel Price arrived at Fort Leavenworth on July 29, and
his force of Missouri volunteers, some twelve hundred men
strong, was sworn into the service of the United States during
early August. On August 10 the first troops of his command—
the Second Regiment company of Capt. Napoleon B. Giddings and the "extra" battalion company of Capt. Jesse B.
Morin—began their march. They reached Cottonwood Crossing by August 22, passed beyond the Upper Crossing of the
Arkansas by September 2, and were in camp at Bent's Fort by
September 9. Giddings's company arrived in Santa Fe on
October 7, but Morin's company, which had to escort and
assist a commissary train in its crossing of the Raton Mountains, did not reach there until October 12. These were the
only companies of Price's command to travel to Santa Fe by
way of the Bent's Fort Trail over the mountains.[15]

The remaining companies of Price's regiment, and those of
the "extra" battalion, departed from Fort Leavenworth between August 11 and August 22. Last to leave were Colonel
Price and his staff, who left on August 23. They experienced
difficulties similar to those of Kearny's troops during their
march, including the problem of availability of supplies as
needed. On September 10, as Price and his men were reaching the Middle Crossing, an express arrived from Santa Fe,
announcing Kearny's entry into that city and advising Price
and the commander of the Mormon battalion, following in
their rear, to take the Santa Fe Trail rather than the Bent's Fort
Trail. They did, but by the time they reached the Lower
Cimarron Springs, their rations were so short it was necessary
to send an express rider to General Kearny at Santa Fe
requesting urgently needed supplies. These were sent as
promptly as possible. Price and the vanguard of his troops
reached Santa Fe on September 28, and by October 12 the

entirety of his command was in camp outside the city.[16]

The Second Regiment of Missouri Mounted Volunteers and the "extra" battalion provided General Kearny with an additional mobile striking force, but he also believed a supplemental body of infantry would be needed to aid in the conquest of the northern Mexican provinces and to garrison a conquered California. To this end, on June 19, 1846, he had ordered Capt. James Allen of the First Dragoons to proceed to Council Bluffs, Iowa, and there recruit four or five companies of volunteer infantry from among the Mormon immigrants then arriving at the Missouri River. The Mormons were in the process of moving themselves from their former headquarters at Nauvoo, Illinois, westward to Utah. President Polk and General Kearny both thought such a large number of uprooted people would be a likely source of recruits, and that judgment proved right. Arriving at Council Bluffs on July 1, Allen began to enlist men for a twelve-month term of service. General Kearny had authorized him to inform the recruits they would be permitted to retain their weapons and accoutrements when discharged and that each company could take along four women as laundresses. The promises worked, primarily because they provided the Mormons with badly needed cash and a means of moving a large number of people westward toward the "promised land" at government expense. The five companies of infantry were raised by July 16. These units were to follow General Kearny to California, to fight if necessary, and to be discharged there at the end of the term of their enlistment.[17]

Once organized, the men of the Mormon infantry battalion marched to Fort Leavenworth by way of St. Joseph and Weston, Missouri, arriving there by August 1. With them went thirty-one women and more than thirty children, all riding in wagons. At Fort Leavenworth they were issued tents and went into camp on the west side of the parade. They had been there but a short time when Captain Allen, by then promoted to lieutenant colonel, as befitted the command, fell seriously ill. He died on August 23 and was replaced as battalion commander by Lt. Andrew J. Smith of the First

Dragoons. Meanwhile Companies A, B, and C had departed the fort on August 13, with Companies D and E leaving on August 15. Following the route of the Army of the West, the men of the Mormon battalion reached the Council Grove on August 27, where they were overtaken by Lieutenant Smith, their new commander. They left the grove on August 31 and, marching at the rate of about fifteen miles per day, reached Cow Creek on September 4, where they caught up with a commissary train filled with their provisions. They crossed Walnut Creek on September 7 and crossed and camped by the Pawnee Fork on the ninth. On the tenth they encountered the express bringing news of Kearny's entry into Santa Fe and his advice that the following troops proceed by way of the Santa Fe Trail rather than going to Bent's Fort and then over the mountains.[18]

The Mormon battalion reached the Middle Crossing of the Arkansas on September 15, finding some of Price's volunteers in camp on the south side. Because of the great animosity then existing between Mormons and Missourians, there was some apprehension of difficulties, but none occurred. While there, ten men were detailed to conduct a number of the women and children along the Arkansas to a good wintering site where modern Pueblo, Colorado, now stands. They left on September 16. The battalion itself crossed the river and resumed its march on September 17. They traveled twenty-five miles into the Jornada the first day, "across one of the most dreary deserts that ever man saw, suffering much from the intense heat of the sun and for want of water." By October 3 they were on the Red River, and the first companies entered Santa Fe on October 9, receiving a one-hundred-gun salute at the order of Colonel Doniphan. The balance of the battalion reached the city on October 12.[19]

After taking Santa Fe on August 18, 1846, Colonel Kearny spent the next month diligently organizing a democratic code of laws, establishing a civil government with Charles Bent as the first territorial governor, and appointing the remaining territorial officers. In preparation for his march to California, Kearny placed Colonel Doniphan in command of all troops in

New Mexico until the arrival of Colonel Price and his reinforcements. On September 23, acting under instructions from
the War Department, Kearny issued further orders that on
arrival of Price and his troops, Doniphan was to proceed with
his regiment to Chihuahua and join the command of Brigadier
General Wool. As Kearny marched west, however, he learned
of attacks on Mexican settlements by a band of Navahoes.
When he decreed American sovereignty over the territory,
Kearny gave his word to the native New Mexicans that the U.S.
government would protect their settlements from Indian depredations, and he therefore sent an order back to Doniphan
directing an expedition against these Indians. Price reached
Santa Fe on September 28, and Doniphan left on October 26,
taking with him a good part of Price's troops. Price and the
rest of his men remained in Santa Fe as the military authority,
a duty the undisciplined volunteers performed harshly and
arrogantly, causing considerable ill will and resentment among
the native population. The Mormon battalion, in the meantime, had been placed under the command of Lt. Col. Philip
St. George Cooke of the First Dragoons, a true Virginia
gentleman and devout Episcopalian. Cooke led the approximately 450-man Mormon battalion on a difficult cross-
country journey in an effort to catch Colonel Kearny and
participate in the conquest of California. They left Santa Fe
on October 21, 1846, charted an overland route to southern
California as they marched, and reached their destination on
January 29, 1847, well behind Kearny and his men. The
Mormon battalion did not have to fight after all, and most of its
men were discharged at Los Angeles on July 16, 1847, having
completed the twelve months of service they had signed up
for.[20]

The march across the plains by the Army of the West and
the successive reinforcing units had been accomplished
with little interference by Indians. Except for stealing a
few horses and mules, the natives had been too awestruck
by the large, relatively compact bodies of heavily armed men
to directly challenge them. They wanted the whites out of
their country, but they were not so foolish as to attempt an

attack on so many troops when they would surely pay a heavy price. So they watched and bided their time, waiting for an opportunity to present itself without such great danger. That opportunity finally came in the form of unescorted commissary and supply trains, driven by inexperienced teamsters who were often fearful of Indians without real cause. On August 13 the eastbound Norris Colburn, once again returning from Santa Fe with his train of wagons, reached the Middle Crossing of the Arkansas. There he found in camp a government supply train bound for Bent's Fort, with forty-three wagons and fifty-four men. They were in distress and "lying by for repairs." Many of the teamsters were sick, their ammunition was low, and they had lost fifteen yoke of oxen, probably to marauding Comanches. They were extremely fearful of the hostile Indians who frequented the area and seemed unable to cope with their own needs. Colburn gave them all of the powder he could spare, then continued his journey. The government train finally reached Bent's Fort on August 25, but the teamsters refused to continue beyond to Santa Fe.[21]

When Colburn and his party reached the crossing, they also found Simeon Turley there with three wagons, bound for Taos and beyond to his home at Arroyo Hondo. Also passing the crossing at the same time was Charles Bent and a mounted party en route from Independence to Bent's Fort. Shortly thereafter Bent moved on to Santa Fe to assume office on September 22 as the first governor of New Mexico Territory, in which capacity he served until his death during the Taos uprising. Colburn continued east along the trail, meeting successive trains as he traveled. Most had similar stories to tell of Indian attacks or raids. On August 15 he met another Santa Fe–bound government supply train, this one with twenty-two wagons, moving along the trail west of Coon Creek. It had been attacked the previous night while in camp, probably by a Comanche raiding party. Colburn's party went into camp near Coon Creek Crossing the same day and suffered a raid on their livestock that very night. Fortunately they thwarted the raiders, and no animals were lost. The party moved out rapidly and on August 16 passed a train of sixty wagons belonging to Armijo, Magoffin, and others, then in camp at the Pawnee Fork. This train too had just endured an Indian raid. At the Pawnee, Colburn was joined by Maj. George Rogers Hancock Clark, the brother-in-law of Edward J. Glasgow, who had been in the company of another party. Clark traveled with Colburn for the remainder of the trip to Independence. Reaching Cow Creek on the seventeenth, Colburn met yet another government train with thirty-one wagons and forty-three men under "Messrs. Barnes and Allen" bound for Santa Fe. They had been struck by a raiding party, and the teamsters, in a state of near panic, were insubordinate. Eventually they also refused to go on to Santa Fe. That evening Indians again raided Colburn's train and made off with three of Major Clark's mules. On August 18 Colburn crossed Owl Creek, where he found "Mr. Horner's company" of eighteen government wagons in camp.* They had been attacked by a large body of Indians at 3:00 A. M. that morning, shattering the myth that Indians would not fight at night. The train lost no livestock, but they were nearly out of powder. Colburn gave them what he and his party could spare, which was precious little for men just then moving into the most dangerous segment of the trail. During the remainder of their trip, Colburn and Clark met a number of other westbound wagons, passing on to them what they knew of trail conditions to the west. Colburn's train reached Independence on August 27, after a trip of twenty-four and one-half days, and logged the fastest time from Santa Fe to the Middle Crossing (ten days) recorded to that time.[22]

Other trains traveling the trail also suffered Indian raids. On August 11 or 12, a party of mounted travelers moving east from Bent's Fort, some returning from Santa Fe and some from Fort Laramie, was struck by a band of Cheyenne raiders near Chouteau's Island. A man named William L. Swan was killed

---

*Owl Creek was later called "Chávez Creek" and was finally corrupted to "Jarvis Creek" by Anglo-Americans. It was the scene of the murder of Don Antonio José Chávez by John McDaniel and seven followers in April 1843.

within seventy-five yards of camp and was given a prairie burial before the party pushed on. After the traders left, the Cheyennes dug up the body and scalped it. Swan was found two or three days later by the trading party of William Magoffin, who reburied him. On August 14 a westbound government train with twenty-two wagons under the leadership of "Mr. Cambell and Mr. Coons of St. Louis" (probably B. F. Coons) was attacked during the night. The teamsters claimed they killed one Indian and wounded another while fighting off the assault.[23]

Among the interesting events occurring along the Santa Fe Trail during the latter part of the 1846 travel season was the meeting of two caravans that included two men later noted for what they wrote about their experiences. On September 15 the train of Ceran St. Vrain left the vicinity of Westport, Missouri, bound for Bent's Fort. The caravan included twenty-three mule-drawn wagons under the command of Frank DeLisle as wagonmaster, a clerk, a trader, twenty-three teamsters (mostly French-Canadians), and three Mexican herdsmen. Traveling with St. Vrain were a number of prominent traders and frontiersmen, including Charles Beaubien, Jared W. Folger, Elliott Lee, Lancaster P. Lupton (the former owner of the trading post on the South Platte known as "Fort Lupton," which he closed in 1844), Edmund Chadwick, T. B. Drinker, and seventeen-year-old Lewis H. Garrard. Drinker and Garrard were both from Cincinnati and traveling the trail for pleasure. Later Garrard would write of this trip in his well-known book *Wah-to-Yah and the Taos Trail*. On September 16 they camped at the Lone Elm and by the twenty-third were on the move a short distance east of 110-Mile Creek.[24]

While the St. Vrain train was moving slowly westward from Westport, another group of mounted travelers was eastbound along the Arkansas. Francis Parkman, who later authored *The Oregon Trail*, as well as his cousin Quincy Shaw, their guide Henry Chatillon, and their muleteer Antoine De Laurier, were returning to Westport following their trip along the Oregon Trail. In their company were four other men who had joined them at Bent's Fort. Parkman and his party left the

Oregon Trail at Fort Laramie and traveled south on the old
Trappers Trail or Taos Trail as far as Pueblo, then followed the
Arkansas east to Bent's Fort and beyond. By the time they
reached the Middle Crossing, the party was encountering
great herds of buffalo, numerous trading caravans, various
companies of Price's Second Regiment of Missouri Mounted
Volunteers and of the "extra" battalion, many government supply trains, and the Mormon battalion. Fortunately they met no
hostile Indians. They traveled the Dry Route, or "Ridge
Road," and reached the Pawnee Fork on September 12,
crossing Walnut Creek on the thirteenth and the Little Arkansas on the fifteenth. On the sixteenth, Parkman celebrated
his twenty-third birthday in camp on Turkey Creek. By the
nineteenth they were at Diamond Springs and on the twentieth
at Council Grove. On the morning of the twenty-third, Parkman and his party met the train of Ceran St. Vrain. And so,
these two men, who would gain fame from the narratives they
would write about their travels, passed and probably greeted
each other along the dusty ruts of the Santa Fe Trail. The St.
Vrain train made camp at Council Grove on September 30,
reached the Middle Crossing on October 23 and Chouteau's
Island on the twenty-sixth, arriving at Bent's Fort by the end of
the month. They also had the good fortune to encounter no
Indian raiders. Parkman and his companions reached Westport, Missouri, on September 26, sold off their livestock and
equipment, and boarded a riverboat for St. Louis.[25]

Only a few of the traders from the States made more than
one trip to Santa Fe in a single season. But on October 1,
1846, Norris Colburn, the intrepid veteran trader, began his
second round trip of the year. He had nineteen wagons loaded
with trade goods, including plows and other agricultural
equipment. He had reached Pawnee Rock by October 20 and
the Lower Cimarron Spring on October 31. He probably
reached Santa Fe in mid-November. Sadly, it was to be his
last trip. In late March 1847, while on his return trip to
Independence, he was murdered near Hickory Point by two
Sac or Fox Indians. His body was not found until early May,
when a search party came across it in a ravine, wrapped in a

blanket and weighted down by stones.[26]

Traffic along the trail continued during the fall and winter of 1846–47, albeit at a much reduced volume. Those traveling during the fall found the plains to be in the grip of a great drought, with no water in the Cimarron and none in the Arkansas from the crossings to the Great Bend. On October 12 or 13, a twenty-eight-wagon train belonging to Bullard, Hooke and Co. of Lexington, Missouri, left the Missouri border for Santa Fe. This was the latest a company of traders had ever left from Independence for a crossing of the plains. Late in November the men experienced disaster when an early winter storm struck them in the sand hills south of the Cimarron. During the storm, twenty head of oxen were lost in a stampede, and a number of mules died. The men were forced to cache some of their goods along the river, then return to the Arkansas, intending to winter at Bent's Fort.[27]

Bad weather was not the only culprit bringing trouble to traders along the trail during late 1846. On or about October 13 a government mule train, under the command of a Mr. Harlowe, was attacked by a party of Indians at the Pawnee Fork crossing. The teamsters were surprised while they were eating their supper; one of them was killed, and the wagonmaster was slightly wounded by an arrow. The teamsters attributed the attack to Pawnees, but considering the season, the great distance from the Pawnee villages, and the location in the country of the southern Plains tribes, it seems more likely that one of those tribes was responsible, probably Comanches. In mid-October another wagon train was attacked and captured about twenty miles below the Middle Crossing, again allegedly by Pawnees. The Indians destroyed nineteen wagons and those supplies they had no use for. They ripped open sacks of flour and frolicked with it, throwing it at each other and generally enjoying themselves. They carried off all arms and clothing and about fifty mules. The teamsters were left, naked and afoot, in the middle of the plains.[28]

Shortly after the attack on the government wagon train in mid-October, and no more than five to ten miles east of the site of that attack, a Santa Fe–bound government supply train with twenty-four wagons under the command of Daniel P. Mann as captain, and a Mr. Buchanan as wagonmaster, was struck by Indians on October 28. The forty teamsters had only twenty-nine guns and eighty cartridges between them. They corralled their wagons, except for Mann's wagon, which was captured and burned, and fought back. One man was killed, one seriously wounded, and three slightly wounded during the attack, which ended when the Indians succeeded in capturing all but a dozen of the train's horses and mules. Like the previous attack, this one was attributed to Pawnees. Most of the circumstances would point to Comanches, not Pawnees, but the following spring the agent for the latter tribe did claim that it had been the work of a raiding party from the Grand Pawnee band and that they had stolen about 160 mules. Although the time and place would seem to dictate otherwise, it may well be that these had in fact been Pawnee raiders.[29]

On October 14 Thomas Fitzpatrick, the famed mountain man known to the Indians as "Broken Hand," left Santa Fe en route to Washington, bearing dispatches from Commodore Robert F. Stockton in California, along with letters from Lt. Col. John C. Frémont. During the course of his journey east he was first informed of his appointment as agent for the newly created Upper Platte, Upper Kansas, and Upper Arkansas Indian Agency. He continued on, reaching St. Louis on November 15 and Washington before the end of the month.[30]

As the year wore on, and winter began to displace the dry winds of fall across the plains, traffic along the trail slowed even further in anticipation of severe weather. The first of the infamous "blue northers" for which the plains are well-known struck on December 9 and 10, with severe winds, very heavy snowfall, and bitter cold. A party of twenty-seven men, including a sergeant of the First Dragoons and twenty-six teamsters, had left Santa Fe on November 2 and had reached the Little Arkansas by the time the storm struck. They had one wagon and seven mules and were hiking most of the time. Three of them — Messrs. Bartlett, Thompson, and Long — had become ill from dysentery several days previously and were in a precariously weakened condition when the sudden drop in temperature occurred. It was more than their bodies could withstand, and they quickly succumbed to the cold. Bartlett died on the eleventh, Thompson the following day, and Long on about the sixteenth. The wagon had to be abandoned, and several of the mules died. A party was sent from Fort Leavenworth to aid them, and by mid-January most of the survivors had reached either the fort or Independence, Missouri.[31]

On January 8, 1847, with snow covering the plains, Solomon P. Sublette and three others left Fort Leavenworth bound for Santa Fe with dispatches from Washington. They reached the Pawnee Fork on January 23, in "very cold and stormy" weather, and there found twelve teamsters from the company of Mr. Harvey of Booneville, Missouri. They were afoot, and two had frozen feet. The party was then forty-six days out of Santa Fe and had lost all their mules, some stolen by Indians and the rest frozen to death. Sublette and his party gave the teamsters some of their provisions and directions for the return route to Independence, then continued on through the third storm they had encountered during their journey. They finally reached Santa Fe and delivered their dispatches to Colonel Price on February 23.[32]

The eastbound mail express from Santa Fe, consisting of Thomas O. Boggs and two assistants, left that city on December 15, 1846, in the company of a five-man party headed by a Mr. Seymour of St. Louis. They traveled by way of the Bent's Fort route through some exceedingly severe cold weather. At Chouteau's Island they came across some eighty teamsters, afoot, many suffering frostbite and unable to travel. The teamsters were short on supplies, but the Boggs party was without enough of their own to be of much assistance. They pressed on, and on the night of January 8 they were caught in a blizzard along the Arkansas. When the storm passed they discovered that several of their mules were dead and most of the others gone—taken by Indians or lost in the storm. Boggs and the others in the party struggled on, sometimes traveling through snow a foot and a half deep. At Coon Creek, Indians stole their last nine mules, and they were forced to walk most of the rest of the way to Independence, stumbling along through deep snow. Near Council Grove they found the bodies of two men at the base of a tree. The bark had been eaten all around the trunk. The dead men appeared to be Missouri volunteers, one of them having "D. B." marked on his canteen. After two weeks of wandering, "half frozen and nearly starved," the party came on a camp of Osages. When Boggs and his companions were sufficiently rested, the Osages gave them a few ponies, and with them they moved north to the Kansas River, which they followed down to the Kansa villages.* There they engaged the services of two young Indian boys as guides, who escorted them the rest of the way to Fort Leavenworth. Boggs and his men reached the fort on February 9 or 10. Seymour and his party continued on and arrived in Independence on February 10, looking "more like icicles of the North Pole than human beings."33

Other stories of hardship and sometimes tragedy continued to filter in from the plains for the remainder of the exceptionally harsh winter. In early February a rescue party from Fort Leavenworth brought in two men some Kansa Indians had found lost on the plains "half starved and frozen." On February 15 Marvin L. Kritzer of Independence, Missouri, and three other men returned home from Santa Fe. They were plagued by severe weather the entire distance but saw no other humans, white or Indian, while en route. B. F. Coons and three others, all from St. Louis, left Santa Fe on January 14 and reached the Missouri border about February 22. Their mules gave out when still some two hundred miles from their destination, and they were forced to walk the remainder of the distance through deep snow. Lt. James W. Abert of the topographical engineers arrived at Fort Leavenworth on March 1, following a difficult trip from Santa Fe by way of Bent's Fort. He had left the Bent's trading post on January 20 with two mule-drawn wagons and fourteen companions, all well armed. Four of the mules froze to death during a norther on February

*These villages would have been a few miles east of present-day Manhattan, Kansas.

1, and the rest were stolen by Indians (reportedly the ubiquitous Pawnees) on the sixth. Since the raid took place at their camp near Jackson's Grove, probably Comanches, not Pawnees, were responsible. Abert's companions found two "broken down" oxen left on the trail, and these they hitched to one of the wagons. With some of the men also in harness, they pulled this wagon (which was loaded with essential provisions, Abert's mineralogical specimens from New Mexico, and a sick man named Pilcher) some sixty-five miles along the Wet Route to the Pawnee Fork. At that point they left Pilcher with two other men to await the expected arrival of the mail express for Fort Leavenworth, and the rest pushed on. The express, in the person of James Brown, arrived and picked up the three left behind and ultimately overtook Abert and the others. But on February 19 they were all caught in a blizzard while camped on Turkey Creek, and eight of the mules belonging to the mail party froze to death. Pilcher too succumbed to the storm. He was taken to Cottonwood Crossing and buried. The survivors continued on with great difficulty, reaching Fort Leavenworth on March 1.[34]

Arriving at Independence on March 1 were H. Hoffman of Baltimore, Maryland, Henry C. Miller of Saline County, Missouri, a Mr. Harris, and one or two others, all of whom had left Santa Fe on January 13. They traveled the Bent's Fort route and brought with them the first news of the uprising at Taos, which had claimed the life of Charles Bent, the territorial governor. The party was forced to abandon their wagon east of Turkey Creek because of a blizzard, and they packed their remaining property and equipment on their mules. There were a few other such travelers who experienced similar difficulties and who finally reached their destinations during early March. But it appears that after March 10, the weather began to moderate as the spring equinox approached. By the latter part of April, the cold was gone and the grass sufficiently advanced that the first trade caravans of the year began their long trek across the trail. Now the concern would once again be the heat of summer and the danger of attack by Indians.[35]

3

Fort Mann: Its Genesis
and First Abandonment

The lack of adequate protection for the military supply trains
traveling the Santa Fe Trail, and the serious losses to the
government resulting from increasing attacks by Plains Indians, finally caused the military authorities to search for more
effective means of providing security. Fort Leavenworth,
built in 1827 near the trail's eastern terminus, and Fort
Marcy, the new fort constructed at Santa Fe in 1846 after the
conquest of New Mexico, were too far removed from the
dangerous middle stretches of the trail to provide meaningful
assistance to travelers. Moreover, there were no facilities to
repair any damage suffered by wagons between Council
Grove* and Las Vegas, New Mexico, on the original trail.
Only Bent's Fort afforded help along the trail to the mountains.[1]

In 1846 the government had appointed the famed mountain man and guide Thomas Fitzpatrick as agent for the tribes
of the upper Platte, upper Kansas, and upper Arkansas
rivers. This vast agency included the Cheyennes, Arapahoes,
Kiowas, Plains Apaches, northern bands of Comanches, and
southern bands of the Oglalla, Brulé, and Miniconjou Sioux.
In January 1847, while at his winter headquarters at Fort

---

*A blacksmith shop, but not a wheelwright shop, had been established at
Council Grove during late July 1846. Except for this limited facility, however,
Westport, Missouri, and Fort Leavenworth were the westernmost points at
which repairs were then available at the east end of the trail.

Leavenworth, Fitzpatrick wrote his annual report, recommending that forts be established at key points along both the Santa Fe and Oregon trails as the best means of protecting travelers. For the safety of the Santa Fe Trail, he recommended that an adobe fort be built at the Great Bend of the Arkansas. In 1848 Lt. Col. William Gilpin made a similar recommendation for the defense of the Santa Fe Trail and the trail to the mountains, suggesting six forts: one at the Pawnee Fork, one at the Middle Crossing, one at Pretty Encampment, one at the crossing of the Canadian, one at the junction of the Mora and Sapello rivers, and the sixth by purchase of Bent's Fort. In time the army followed their advice, at least in broad principle. Because of the hostility of Comanches, Kiowas, and Plains Apaches, Fitzpatrick had also suggested that the original trail be abandoned south from the Upper and Middle crossings, and thereafter to follow the Kearny route to Timpas Creek and south over Raton Pass — the "Mountain Branch" of later times. For the defense of that portion of the trail, he recommended that an adobe fort be built at the mouth of the Purgatoire. Because of the greater distance, travel time, and difficulty involved in any route through the mountains, however, this recommendation was not adopted.[2]

Even before the suggestions of Fitzpatrick and Gilpin were received or acted on, others took limited steps to deal with the problem. On February 16, 1847, Capt. William M. D. McKissack, assistant quartermaster at Santa Fe, wrote to Q. M. Gen. T. S. Jesup and suggested that a repair station be built approximately halfway between Fort Leavenworth and Santa Fe. The idea was evidently approved because during late March or early April, McKissack dispatched about forty teamsters headed by a master teamster, Capt. Daniel P. Mann, with instructions to construct such a station near the Middle Crossing. It was originally intended not as a combat military post but solely as a station where wagons could be repaired and where travelers and their animals might find safe haven in the heart of Plains Indian country. It was, McKissack later stated, the large number of wagons abandoned on the plains that prompted the decision to build the post.[3]

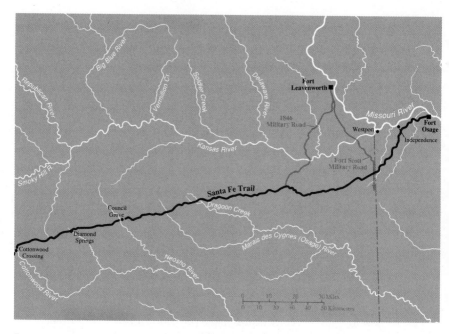

Route of the Santa Fe Trail in detail: Fort Osage–Independence to Cottonwood Crossing

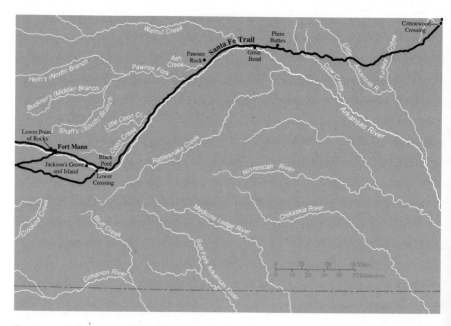

Cottonwood Crossing to Fort Mann

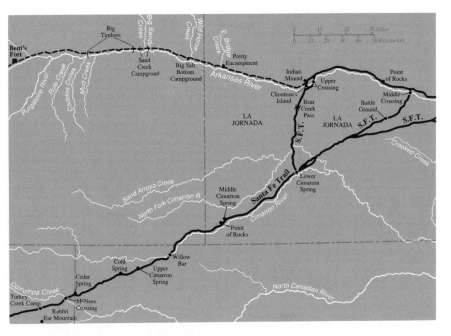

Fort Mann to McNees Crossing

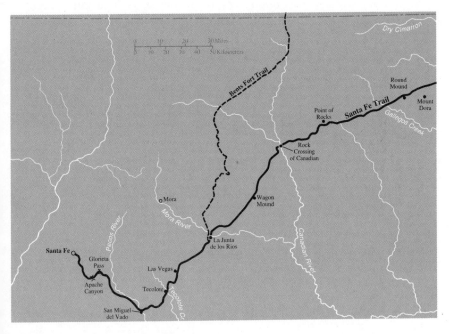

Rabbit Ear Mountain to Santa Fe

The site selected was about twenty-five miles below the
Middle Crossing, within sight of the Caches and near the
location where Captain Mann had been attacked on October
28 of the previous year. Whether the attack played any part in
Mann's decision is unknown, but it is possible that hard
experience convinced him it was a superior location. Being
close to the famous Caches and the lower Point of Rocks, it was
a well-known and readily identifiable site. The valley on the
north side of the river was somewhat broader than it was a few
miles farther east or west. To the north and east about ten
miles were the upper reaches of the Lower or Shaff's Branch of
the Pawnee Fork, known in later times as Saw Log Creek
because it provided the only reliable wood supply (mostly
cottonwoods and scrub trees) in the vicinity. Finally, it was
above the junction of the Wet and Dry routes and below the
principal crossings, which would require through traffic to
pass immediately by its gates. Any or all of these factors may
have influenced Mann in locating the post where he did and
other army officers in constructing the later Forts Atkinson
and Dodge in the same area. *4

The station the teamsters built was a rude affair constructed with adobe bricks and cottonwood logs cut on the
Arkansas River and Saw Log Creek. It originally consisted of
four log buildings (later expanded to eight) built in a square
and connected by log palisades or walls at the angles.
Loopholes for cannons and small arms were cut in these
connecting walls. The cabins had adobe chimneys and fire-
places and flat roofs made of small poles, laid parallel, with
"six inches of mud piled on," probably adobe, sod, or both.
The cabin walls were encased in "breastworks" of adobe
bricks to deflect arrows and keep out weather, those on the
northwest and southeast corners being the first completed.
Two large wooden puncheon gates, a foot thick, were installed

*Fort Atkinson was constructed in 1850 about three-quarters of a mile or a
mile to the west of the site of Fort Mann. Fort Dodge was built in 1864 about
seven or eight miles to the east, one mile west of the point where the Wet Route
and the Dry Route converged.

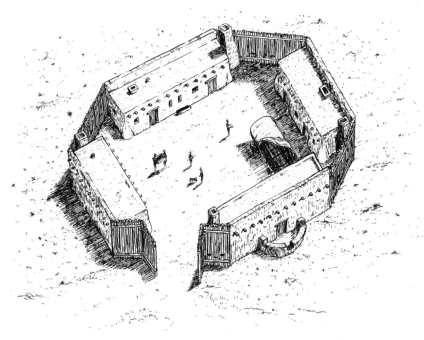

Fort Mann was constructed during the spring of 1847. The four initial buildings in the enclosure were eventually increased to eight. Originally built as a station to provide safe haven for travelers and their livestock, and repairs for their wagons, it was abandoned on June 22 because it was too hazardous and difficult to supply. The fort was reoccupied by the Indian Battalion on November 6, 1847, as a military post. On orders from Lt. Col. William Gilpin, the battalion repaired and enlarged the fort to accommodate its new garrison of two companies of infantry and one of artillery. It was again abandoned in October 1848.

by May 16. The inner courtyard or plaza was about sixty feet in diameter, and the outer walls were somewhere between ten and twenty feet in height.* Within the enclosure, the cabins

*Lewis Garrard said the walls were twenty feet high, but Thomas Fitzpatrick, who visited in early July 1847 while the fort was in a derelict state, said in his report of December 18 that the walls were only eight or ten feet high. See Louise Barry, *Beginning of the West*, 670.

provided storage rooms, a blacksmith shop, a wheelwright shop, and accommodations for the fort's inhabitants, never expected to be more than a small force of civilian employees and temporary guests.[5]

Construction of Fort Mann began in late March or early April 1847 and continued until June, at which time the breastworks were completed for the northwest and southeast cabins, and a large number of adobe bricks had been made to complete the rest. But the work was performed under extraordinarily difficult conditions, and this took a heavy psychological toll on the men. In late April, when the little post was hardly more than piles of logs and stacks of supplies and equipment, a small party of traders returning from Santa Fe was attacked by ninety Comanches approximately nine miles to the east. The raiders made off with ten animals and forced the travelers back to the construction site. The party included Lt. William G. Peck, of the topographical engineers, with a small wagon train owned by "Messrs. Sanford and Woods," and John McKnight, a trader returning from Chihuahua with his own small train. These two parties had met while traveling across the Jornada between the Cimarron and the Arkansas and had joined for safety. After the attack, they set up their camp adjacent to the fort, but the next day the Comanches struck again. This time they ran off all remaining livestock, some thirty-nine horses and mules, owned for the most part by Sanford and Woods. Fortunately for the traders, a party from California, headed by Kit Carson, Lt. Edward F. Beale, U.S.N., and Theodore Talbot (recently a lieutenant and adjutant in Frémont's California Battalion), arrived that evening. The three carried dispatches and letters for delivery to Washington, D.C., and had left California with an escort during early March. They had reached Santa Fe in April and left again about April 19, bound for Missouri by way of the Bent's Fort route. Their party reached Fort Mann only hours after the second Comanche attack, and their extra livestock made it possible for the Sanford and Woods and the McKnight trains to continue their journey. The three groups joined for the remainder of their trip to provide greater security but were once again attacked at the Great Bend of the Arkansas by a band of raiders believed to be Pawnees.* This time they lost only two horses.[6]

The days following the departure of the combined Peck, McKnight, and Carson-Beale-Talbot parties saw feverish activity in an effort to complete the cabins and connecting walls of the little installation on the Arkansas. The pace of construction was critical because the post was almost constantly surrounded and in effect under siege by large bands of hostile Comanches and Arapahoes roving the area. On May 9 Comanches killed and scalped one of the teamsters building the post. The man was fishing in the river, and his death occurred as his comrades looked on from within the stockade. Two days later the Indians struck again, this time stampeding and driving off fifteen oxen and forty mules grazing nearby. Progress in construction slowed as panic stalked the teamster camp. Men were afraid to venture far beyond the immediate precincts to cut wood for building materials or for fuel. Even trips to the river to get water or to find clay and mud to make adobe bricks were filled with hazard.[7]

While the teamsters, under the leadership of Captain Mann, struggled to build their post, another party prepared to leave from Bent's Fort bound for Fort Leavenworth. Capt. A. W. Enos, a Missouri Volunteer serving with the army's quartermaster department, left during early May, taking with him about twenty empty government wagons, a six-pounder cannon, and a motley crew of "wagonmasters, teamsters and amateurs." Included as "amateurs" were Lewis H. Garrard and T. B. Drinker, both in the West for their own pleasure. Also included were the British adventurer George F. Ruxton and two companions. The trip of the Enos train was beset with ill fortune — many of the teamsters were sick with scurvy, and seven died during the journey. When the caravan moved eastward to the Purgatoire, the first camp beyond Bent's Fort,

---

*This raiding party was probably made up of Comanches or Arapahoes, both of whom were very active in attacking trains in this area during the spring and summer of 1847.

it was joined by a party consisting of Marion Wise, J. C. Davis, Thomas E. Brackenridge, Joseph Steppe, and Aaron Hamilton, former members of Frémont's third expedition and lately with Kit Carson's escort from California. On May 4 they passed the site of the Cheyenne village that Garrard had visited the previous winter, apparently in the Big Timbers. They camped at Big Sandy Creek on the fifth and in the Big Salt Bottom, just above the mouth of Wild Horse Creek, on the sixth. Early on the evening of the seventh they stopped at the campground known to travelers as Pretty Encampment.* About a half mile above it they passed a Cheyenne village, in which they found the mountain man John S. Smith, his Cheyenne wife, and their two children. That same day Captain Enos engaged the services of Smith to serve as "commander" of Fort Mann when Daniel Mann and the teamster construction crew moved on. Enos and his men left the following morning; with them went Smith, his family, their lodge, and seven mules and horses.[8]

The journey beyond Pretty Encampment was grim, with three teamsters dying of scurvy before they reached the Middle Crossing. A terrible heat descended on the land, the ground became cracked and parched, and even the water in the broad shallow river was no more than knee deep and lukewarm. The herds of buffalo were wary, and the best efforts at hunting them were seldom successful. The men felt as if they were crossing an endless desert, and at times their throats were so dry they could hardly speak. Even before reaching the Santa Fe Trail's Upper Crossing, the wagonmasters made certain that no one lagged behind and that hunting parties did not roam far, for now they had entered the territory of the dreaded Comanches. Finally they passed the Middle

*Pretty Encampment was a noted camping ground along the trail to Bent's Fort (eventually the Mountain Branch of the Santa Fe Trail) located in present Hamilton County, Kansas, probably at the mouth of East Bridge Creek. See Louise Barry, *Beginning of the West*, 688; Lewis H. Garrard, *Wah-to-Yah*, 28, 249–51; George Bird Grinnell, "Bent's Old Fort and Its Builders," *KHC* 15:91 and map; George Frederick Ruxton, *Ruxton of the Rockies*, 272–74.

Crossing, and at noon on May 15 they reached Fort Mann. Within its walls they found Captain Mann and his little band huddled anxiously, fearful of moving more than a few hundred yards beyond its walls. The beleaguered garrison greeted Enos and the other newcomers with cheers, clearly impatient to escape their "prairie prison." So many wanted to leave that only by raising their pay half again (a ten-dollar increase, to thirty dollars per month) could eight of the original construction crew be induced to stay. They were joined by Smith, as the new commander, and Garrard, who wanted to remain at this remote place out of a sense of adventure, having never been in an Indian fight. For the present, the garrison of the post would be ten brave men, Smith's wife and two children, the wife of another man, three men so sick with scurvy they were unable to continue with the train, plus the six-pounder cannon, ten serviceable horses and mules, three broken-down horses, five decrepit steers, and an old dog. Captains Enos and Mann, the members of the original train (less Smith and Garrard), and apparently thirty-one from the fort's first garrison left on May 16, bound for Fort Leavenworth. They completed their journey without further encounters with Indians.[9]

The departure of the others must have created a deep sense of foreboding in those remaining. There were no white military facilities closer than Santa Fe to the west and Fort Leavenworth to the east. Should the Indians launch a determined effort to overwhelm the post, there would clearly be no help from any source. With that truth hanging over them, the ten men set about organizing their own defense. First, Smith established the night watch, with the men assigned to it in teams of two. There were to be five watches of two hours each, lasting from twilight to dawn. During the day two men were assigned as full-time sentries and did nothing else. One man served as cook, while the others devoted themselves to continuing the construction of the fort, building chimneys and encasing the crude log buildings with adobe bricks. On May 20 a trader named Callahan, eastbound for the States with a small train, passed the fort. Smith, who as commander had authority to hire additional men, somehow persuaded one young fellow from the train to stay with them. During the afternoon of May 23 another train appeared on the horizon and finally went into camp above the Caches. The following morning it continued eastward, stopping opposite the fort so the men could visit. The train, belonging to Bent, St. Vrain and Co. and under the command of Frank DeLisle, included an Indian trader named William Tharp and his wagons. Tharp and his men had joined the Bent train for security during the trip.[10]

John Smith, the new commander of Fort Mann, was showing signs of considerable nervousness at being confined with his family and animals in such an ill-prepared, ill-defended post at such a dangerous place along the trail. He confided to Garrard his belief that it was folly and madness to stay there at the mercy of the Indians and that his pay was nothing compared with the prospects for loss of life and property. Now, with the train offering a means of escape from his dilemma, he resigned his position and prepared to leave. He quickly collected his possessions and turned command of the post over to Thomas Sloan. When the train departed a short time later, Smith, his family, and his livestock left with it.[11]

The morning of May 26 brought other guests, this time unwelcome ones. As the garrison took its ease, the sentry suddenly cried out: "Indians! Indians!" The men ran the cannon to the gates and prepared for action. Beyond, eight or ten mounted warriors attempted to stampede the picketed horses and mules belonging to the post, another party dashed toward the fort, and yet others advanced from the river. At first it seemed there would be a serious fight. But as the Indians drew near, the men assigned as the crew for the six-pounder fell back before firing, and the cannon was easily seen by the charging warriors. They turned sharply, anxious to be out of range of this powerful weapon. When another attempt by a single warrior to stampede the livestock was unsuccessful, an older Indian dismounted and indicated a wish to parley. The raiders were Arapahoes, and though they had clearly come with hostile intent deterred only by the cannon, they now professed friendship. The Comanches, they said, were en-

On May 27, 1847, one of the ten-man garrison left Fort Mann to stalk a buffalo that had appeared on a hill north of the post. After killing it, he returned for a horse with which to pack the meat, but on his return to the carcass he was suddenly attacked by three Comanche warriors. They chased him nearly to the walls of the stockade, and he barely escaped with his scalp.

camped in great numbers on a small stream a day's ride to the east and had intended to take the fort but were dissuaded by the Arapaho chiefs. After receiving a few gifts of coffee, bread, and tobacco, the party left.[12]

On May 27 the garrison was again reminded of its precarious position. During the day a buffalo suddenly appeared on the crest of the hill to the north of the post, moving southward against the wind. The great beasts seldom traveled into the wind unless there was trouble, and since there was water in the buffalo wallows and small streams on the high plains from a recent rain, it was unlikely that any would come to the river to drink. It was a sure sign of the presence of Indians. Heedless of danger, one of the men left the safety of the fort and stalked the animal, finally killing it. He returned for a horse to get the meat and had scarcely reached the carcass when those watching saw him turn his mount and head for the

post at a dead run. Hard on his trail were three yelling
Comanches brandishing their lances. Fortunately, he reached
the safety of the stockade just in time to avoid losing his
scalp.[13]

The Indian difficulties at Fort Mann had only begun.
During the morning of May 28, as the men were laboring on
the adobe walls intended to encase the cabins, the sentry
caught sight of a large band of mounted warriors approaching
from the east. Work was stopped, the gate was shut, and
weapons were prepared. Two of the Indians rode up to the
wall, seeking entry. This was denied, as was their request for
whiskey. They were Arapahoes from the band of Warratoria, a
chief usually noted for his peaceable and friendly disposition
toward whites. The two rode away, unhappy at the result of
their conference, but soon the whole band appeared — wom-
en, children, horses, and dogs — and made camp about three
hundred yards above the fort along the banks of the Arkansas.
There were eighty lodges, some three hundred inhabitants,
and eleven hundred horses. The camp routine was quickly
established, but within an hour or so a commotion arose. A
young Arapaho captured by a wagon train during an attack
two days earlier had been released and had caught up with
his village. These Arapahoes had been in league with the
Comanches in attacking trains along the trail between the
Walnut Creek crossing and Fort Mann and were now apprehensive about the approach of the traders' caravan they had
been harassing for the past three days. The Indians promptly
struck their lodges and moved upstream to a new site a half
mile above the fort.[14]

At midday a government train eastbound from Santa Fe,
under the command of Captain Fowler, came into sight and
corralled next to the post, a few steps from the gates. Thomas
Sloan, now commanding at Fort Mann, managed to persuade
one of the men in Fowler's company to join the garrison,
bringing their strength to eleven able-bodied men. Later in
the day Alexander Barclay arrived with wagons from Bent's
Fort and joined the government train. At 3:00 P.M. a trading
caravan bound for Santa Fe arrived and went into camp.

Included in the trading party were James C. Bean, Thomas G. Clarkson, and Mr. Reynolds from Jackson County, Missouri, Dr. G. W. Hereford of St. Louis, and the wagons of McCauly and Shaw of St. Louis and Bullard, Hooke and Co. of Lexington, Missouri—thirty men in all. Their train had been under attack by the Comanches and Arapahoes during the previous three days, with the attack beginning at Pawnee Fork Crossing, where the Indians attempted to steal their live-stock. At Coon Creek they awakened in the morning to find themselves surrounded by about seven hundred Comanches and Arapahoes preparing to attack. They withstood the assault but lost fifty-one oxen. Thereafter they were under attack every day until they crossed the Arkansas. Finding the Arapaho village so close at hand angered the traders and teamsters, and a fight was avoided only with difficulty. The following morning (May 29) both trains left, the traders headed for Santa Fe and the government train for Fort Leaven-worth. Captain Fowler and his men took the three sick men who had been unable to leave with Captain Enos, although their prospects for reaching the States alive seemed slim.[15]

Toward noon on Sunday, May 30, yet another eastbound party arrived. It proved to be Ceran St. Vrain, George Bent, and a number of others who were on their way from Santa Fe to St. Louis via Westport. They had one wagon and twenty-five horses and mules "in prime order." Their party passed the Arapaho village and the fort at a brisk trot, going into camp three hundred yards to the east. They originally feared the Arapaho camp was a Comanche village, and took refuge on an island in the Arkansas for two hours before deciding to chance passing it. Although St. Vrain tried to persuade Lewis Garrard to leave with them, he stubbornly refused, and St. Vrain and the others left the following morning.[16]

The days following the departure of the St. Vrain party were alternately filled with work and construction, the mak-ing of adobe bricks, and idle boredom as rainy weather descended across the plains. When the rain let up, work resumed, only to be once again interrupted by rain. On or about June 11 a small eastbound wagon train owned by a trader named Coolidge arrived at the fort with four large, heavily laden wagons and five men. Because of the known danger along the trail ahead, Coolidge and his party decided to wait at the little fort pending the arrival of other, stronger trains. They hoped to attach themselves to one of these before attempting passage of the "Coon Creeks" area, where Comanche war parties were causing serious trouble. That same day the garrison made 326 adobe bricks. The next day, June 12, was dry and hot, and they made another 210 adobes, then dug a drainage ditch to carry off accumulated rain water. Three men from the fort and one of Coolidge's men hunted for buffalo during the day; when they had not returned by dark, those remaining became apprehensive over their safety. Finally they arrived late at night, much worn following an exhausting and harrowing chase by sixteen Comanches. Because of incessant rain, there was no work on the thirteenth and fourteenth, and June fifteenth started the same way. It was Lewis Garrard's birthday and gave promise of being a drab and lonely one. But in the afternoon the clouds broke, and the day became warm and sunshiny. Some of the men took a swim in the Arkansas under the watchful eye of sentries on the riverbank and the roof of the fort. Then, in mid-afternoon, another eastbound train appeared on the horizon and went into camp near the Caches.[17]

Contact was quickly made with the new arrivals. This party included a returning government train of twenty-five wagons led by Mr. Bell, plus Col. William H. Russell of Callaway County, Missouri, with one wagon and a fifteen-man mounted guard from the California Battalion under the command of Second Lieutenant Brown. Russell was the secretary of state for California under Frémont and was bearing dispatches for Washington. He also turned out to be an old friend and college classmate of Lewis Garrard's father. In a short time he convinced the youthful Garrard of the folly of remaining in such a weak and ineffective post, manned by only ten other men and in the range of the fierce Comanches. Through Russell's persuasive efforts, Sloan gave Garrard his discharge, and the young man settled his accounts and gathered his belongings. When the Bell-Russell party departed on June 16, he left with it. Unfortunately, further encounters with the Comanches awaited Garrard and the others before they reached the Great Bend of the Arkansas.[18]

While the Bell-Russell train made its precarious way eastward, the ten men remaining at Fort Mann faced a crisis of their own. On Saturday, June 19, an estimated four hundred Comanches, attacked the post, beginning a series of intermittent forays lasting until June 21. Three of the garrison were killed and scalped within three hundred yards of the gate when they left the confines of the walls, presumably to obtain wood or water or to hunt for meat. The remaining seven saved themselves by the effective use of the six-pounder cannon, with which they managed to kill fifteen and wound thirty or forty of the enemy. But their position was now so tenuous and the danger of being overwhelmed by another attack so great that they decided to abandon the fort at their first opportunity. That presented itself on June 21 with the arrival of two large government trains en route to Santa Fe. Sloan and his men made their arrangements, then destroyed most of the contents of value, throwing many of the stores into the well. They rigged up two teams from their remaining livestock, placed the cannon in front, and joined the trains when they left on the morning of June 22. On June 26 Solomon Houck and his party of traders, eastbound for Missouri, passed the garrison and the government trains somewhere in the Jornada, bound for Santa Fe. Fort Mann—small, incomplete, and ineffective—was now derelict, at the mercy of the Indians, the elements, or whatever other forces might appear to determine its fate.[19]

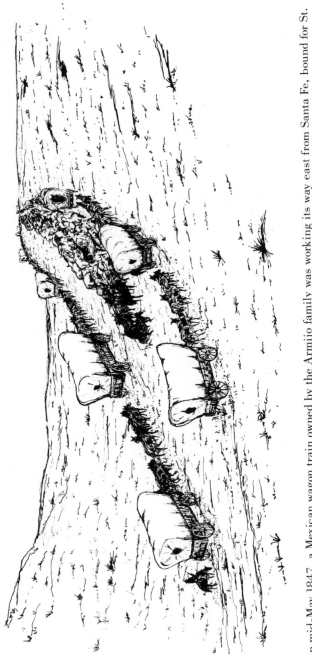

In mid-May 1847, a Mexican wagon train owned by the Armijo family was working its way east from Santa Fe, bound for St. Louis. There were eighteen wagons pulled by mule teams, about fifty-four men, and a large remuda of horses and mules. By May 12 they were approaching the crossing of the Pawnee Fork, unaware of the danger that lay ahead.

4

The Death of Red Sleeve

During mid-May 1847, while the garrison at Fort Mann still struggled to survive amid large bands of Comanches and Arapahoes, both of whom were harassing traffic along the trail, a mixed war party of Comanches and Kiowas was encamped on the lower reaches of the Pawnee Fork. There were about one hundred Comanches under the leadership of a war chief named Ikanosa ("Red Sleeve," or "Red Arm") and perhaps nearly as many Kiowas with their leader Setangya ("Sitting Bear"), commonly known to whites as Satank. Satank was a prominent war chief and headman of the Kaitsenko, a select body of ten of the bravest warriors holding the highest order in the Kiowa military society. The combined war party planned to proceed east to the mouth of the Pawnee, then north and east along the Arkansas to Walnut Creek and beyond in search of enemies. They hoped to find Pawnee raiders who might have come south from their villages along the Platte and the Loup Fork to steal horses from the southern Plains tribes or to raid whites along the trail. The Pawnees were traditional enemies of nearly all Plains Indians; whenever they went south of the Platte and were discovered, a bloody fight ensued.[1]

At dawn on Wednesday, May 12, the Comanche-Kiowa war party filed out of camp and moved east along the Pawnee Fork. As it did, another party stirred itself into action along the banks of the Arkansas River some twelve or thirteen miles southwest of the place where the Wet Route of the Santa Fe Trail crossed the Pawnee. A wagon train of Mexican traders in the employ of the Armijo family was eastbound for St. Louis with eighteen wagons pulled by mule teams, about fifty-four men, and a large number of horses and mules. Accompanying them were fourteen former Missouri Volunteers who had served with the Army of the West and had recently been discharged because of poor health. These men, who were carrying mail from Santa Fe, had left in separate parties, the last departing on April 21. Each overtook the trading party, joining it for safety while traveling through Indian country. The Mexicans had various commodities for trade in the States but, more important, were taking with them nearly sixty-five thousand dollars in specie for use in purchasing merchandise to resell in New Mexico. They proceeded east along the Santa Fe Trail, apparently without any serious problems, and probably camped at or near Plain Encampment, about four or five miles southwest of the crossing of Coon Creek (the next major camping ground southwest of the Pawnee), on the evening of May 11.[2]

It was approximately twelve miles from Coon Creek Crossing to the Pawnee Fork. With mule teams, the Mexican train could move faster than the lumbering ox trains commonly used by American traders, and they likely reached the Pawnee after traveling only three or four hours. The Comanche-Kiowa war party, with their tough, fleet horses, would have made much faster time and doubtless arrived near the crossing of the Pawnee before noon. It was a clear, hot day, and the prevailing south breeze was gathering force as they arrived on the high ground overlooking the north bank of the stream. The wolves (scouts) had soon assured themselves there were no Pawnee raiders in the vicinity, and the leaders made plans to move northeast along the Arkansas in search of their foe after a brief stop to eat and graze their horses. Then in the distance, along the southern horizon close to the line of the Arkansas, appeared the minute outlines of the traders' wagons, the white covers brightly reflecting the noonday sun. If there were no Pawnees to kill, no Pawnee scalps to take,

Ikanosa thought the next-best thing would be to capture the large herd of mules and horses accompanying the approaching train. And so they watched in silence from the top of their ridge as the long, strung-out line of wagons slowly drew closer.[3]

The men with the Armijo train saw no indication of imminent danger as they neared the Pawnee, although Indian signs were abundant along the Arkansas and they had heard stories and warnings from a number of west-bound trains that had suffered Comanche and Arapahoe raids or attacks at Walnut Creek Crossing and beyond. So they continued steadily northeasterly along the trail, unaware of the war party observing them. The Indians, remaining well away from the crest of the hill to avoid revealing their presence until the train reached the crossing, watched the approach of the wagons and livestock of these alien intruders in their land with keen interest. Then Ikanosa turned to Satank, who was next to him, and proposed an attack on the train to take its valuables, particularly the horses and mules. Satank promptly refused. The whites, he said, were friends of the Kiowas. The tribe had signed a solemn treaty in 1837, promising peace and friendship with the United States, a treaty they had kept with the Americans north of the Pe p'a edal (Red River).* Ikanosa laughed scornfully, calling the Kiowas fools and cowards. The Comanches, he said, were great warriors and raiders, and they would fight and take what they wanted. He invited the Kiowas to watch and see how brave his men were. Satank, stung by the taunts and insults of the Comanche chief, quietly indicated that the Kiowas would watch.[4]

Ikanosa turned his back on the Kiowas and, riding to the front of his Comanches, made medicine and donned his great warbonnet with its long trailer of eagle feathers that cascaded down his back. Then they boldly rode up to the crest of the

---

*After the annexation of Texas, neither Comanches nor Kiowas equated Texans with Americans, and both tribes had difficulty in understanding the outrage of the United States for raids and attacks made on Texans and their property.

ridge. As they reached it, they were silhouetted against the horizon in a long line, one hundred strong and clearly visible to those in the valley beyond. For a moment they halted and stood motionless, their war lances held threateningly toward the sky and their fierce, painted faces arrogantly mocking the oncoming whites. The south breeze caused the feathers on their lances to flutter, as if warning of impending battle. Below, men in the small advance party from the train stopped in their tracks as the long line of Comanche warriors suddenly appeared on the hill to the west of the trail and north of the Pawnee. Then they turned, shouted the alarm, and galloped back to the wagons. With a hurried cry from the wagonmaster, the men circled their wagons into a hollow square, the flankers and other horsemen entered within, and all prepared themselves for a hard fight. Above, Red Sleeve raised his arm, brought it down with a flourish, and the line of warriors, each shouting his war cry, swept down the hill, crossed the Pawnee, and began to circle the traders. At first they kept a safe distance from the train, hoping to draw an ineffectual fire and deplete the ammunition of their quarry. But gradually they tightened the ring around the wagons.[5]

The men of the Armijo train and the accompanying Missourians watched warily as the Comanches galloped down the hill and began to circle them. Though in a distant land and far from help, both the Mexican traders and the former soldiers were experienced fighters and marksmen, and they knew how to defend themselves. For the moment they withheld their fire, awaiting the right opportunity for an effective volley. On the large hill to the north, Satank and his Kiowas were now visible, strung out along the ridge and watching impassively from their horses as the action unfolded below them. Then a few of the Comanche warriors began to make short dashes toward the wagons, turning abruptly and moving quickly back out of range. Still the men inside the circled train held their fire.[6]

As the sun approached its zenith and the land warmed under its rays, events at the crossing of the Pawnee took a dramatic turn. The Comanches suddenly wheeled their horses

At a signal from Ikanosa ("Red Sleeve"), a war chief of the Yamparika Comanches, his men swept down the hill north of the Pawnee Fork, crossed the stream, and began to circle the Armijo train. From the crest of the hill, Satank and his Kiowas watched the action unfolding below.

and made a dash directly at the train. With their approach, a volley of rifle fire rang out, then another. Men stiffened in their saddles as balls from the traders' rifles hit them, and terrified horses screamed in agony as they too were struck. The line of charging Indians wavered, then broke. In their center the action was reaching its climax. The first to be hit was their leader, Ikanosa, Red Sleeve. A ball struck his thigh, passed through it, and smashed into the spine of his horse. Down went horse and rider, with the body of the dying animal coming to rest on top of one of Red Sleeve's legs, pinning him to the ground. His followers broke off their charge and retreated across the Pawnee and up the hill from where they had begun their attack. They took with them their other wounded, but Red Sleeve was too close to the enemy to be rescued safely. The dead horse that held him fast could not be moved without sacrificing the lives of others, so he was left to the mercy of bitter foes. The charge was not without profit, however, for while the whites were occupied with their defense, a few of the Comanche raiders stampeded the remuda of horses and mules away from the train and the valley of the Arkansas. [7]

When he saw his warriors returning across the Pawnee and realized his plight, Red Sleeve shouted to Satank for help. But Satank, who had remained with his warriors on the hill throughout the fight, was in no mood to do so. The stinging insults of Red Sleeve still rang in the ears of Satank and his Kiowas. The Comanche had called them cowards for not wanting to attack the white train and told them to watch his brave warriors do what the Kiowas feared to do. They had, and now they would watch to see how bravely a Comanche war chief died. Red Sleeve squirmed and twisted, trying to free himself, but he could not. When the men of the Armijo train were certain the raiders had gone, not to return, several ran out to kill the trapped chief. Seeing them coming, Red Sleeve redoubled his efforts to escape, at the same time bawling out to Satank to save him. But there was to be no help. When the New Mexicans reached him, several shots rang out, and the great Red Sleeve, Ikanosa, war chief of the Yamparika

Comanches, died an inglorious death pinned beneath a horse.
They left him where he lay.[8]

On the hill above, Satank and his men wheeled their
horses and returned to their camp. The accompanying Comanches could make no complaint and rode in silence. Red
Sleeve himself had told the Kiowas to watch, and his own men
had done nothing to save him. Though Satank's lean face with
its scraggly mustache* probably remained impassive, his
inner countenance no doubt bore an ironic smile.[9]

After the Indians left the area of the fight, the teamsters
regrouped themselves and counted their losses. None of the
men were hit, but they had lost 105 horses and mules, 100 of
which belonged to Emanuel Armijo. Other than that they were
intact. Their train probably completed the crossing of the
Pawnee, then went into camp on the north side of the stream to
rest and graze their animals. No more Indian attacks occurred during the remainder of their journey, and the men
reached St. Louis on May 28, having taken a riverboat from
Independence.[10]

The remains of Red Sleeve and his horse lay moldering
near the banks of the Pawnee Fork for some days, the bones
occasionally gnawed by wolves, coyotes, and other scaven-
gers, bleached by the sun, and parched by the dry south
winds that swept across the arid plains. Men from passing
wagon trains doubtless noticed and wondered about them.
Finally, on June 22, an eastbound party of some eighty-five
men reached and made camp on the right, or south, bank of
the Pawnee. It included the government train of twenty-five
ox-drawn wagons under Mr. Bell, the fur trader Coolidge with
four loaded wagons, and Col. William H. Russell's mounted
party of sixteen or seventeen men and one wagon, accom-

---

*During the winter of 1846–47, the Kiowa band to which Satank belonged
encamped for the winter on Elk Creek, a tributary of the north fork of the Red
River. While there, a band of Pawnees came on foot to steal horses. The Kiowas
pursued them northward, overtook them on the Washita, and recovered their
horses in a fight in which one Pawnee was killed. In this action Satank was hit
in the upper lip by a Pawnee arrow, which left a scar that he covered by growing
a full mustache, albeit a scraggly one.

panied by Lewis H. Garrard. The stream was in flood
because of heavy rains upstream, and it was not possible to
cross until the turbulent waters subsided. As they explored
the area around their new campsite, some of the men,
including young Garrard, came upon the body of an Indian.
Garrard later wrote, "the sinews, well gnawed by the wolves,
were not yet dry, and the skin and hair still graced the head."
The head was passed from hand to hand by curious teamsters
and freighters until, tiring of this diversion, one of them
tossed it into the churning waters of the Pawnee Fork.* Thus
did an inglorious death become an inglorious end.[11]

After the spring of 1847 the Pawnee Fork, which was
originally known to the Kiowas and other tribes of the southern plains as "Dark-timber River," was commonly known to
them as "Red Sleeve's River" or "Red Arm's River." Sto-
rytellers among the Comanches, Kiowas, Plains Apaches,
Cheyennes, and Arapahoes recounted the tale whenever they
camped along the banks of the little stream, and the Kiowas
recorded it in their calendar history. It marked a year in
which a great war chief, filled with pride and arrogance, had
died a coward.[12]†

---

*Although no one identified the body of the dead Indian as that of Red
Sleeve, this was the only death of a warrior, left behind by his party, recorded
during the spring or early summer of 1847.

†George Bent claimed that Red Sleeve was killed by either John S. Smith
or Thomas Murphy while accompanying the eastbound Bent, St. Vrain and Co.
train during the summer of 1847—both men apparently claimed the honor.
There is no evidence that the Bent train suffered any attacks before its arrival
at Walnut Creek on May 27, at which time the trader William Tharp was
killed. The attack on the Mexican train, in which the Comanche war chief was
killed, occurred on May 12 while John Smith remained in command at Fort
Mann. The Bent train departed Fort Mann on May 24, with John Smith
accompanying it, and likely passed the remains of the slain Red Sleeve while
approaching Pawnee Fork. The story evidently evovled thereafter. George E.
Hyde, *Life of George Bent*, 265.

5

A Hazardous Trip

From the beginning of a trip to its end, during at least the first fifty years of its existence, those traveling the Santa Fe Trail faced the prospect of great danger to themselves, their livestock, their wagons, and their property. They might freeze in a winter blizzard, perish from sunstroke or thirst in the summer, die from the venom of a rattlesnake bite or under the hoofs of a stampeding herd of bison, succumb to illness for want of medical treatment, or meet an untimely end from any number of other causes. But the death they feared most was at the hands of the fierce warriors of the plains.

From the time they first encountered horse Indians until the tragic end of the Indian wars, most European whites who came west considered them nothing less than barbarous marauders and murderers, lusting for blood and booty, descending without provocation on innocent white caravans or settlements. Seen from the perspective of the Indians, however, it was quite a different matter. It was *their* country the whites had entered uninvited, taking what was found of value, wantonly killing game, destroying what was not needed, and making little effort to befriend or respect the natives, their culture, or their rights. Faced with this invasion, the Indians did what all brave people have done throughout human history—they fought back courageously, ferociously, and well. And on the southern plains, the first Americans they struck were those traveling the road to Santa Fe.

When the war with Mexico began, there was a serious shortage of experienced teamsters to take the long wagon trains of supplies westward in support of the army. As a result, many of these trains had no competent or knowledgeable persons to guide them through the areas of greatest danger, and most of the men had neither the weapons nor the know-how to use them in their own defense if attacked. Stories, usually exaggerated and often untrue, filtered back across the trail to fill the minds of apprehensive young men with an unnecessary dread of any Indian raiders they might encounter. Faced with a determined defense, most Indians were reluctant to expose themselves needlessly to the terrible danger of the white man's firearms. But the inexperienced and terrified teamsters now manning the trains frequently gave Indian raiders new opportunities, ones not to be found with the wagons of longtime traders. The result was that, except for attempted theft of livestock, few large trading caravans suffered direct attacks, but nearly all of the government trains did. There were many such incidents reported, but none more vividly than the attacks on the train that the eighteen-year-old Lewis H. Garrard accompanied en route home after his service at Fort Mann.

On the afternoon of June 16, 1847, Garrard left the little outpost on the Arkansas in the company of Col. William H. Russell, Frémont's secretary of state for California, and his fifteen-man guard from the California Battalion, commanded by the nineteen-year-old Second Lieutenant Brown. Russell carried dispatches to Washington from Commodore Robert Stockton. He and his men had one wagon in which to carry their clothing, supplies, and equipment and were mounted on horses and mules. Also leaving with them were the twenty-five wagons of the government train under Mr. Bell, the wagonmaster, along with Mr. Coolidge, his five men, and his four large wagons filled with robes and hides. The wagons of the government train and those of Mr. Coolidge were pulled by oxen, that of Colonel Russell by mules. In all there were eighty-five men and thirty wagons. On the night of June 15, the Russell-Bell train had camped near the Caches, a half mile or so west of the fort. Because of a late start on the sixteenth, following a lengthy visit with those at the fort, the train continued only another three miles east before going into camp along the banks of the Arkansas.[1]*

They were a colorful crew. Colonel Russell wore buckskin trousers of the California style, split to the knee, with a light summer jacket, a white wool hat, and yellow California-style riding boots. Lieutenant Brown was clothed in the garb of an Apache Indian, and doubtless most of his men were attired in a similarly unconventional manner. Garrard himself wore buckskins and an old wool hat, making him look the part of a plainsman and Indian trader. The most "civilized" clothing was probably that of the teamsters from the government train, but they were a rough-looking lot, and green to the duties they now performed.[2]

When dawn broke across the plains on the morning of June 17, the men of the Russell-Bell train rose early, breakfasted, and commenced their eastward trek. Their ox-drawn wagons moved slowly, averaging only about eleven and one-half miles per day en route to the Pawnee Fork, although this varied daily because of changes in terrain, location of good campgrounds, Indian attacks (or the anticipation of such), and other similar factors. They followed the Wet Route, which stayed in or near the valley of the Arkansas nearly the entire distance to the point it rejoined with the Dry Route south of the Pawnee Fork. Although the Wet Route was about five miles longer, there was better grass and it kept the livestock near the life-giving waters of the Arkansas the entire distance, an important consideration with the heat of summer coming and the grasses of the high plains shriveling for want of rain. The river itself had a broad sandy bed, but the water in it was shallow and braided into small rivulets, which carved out a number of sandy islands. Though some scrub brush grew on a few of the better-defined islands, there were almost no trees, except for an occasional cottonwood that had somehow escaped the

*This camp would have been located approximately on the townsite of the later Dodge City, Kansas.

wildfires that periodically swept across the plains. There was, however, one notable large stand of cottonwoods on an island and along the south bank near the south bend of the river. This was "Jackson's Grove," famous as the location of the 1843 confrontation between the dragoons of Capt. Philip St. George Cooke and Texas freebooters under Jacob Snively. It provided firewood as well as relief from monotony and was therefore a favorite place near which to camp. This was probably the evening camping destination for Russell and the others, since it was only about eleven or twelve miles beyond their previous encampment.[3]

When they resumed their journey on the morning of the seventeenth, the wagons were placed in double file, and the remuda of horses and mules and the ox herd were driven between. In the event of Indian attack, this made it possible to circle or corral the wagons more rapidly than if they were strung out in a single column, and it protected the animals from easy reach by raiders. In this formation the men proceeded eastward, with the river to their right and, beyond, the range of sand hills that paralleled the opposite bank. In front of them lay the broad valley of the Arkansas, broken occasionally by the dry bed of some small intermittent stream that fed into it and more frequently by the deep paths incised into the earth by the great herds of bison coming to the river to drink or to cross to the other bank. On the left the valley floor gradually rose until it merged into the seemingly unending expanse of the high plains. The turquoise-green of the shortgrasses of the plains in spring had changed to the bleached brown that would remain until the following spring. Here and there small herds of bison or antelope moved to and fro in dark clumps dotting the plains. It was a strange and beautiful wilderness, untouched by the hand of man, free of his litter and debris, as the Creator had made it. They were passing through a world different from anything the men had known in their eastern homes. The more thoughtful among them must have been awestruck by the immensity surrounding them and probably pondered their own puny condition.[4]

The caravan stopped for a noon meal somewhere along the

Late in the afternoon of June 17, 1847, a scouting party from the eastbound Russell-Bell-Coolidge train spotted a large number of dark, moving objects on a rise about a mile ahead. Col. William Russell, Lieutenant Brown, Lewis Garrard, and two others rode to within a quarter of a mile of what turned out to be approximately four hundred mounted Comanche warriors, painted for war.

trail, then continued. A small party of mounted men rode about a quarter of a mile in advance (as was customary), scouting the trail ahead for signs of an Indian raiding party and looking for a suitable evening campsite. Late in the afternoon, when the sun was beginning its downward slide, the scouting party reached the crest of a small hill and abruptly stopped. Ahead of them, directly on the trail at the opposite rise perhaps a mile ahead, were a large number of dark, moving objects. At first the men were uncertain whether the objects were buffalo, antelope, or some other form of wildlife. Then a man named Barton, keener-eyed than the others, blurted out one word, "Injuns!" Colonel Russell, leading the party of eight or ten men, wanted a closer look to verify that the distant shapes really were Indians. He put spurs to his large, brown California mule and led his men directly toward the moving objects. It was soon apparent they were looking at a band of mounted Indian warriors, astride their horses and observing the white men charging toward them. All but five of the men then wheeled their horses and galloped back to the train. The others—Colonel Russell, Lieutenant Brown, Garrard, McCarty, and Barton—continued riding forward until they were within less than a quarter of a mile from what they could now see was a force of perhaps four hundred mounted Comanche Indians.* With painted faces, wearing buffalo-horn helmets or their hair adorned with feathers, and carrying long glittering lances with feather pennons, white shields, and all of the other colorful accoutrements of Indian warfare, the Indians sat passively watching the five white men riding toward them, doubtless surprised and puzzled by such an audacious display by so few. As the whites drew closer, a number of the young warriors rode their restless mounts to and fro, impatient for action. Russell quickly ordered his men back, and they returned to the train at a gallop.[5]

Reaching the two halted columns of wagons, Russell and

---

*This war party was probably the same one that moved westward and attacked Fort Mann June 19–21, causing the garrison to abandon it on June 22.

the others found matters in great confusion and the teamsters from the government train in a state of panic. Thirty of their sixty-one men had no weapons at all, and the rest were inexperienced and frightened. The colonel calmed them and gave orders for corralling the wagons, confining the animals inside, and organizing firing parties. The train was hurriedly moved to the brow of the hill from which the Indians had first been seen and was circled into an oval-shaped corral. The two front wagons were brought together, and those behind were brought in close so that the inside front wheel of each touched the outside rear wheel of the wagon ahead. The oxen, mules, and horses were driven into this enclosure for protection, and the opening was closed behind them. That done, Russell drew up those of his men with weapons in a line in front of the wagons, facing the oncoming Indians, who were charging down the trail by this time. Preparations were barely complete when the action began.[6]

As the Comanches neared, Colonel Russell gave orders that only half of the men were to fire at a time, providing protection and firepower while the other half reloaded. The warriors were bearing down on them, charging furiously with lances poised. When they were about 250 yards distant, several volleys were fired at them, breaking up the charge and scattering the warriors. The Indians then began to circle the corralled wagons, looking for an opening or a target. Those warriors with firearms, and there were a surprising number, carried them unslung and ready for action. While they circled, just beyond effective range of fire, they continuously shifted their white-painted buffalo-hide shields to protect their bodies. These shields were usually made of hide from the hump of a tough old buffalo bull and were often effective in stopping or deflecting the bullets of that day. Finally the warriors quit circling and began firing their old rifles and muskets into the corral from opposite sides. Russell, meanwhile, had dissolved the firing party and ordered the men to post themselves around the wagons, providing some protection to all sides. The balls from the Indian weapons were singing overhead, perforating the wagon sheets, and occa-

Colonel Russell corralled the wagons on the brow of a hill, with the livestock herded into the enclosure for protection. After circling the wagons for a time, the Comanches began firing. Finally, individual warriors, hanging on the opposite side of their horses, began making dashes at the wagons.

sionally striking one of the oxen, causing the beast to rear and buck, bellowing in pain.[7]

When Colonel Russell posted the men among the wagons, Lieutenant Brown took five of his Californians and moved to a small knoll fifty yards beyond the train. From there Brown and his men kept up an incessant fire at the Comanche snipers and those circling. This called heavy fire from the Indians down on his position. Then individual warriors began making dashes at the corralled wagons, hanging from the opposite side of their horses with only a heel and part of a leg visible, slung across the cantle of the saddle. In this manner they fired their weapons from under the neck of their horse while at a gallop, a tell-tale puff of smoke appearing to announce the bullet, which then sighed overhead or kicked up a cloud of dust from the dry plain. Such individual rushes were greeted by heavy fire from within the corral, but the efforts of both sides were ineffectual, and there were no casualties other than a few injured oxen.[8]

The attack lasted about an hour. Then the Comanches, evidently concluding that they were wasting precious ammunition and that no scalps or booty were to be had without paying an unacceptably high price, broke off the engagement and moved to the west toward Fort Mann. They left behind no dead or wounded whites and no seriously damaged property. But they did leave in the minds of their intended victims a vivid impression of the wondrous horsemanship and bravery they had displayed. As the Indians disappeared to the west, the men of the Russell-Bell train assessed their own condition. They were unhurt but were exceedingly hot, tired, and thirsty. There had been no water for men or animals since their noon stop, and it was now beginning to tell on all of them. The teamsters yoked up the oxen, the wagons moved out in their two files with the remuda and ox herd between, and they continued on to whatever nearby site they had chosen for their evening's camp. While grateful to have come through intact and unhurt, they were irritated that they had inflicted no apparent harm on their attackers. Doubtless the Comanches harbored a similar irritation at an unsuccessful effort. Ironically, had the Indians charged the train when they first sighted it and before it could be corralled, they would probably have overwhelmed the white men and taken eighty-five scalps, all of the livestock, and any of the contents they found useful.[9]

For the next two days the train continued moving northeasterly along the trail, though now more cautiously. The scouts were out as usual, but all men were keeping a wary eye on each horizon. It was obvious the Comanches were not finished with them. Across the river, on the bleached-yellow sand dunes that obstructed the view beyond, an occasional motionless Indian scout would be spotted. More ominously, the sun frequently glinted on the tip of a lance held by a warrior screened by the dunes on the opposite bank, and a number of warriors could be seen some distance behind them, following their trail like wolves waiting to cut out a weakened member of the herd. Flank guards were out, and all expected an early attack. They were now in the region known as the "Coon Creeks," a dangerous place where nearly every train that year had experienced some kind of raid or fight. The Comanches and Arapahoes were known to be there in force, and a few Kiowas and Cheyennes were probably also present, riding with the raiding parties of friends. The days were almost unbearably hot and dry, and a searing south wind added to the misery, causing the wagon sheets to flap and making everyone more nervous. Imagination was fast becoming an enemy. The green teamsters of the government train were edgy and frightened, near panic. Still, there was no attack on the eighteenth or the nineteenth.[10]

The morning of June 20 gave promise for a good day's travel. By the standards of the plains, the morning air was brisk and cool and the sky cloudless. After a quick cup of coffee, the men yoked the oxen, hitched the mules, and saddled the horses and riding mules. Then the train organized itself into the two customary files, and their movement began. The scouts and flankers were out, but the day continued peacefully. Though there was great apprehension, spirits were generally high. They moved along well enough and by noon reached the site selected for the evening camp — a large horseshoe-shaped bottom circumscribed by the river for a distance of three or more miles. As the wagons entered the campground, a party of six riders, including Colonel Russell, Garrard, and the trader Coolidge, rode downstream along the riverbank looking for driftwood as fuel for the cooking fires. Garrard, Russell, and Coolidge had just collected a small supply and laid it across the pommel of the colonel's saddle when the three accompanying horsemen bolted directly for the wagons. They made no audible response to the shouted inquiries of the others as to the cause of such a rapid departure but pointed to the southwest along the Arkansas. In the distance, approaching at full speed, was a party of about forty Comanche warriors, obviously intending to cut off the route to the train for the men of the wood detail.[11]

When a party of Comanches attempted to cut them off from their train, Garrard, Russell, and a trader named Coolidge made a desperate dash for safety on their mules. Coolidge soon fell behind, and it was only the quick action of Garrard in providing cover that enabled him to escape.

Realizing what was about to happen, Russell and his two companions jumped on their mules and hastened after the others. In the distance, puffs of smoke were seen as other mounted warriors began an attack on the train, which even then was forming its corral. The forty Comanches trying to cut off the men of the wood detail were on a course that would join theirs at or close to the train; the only question was whether the white men would reach the corral or lose their scalps. Mules are not noted for speed, but the three men beat their poor mounts so unmercifully that they outdid themselves, fairly flying across the plains. When they were within three hundred yards of the corral, Garrard, who was in the lead, looked back and saw that Coolidge was straggling far behind and several Comanches were closing on him fast. He shouted to the colonel, and both jerked their mules to a halt, then turned and fired at the closest of the following Indians. Russell then galloped back to the corral to take charge of the defense while Garrard stood by to cover Coolidge's escape. Placing his rein between his teeth, Garrard took steady aim at the nearest of the pursuers and kept the warrior in his sights until the man passed to his left, close on the heels of Coolidge. The warrior was an older man with a large belly, and as he passed Garrard fired at that largest of the available targets. The Comanche's leg twitched in pain, but he uttered no sound. He wheeled his horse, galloped off to the river, and was not seen again. Garrard quickly followed Coolidge into the relative safety of the corral, just then being closed, and dismounted.[12]

Inside the corral Colonel Russell had organized a defense, and his firing parties were blazing away at the charging Comanches. There was a great din, with the boom of muskets, the crack of rifles, the ear-splitting war cries of the Indians, the shouts and curses of the whites, and the whinnies, braying, and bawling of the frightened animals. Amid all the confusion, smoke and dust mixed with sweat and gunpowder as Russell's men did their best to turn back the charging warriors. Their hearts sank when, in the distance, close to the place where they had been gathering firewood, they saw another large band of Indians coming down the sand dunes and crossing the river at a trot. The blazing midday sun glinted on gun barrels and lances as the warriors crossed, showing them to be very well armed. Once they reached the west bank, they broke into a gallop as they charged directly at the circled wagons. When they had come to within 150 yards of the train they opened fire, and the air exploded with the sounds of battle.[13]

Russell's firing teams did their work well, pouring a withering fire into the charging Indians. Riders stiffened in their saddles as they were struck by shot. True to their code, not one showed pain or cried out. The only way of knowing that firing from the train was having any effect was by observing the sudden jerk of a warrior who was struck, then seeing him gallop precipitously away from the scene of action. None were seen to fall from their saddles; if any were mortally wounded, their fellows immediately carried them away, and not one was left on the field. The charge of the Comanches broke before this solid defense, and they retired beyond the reach of the white men's bullets. After a time they rallied and began to circle the train, always keeping their white shields between their bodies and the line of fire. In this manner they kept steadily moving, then suddenly one or more would rush in and throw their long war lances and just as rapidly dash back out of the range of fire. Looking for a weak point where they could make a charge, they found none. After many such feints, they fell back again, finding the corral too well guarded.[14]

A few more individual warriors dashed at the corral, each one greeted by the crack of rifle fire from within the circle of wagons. But the fight for this day was over. After a two-hour combat, the Comanches finally left the field, crossing the river and filing slowly up the sand dunes beyond. Then, as if in a dream, they were gone. A strange silence descended on the camp. The sounds of battle subsided, and the exhausted men realized the ordeal was over and they had once again survived. After a time they stirred themselves and proceeded to the campsite. Here there was much conversation as each man bragged or speculated about his own shots. Many expressed scorn too, for some of the more frightened and cowardly teamsters had tried to hide in the wagons during the fight. It was a natural release of emotions for young men who had been fighting for their lives. As good as they felt, however, there was the sobering realization that many more dangerous miles lay ahead and the Comanches were likely still out there, beyond their range of vision, waiting for the right opportunity to strike again.[15]

The rest of the twentieth passed uneventfully, except for a nervous apprehension that caused each man to keep his eyes on the horizon, fearful of what might appear. The twenty-first

was much the same—hot dry weather, a burning sun that
drained the moisture from the land and those upon it, fatigue
and thirst for man and beast, and a dread of what they might
encounter beyond what they could see. That night they
probably camped near the Coon Creek crossing. On the
twenty-second the train once again started its movement
early, following the trail north-northeasterly toward Walnut
Creek and beyond to the Great North Bend of the Arkansas,
where they would leave the river. They expected to reach the
crossing of the Pawnee Fork by noon, but there were bluffs
nearby and dry arroyos between, good places for an ambush.
They moved slowly and cautiously, ready to corral the wagons
on a moment's notice and half-expecting to hear the Comanche
yell at any time. But no enemy appeared, and when the sun
was overhead, they reached the Pawnee. A heavy rain far
upstream to the north and west had raised the water to flood
stage, and Russell and the others had to camp on the south
bank until the waters receded sufficiently to permit a safe
crossing. Near their campsite, young Garrard discovered the
remains of the Comanche war chief Red Sleeve. Two westbound trains were in camp near the opposite, or north, bank
of the Pawnee, also waiting for the stream to become fordable.
The sight of so many others doubtless gave the men of the
Russell-Bell train a feeling of security and confidence. Yet
the danger was not over, and for them, more adventures lay
ahead. [16]

6

Lieutenant Love's Defeat

It was during the evening of Wednesday, June 23, 1847, that 1st Lt. John Love and Company B, First Dragoons, reached the place where the Wet Route of the Santa Fe Trail crossed the Pawnee Fork. From afar the Pawnee seemed no more than a thin line of scrub trees and a sprinkling of cottonwoods set against the distant horizon. But as they drew closer, it took on the appearance of a typical small stream of the plains, with a winding course and steep banks to which the straggling growth of trees clung tenaciously. The trail ruts followed by Love and his men ran parallel to and a short distance west of the Arkansas, crossing the Pawnee a few hundred yards above its mouth. Southeast of the river a line of sand dunes radiated a golden glow from the dying rays of the setting sun, while north of the crossing the fading light struck the white tops of two government supply trains, outlining the circles of their camps. Nearby, and next to the trail, an eastbound party with four wagons had just crossed the Pawnee and was hitching up to travel by night in hopes of avoiding Indians.[1]

Company B consisted of approximately eighty men, mostly young recruits from eastern Missouri. After a brief period of training at Jefferson Barracks, they had paraded at St. Louis Park on May 15, then marched for Fort Leavenworth under orders to Santa Fe as escort for the paymaster en route to pay troops in New Mexico. The British adventurer George F. Ruxton, returning to the States, passed them on the Santa Fe

Trail near the western border of Missouri at the end of May. He thought them superbly mounted on blooded horses about fifteen hands high, but the dragoons themselves he found to be "neither soldier-like in dress nor appearance." After a short stay at the fort they departed on June 7 as guard for paymaster Maj. Charles Bodine, his train of twelve wagons, each pulled by six mules, and nearly $350,000 in specie. On June 10, about seventy-five miles beyond Fort Leavenworth, the column was joined by Thomas Fitzpatrick, Indian Agent for the Upper Platte, Upper Kansas, and Upper Arkansas Agency, and Maj. John Dougherty, who was delivering 550 head of beef cattle to Santa Fe under contract with the army. Near mid-June Dougherty's herd stampeded at Council Grove. Although most were eventually recovered, he left them there to be taken on to Santa Fe with Missouri volunteer infantry troops under Lt. Col. Alton R. Easton while he returned to Fort Leavenworth.[2]

Beyond Council Grove, Lieutenant Love and his troops traveled rapidly and without difficulty until they reached the Pawnee Fork. Indian signs were all around them after they crossed the Little Arkansas, but the first real indication of danger appeared at Walnut Creek. Here they found two fresh graves, one that of the young trader William Tharp,* killed on May 28, and the other that of an American named McGuire, killed on June 3. Tharp and his wagons had been accompanying Bent, St. Vrain and Co.'s eastbound train when they were attacked at Walnut Creek, apparently by Arapahoes or Comanches, and Tharp was killed. McGuire had been mortally

*William Tharp was one of the most respected of the Indian traders on the Arkansas. A first cousin of Ceran St. Vrain's, he had come west from St. Louis in about 1841 to become a trader at Bent's Fort. By 1844 he was trading on his own at Pueblo. The winter of 1846–47 he spent trading with a band of Cheyennes camped at the Big Timbers, where he and his family lived in an Indian lodge. He left on his last ill-fated trip from Pueblo on May 5, 1847, taking with him a large herd of mules and several wagons filled with buffalo robes. It is said that had he reached market, he would have cleared a profit of at least five thousand dollars. See Janet Lecompte, *Pueblo, Hardscrabble, Greenhorn*, 160, 199–201.

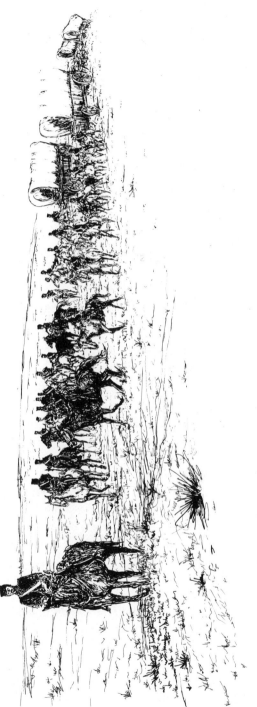

On June 7, 1847, 1st. Lt. John Love led his Company B, First Dragoons, westward from Fort Leavenworth en route to Santa Fe as escort for paymaster Maj. Charles Bodine, his train of twelve wagons, and nearly $350,000 in specie to pay troops in New Mexico. For Love and his men, the journey would lead to a tragic encounter with the Comanches, which became known as "Love's Defeat."

wounded by Comanches at Ash Creek on June 3 during an
attack on a government train commanded by Captain Fowler,
the same train that had reached Fort Mann on May 28. He
died later and was buried at Walnut Creek.[3]

When the paymaster and Fitzpatrick, with their escort
under Lieutenant Love, reached the Pawnee Fork, the danger
of Indian attack became apparent. The two westbound trains
encamped on the left or north, side of the Pawnee carried
commissary supplies for the army at Santa Fe, supplies that
along with the livestock, made them highly desirable prizes
for raiders. One train of about thirty wagons was in the charge
of a Mr. Hayden and was corralled nearest the crossing of the
stream. Accompanying him was a trader named Henry C.
Miller, of Arrow Rock, Missouri, with two wagons. The other
train, with about an equal number of wagons, was headed by a
Mr. Fagan of Platte City, Missouri. Traveling with Fagan's
train for protection were several traders, including James S.
Wethered. They had reached the crossing two or three days
earlier and, finding the Pawnee in flood stage because of
heavy rains upstream, had been forced to make camp and
wait for the waters to recede. On the opposite bank Colonel
Russell and his escort, accompanied by Lewis Garrard, and
another large government train, eastbound under the control
of Mr. Bell, and the trader Coolidge and his men, had gone
into camp on June 22 to wait for the water to drop.[4]

On the morning of June 23, before Lieutenant Love and his
men arrived, the Pawnee was slowly receding. As they waited
for it to become fordable, the men of the three camps turned
their livestock out to graze. At about 10:00 A.M. a large herd
of bison suddenly began to stampede across the plains from
the north, moving southwest. Older, wiser heads and experienced plainsmen would have questioned the cause of such a
sudden movement by so many animals. But the teamsters of
all three trains were largely green and untried, having made
only a few trips across the trail and lacking both good
defensive weapons and training in their use. Some of those on
the south side of the Pawnee mounted their horses and went off
at a gallop toward the oncoming herd, hoping to shoot a few for

their mess, while twenty or thirty more ran to the bank of the stream near where they thought the bison might cross. When they were at some distance from their camp, a cry of "Indians!" suddenly rang out from the camps on the north bank. Passed along from camp to camp, person to person, this warning quickly brought a halt to the pell-mell rush to the Pawnee by those on the south bank. Caught in the open, many stopped in their tracks, wavering between hiding in the scrub trees and brush along the stream or returning to camp. After a moment of indecision, they made a rush for the wagons.[5]

Once within the security of the corral, all eyes turned to the sounds of commotion at the farthest camp on the north side of the Pawnee—that of Fagan and the accompanying traders. About fifty Comanches* were charging through the circled wagons with their lances while others were attempting to stampede the oxen and mules. Shots rang out, followed by the telltale puffs of smoke among the wagons as the traders and teamsters fought back. The Indians would wheel away momentarily after a volley, then sweep back through the corral, obscuring the view of those in the other camps. Finally, after a fight of several minutes, the Comanches broke off the combat and carried the body of a dead warrior away with them. They disappeared behind a hill on the north side of the Pawnee overlooking the valley of the Arkansas. The warriors had wounded three or four men in Fagan's camp, one of whom, Mr. Smith of the Wethered party, had been lanced seven times in the neck and chest and was lucky to survive. Although already seriously wounded and down on his back, Smith had somehow managed to shoot and kill his attacker.[6]

Fast-moving action on the opposite side of the Pawnee gripped the attention of those on its south bank. Watching in stunned disbelief, giving no thought to their own oxen, which were grazing some distance upstream under the guard of only three teamsters, most men simply felt relieved to be back in the security of their corral and grateful the attack was not

*Fitzpatrick later stated that there were both Comanches and Kiowas in the raiding party.

against them. Suddenly shouts from the guard made it clear the Comanches had reappeared. They were swimming the stream on their horses, then charging into the herd. More than half of the men from the Bell-Russell party made a dash toward the grazing oxen, but by the time they turned a bow in the stream, at least sixty Indians were among the animals, yelling and goading them into a gallop toward the high plains and away from the camp. The teamsters from Bell's train, inexperienced and frightened, hung back and failed to support Colonel Russell and his men in their effort to thwart the raiders. Without their help, those in the lead could do nothing, and the cattle lumbered off to the southwest. Cursing the teamsters' cowardice and negligence, Russell and his men (including young Garrard) ran back to camp, mounted their horses, and dashed off for one last attempt to save the herd. The gallant effort did rescue 30 oxen, but the Comanches still managed to drive off 160 others, which they killed when they had gone about two miles and were beyond the range of the white men's guns. With relatively little danger to themselves, the Indians had effectively destroyed one of the hated white trains. [7]

When the melee was over, Colonel Russell inventoried the losses. The fur trader Coolidge had lost twenty-seven animals and had only two left. His big wagons were laden with robes and hides, and he now lacked the means to haul them. To help him, Russell took as many packs as he could carry in his single wagon. Then Coolidge struck a bargain with one of the westbound trains to carry some of the packs back to Fort Mann, to be stored until he could return for them. The rest he cached in his own wagons near the crossing. The inept Bell and his green crew were left with only twenty-four oxen (twelve yokes) for their twenty-five wagons and now had no choice but to place their personal property and provisions in three of these. The other wagons, with their accoutrements and some of the government property, were abandoned and burned at the site. The only positive note to this grievous loss was the fact that no one south of the Pawnee had been harmed. This, however, was largely because the teamsters had failed to provide any real defense for their animals. [8]

The Pawnee Fork continued to drop during the day on June 23, and late in the afternoon the eighty-five men, thirty oxen, and four wagons constituting the remnants of the Bell-Coolidge-Russell party crossed the stream to the north bank. Near sundown, while they were hitching up to continue their journey at night, Lieutenant Love and his dragoons reached the Pawnee. Love was promptly apprised of the disastrous Comanche raid, and he promised to exact revenge. Bell, Coolidge, and Russell then moved on to the east with their men, remaining livestock, and wagons. While Love's men were making camp near the crossing, he assessed the condition of the two westbound trains and determined to take them under his protection and travel with them to Santa Fe.[9]

At dawn on June 24 the two trains and Lieutenant Love's command made ready to cross the Pawnee. Before leaving, however, Love gave orders to the two captains, Hayden and Fagan, that for the rest of their journey, or at least until they were beyond the most dangerous part, they were to travel and to camp as close to him each day as would be convenient. Fagan was agreeable, but Hayden, a stubborn, taciturn fellow, was quite the reverse. He remarked that he had been given his instructions by the quartermaster at Fort Leavenworth and would not submit to those of others. Lieutenant Love told Hayden he must obey, because so much valuable government property could not be placed at risk from Indian attack. With that, the fording of the stream began. Because of the high water, the steep banks were sodden, making the crossing slow and difficult, but it was finally completed without accident or loss. The two government trains and the company of dragoons, with the paymaster and his wagons, made separate camps on the south bank, ready to continue their journey the following morning.[10]

At dawn on June 25 the oxen, mules, and horses were turned out to graze under the watchful eye of a dragoon guard. That completed, the teams were hitched to their wagons and brought into line, riders mounted, and the long column slowly strung itself out and began the day's march. Hayden, stubborn and resentful, moved in front and considerably ahead of the others. Before leaving, he was heard to say to some of his men that "if those gentlemen in the rear encamped near him that night they would have to travel after dark." But ox-drawn wagon trains, heavily laden, were never known for speed, and although Hayden's train was out of sight for much of the day, the rest caught up with him before sundown. He had circled his wagons and made camp at the edge of the valley of the Arkansas, nearly a mile west of the river and five hundred yards beyond where the dragoons erected their guard tent. Lieutenant Love put his dragoons into camp next to the river, where grass and water were plentiful and an attack on their camp would be the most difficult.* Fagan's train also made camp near the river, about three hundred or four hundred yards in the rear. Although Love was concerned about the vulnerability of the campsite Hayden had selected, and irked about the wagonmaster's refusal to obey orders, it was too late to require a move. He resolved to force Hayden to abide by his orders in the future, then established a strong guard and directed them to exercise the utmost vigilance. With that, the camps settled down, and the rest of the night passed uneventfully.[11]

The morning of Saturday, June 26, dawned clear, with the prevailing south breeze causing the grasses of the valley to ripple gently, like the swell of the sea. As the first rays of the sun began to break across the horizon, the men at Hayden's camp moved one of their wagons, opening the corral and allowing the penned oxen to leave the enclosure and move onto the plains to graze. The teamsters of Fagan's train also began

---

*This camp appears to have been near the camping ground known as Plain Encampment (or Plain Camp), about 4 miles southwest of the crossing of Big Coon Creek. Today that would be about 5 miles southwest of Garfield, Kansas. See James Josiah Webb, *Adventures in the Santa Fe Trade*, 294. Measurements taken by Randolph B. Marcy in 1849, using an odometer, indicated that Coon Creek Crossing was 11.43 miles from the crossing of the Pawnee Fork. Bvt. Maj. Henry L. Kendrick's table of distances compiled in 1849, also using an odometer, showed the site of "Love's Defeat" as 16.57 miles from the Pawnee Fork Crossing, or 5.14 miles beyond Coon Creek Crossing. See House Ex. Doc. No. 17, 31st Cong., 1st sess., vol. 5 (Serial 573), 92.

to open their corral, and at the dragoon camp, the horses were picketed to be curried and fed their morning grain. Before turning his stock loose to graze, Hayden mounted a wagon wheel and looked up and down the valley of the Arkansas. Except for the picket guards at the edge of the valley, no horses or humans could be seen outside of the three camps. With no apparent danger in sight, the livestock were allowed to file out of the corral, moving slowly and in a string westerly toward the high plains to graze under the guard of their herdsmen. The quiet of morning was broken only by the occasional nickering of horses, snuffling of mules, lowing of cattle, and other sounds of the stirring camps, along with the calls of a few birds greeting the new dawn.[12]

When the oxen reached the edge of the valley, a considerable distance from the train, the herdsmen were suddenly shocked by blood-curdling screams. Like phantoms materializing in the thin light of early morning, Comanches on horses, their shields and long war lances held menacingly, were rising from the grass all around. More of the painted warriors charged without warning from the ravine of Big Coon Creek, their buffalo-horn helmets looming against the low horizon. Many held rattles in their hands, others had them tied to the tails of their mounts, and still others shook buffalo robes. Their cries, the din of the rattles and galloping horses, and the waving robes caused the oxen to mill about, then stampede. Perhaps 250 to 300 warriors charged in among the oxen, lancing a few as they went. The uproar, the smell of blood, and the charging Indians and horses so frightened the beasts that they bolted away from the camps in the valley. The herders made a valiant effort to check their flight and regain control. Failing that, they tried to place themselves in a line between the Indians and the panicking cattle. The warriors charged through the men, wounding three with their lances as they passed.[13]

When the attack began, Lieutenant Love was on a high point of ground overlooking the camps to reconnoiter the surrounding country. He did so each morning before turning the company's horses out to graze. This day his telescope revealed nothing. When he heard the commotion at Hayden's camp and saw what was happening, he returned to the dragoon encampment at a gallop. Once in camp, he issued orders for his men to saddle their horses and mount up, prepared for action. The bugle sounded "to horse," and the men swung themselves into their saddles. Once mounted, Lieutenant Love prepared to lead them in pursuit of the rapidly disappearing herd of oxen. Just as the troopers were formed, however, a new body of Comanche warriors appeared on the southeast side of the river, directly across from the dragoon camp, apparently intending to attack as soon as the soldiers were gone. Initially there seemed to be between fifty and one hundred of them, but more soon appeared, and finally it seemed there were about two hundred. Love's first duty was to protect the paymaster, his train of wagons, and the specie for the troops in New Mexico. He reluctantly gave the order to dismount and fight on foot to all but about twenty-five men. The latter he placed under the command of Sgt. Ben Bishop with orders to pursue the Indians and retake the oxen from Hayden's train. He then deployed the rest of his troopers around the dragoon camp to ward off the expected attack.[14]

Sergeant Bishop and his men lost no time in beginning their pursuit. They galloped west after the livestock, crossing Coon Creek and reaching the edge of the valley about a mile beyond their camp. When they had come within 150 yards of the Comanches, Bishop halted his men and formed them into line for a charge, expecting to "rally" on the teamsters and herders from Hayden's train, who were trying to recover their animals. Once his men were in line, Bishop ordered a charge, and twenty-five brave troopers galloped directly at ten or twelve times as many Comanches, who were driving the oxen onto the plains. At first the Indians seemed to retreat, causing the soldiers to be drawn farther away from the camp and any hope of help. At the same time, the large body of Comanches that had been menacing the dragoon camp crossed the river a short distance upstream and charged after Bishop and his men. Hayden's teamsters, fearful of so many warriors, failed to support Bishop and retreated toward their camp.

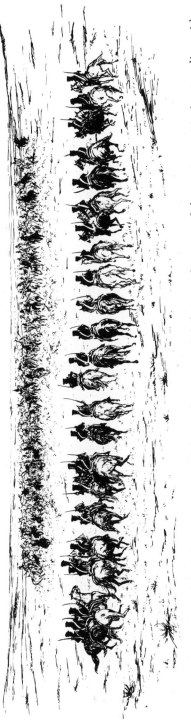

At dawn on June 26, 1847, a large war party of Comanches stampeded the oxen from one of the government trains traveling with Lieutenant Love and his men. Other warriors menaced the paymaster's train, so Love sent Sgt. Ben Bishop and about twenty-five troopers to recover the oxen while the remainder defended the paymaster. When within 150 yards of the Comanches, Bishop formed his men into line, then ordered a charge. Away went the brave men, charging ten or twelve times as many Indians.

Sergeant Bishop and his men were quickly surrounded by Comanche warriors. Their effort to recover government oxen became instead a fight for survival, each man facing six to ten Comanches. When they broke off the fight, five dragoons had been killed and six wounded.

What had been an effort to recover the livestock now turned into a fight for survival by the beleaguered soldiers, who were caught between the two bands of Indians and quickly surrounded.[15]

    Engulfed by waves of horned warriors, the soldiers were forced into hand-to-hand combat with sabers, each man facing six to ten Comanches. They fought bravely, but more than numbers were against them. Their horses, though blooded and beautiful, were new to the service and had never been exposed to the noise and chaos of battle. Some of the Indians began waving blankets, and in combination with the noise and smells of combat, this panicked many of the animals and made them unmanageable. The troopers defended themselves gallantly, but their only hope for survival was in retreat. Five of them had been killed and six more wounded, four severely, when Bishop gave the order to break off the fight and make for their camp as best they could. Bursting through the swarm of Comanche warriors, the surviving troopers galloped east without looking back. Once within gunshot range of the three camps, those Comanches who had followed broke off their pursuit. The Indians, meanwhile, scalped three of the dead troopers, cut the throat of one from ear to ear, and sliced the ears off another. They took the horses, equipment, arms, ammunition, and uniforms of all the dead, then moved away with the oxen from Hayden's train. From the time Sergeant Bishop led his men in the charge to the time of their return, the fight lasted about twenty minutes.[16]

When Sergeant Bishop and his men reached the security of the dragoon camp, Lieutenant Love took stock of their situation. Privates Jonathan Arledge, Moses Short, John Dickhart, George Gaskill, and J. H. Blake had been killed, Sgt. Ben Bishop and Privates Henry Vancaster, John Lovelace, and Thomas Ward were severely injured, and Privates James Bush* and Willis Wilson were slightly wounded. Twelve to fifteen Comanches had been seen to fall but had immediately been carried away by other warriors, and it was impossible to say how many had been killed or wounded. The Indians did leave four dead horses on the field. After it was clear the Comanches were gone, parties from the dragoon camp and Hayden's camp moved out to the site of the fight. The bodies of the dead were recovered and buried in graves at the side of the trail. Some were found to have suffered as many as twelve to fourteen wounds from lances, plus the mutilation inflicted

---

*Lieutenant Love's report gave this soldier's name as "Bush," whereas Sergeant Bishop's letter of July 1, 1847, referred to him as "Burk." Niles' National Register Baltimore, Md., V. 72 (July 31, 1847), 343; James M. Cutts, *The Conquest of California and New Mexico*, 242.

after death. Hayden looked over the area where the Comanches had first appeared to stampede his oxen. There he
found the depressions in the grass where the Indians and their
horses had lain, waiting to rise and charge at dawn when the
livestock were being taken to the grazing grounds. They had
infiltrated the picket lines undetected during the hours before
dawn. They had succeeded in driving off 130 yoke of oxen
from Hayden's train and 30 yoke belonging to the trader Henry
C. Miller.[17]

The severity of the wounds inflicted on Bishop and the
three others forced the dragoons to remain in camp along the
Arkansas. After the injuries were attended to, Lieutenant
Love ordered the teamsters from Hayden's train, including
Miller and his men, to camp with Fagan for safety. Then he
sent an express rider to Fort Leavenworth to report the action
and the fact that a government train with thirty wagons was
stranded. He requested that new teams be sent to Fort Mann
to take the train on to Santa Fe. Pending their arrival, he
intended to divide the teams from Fagan's train, making it
possible to move Hayden's wagons to the safety of that post. On
June 27 Love wrote his report of the affair and sent it to the
office of the adjutant general in Washington. Then soldiers
and teamsters alike simply waited for the wounded to recover
sufficiently to be moved.[18]

Love and his men, along with the two government trains,
remained encamped along the Arkansas near the battle site
until July 2. During the morning of June 27 they spotted a
small eight-wagon train belonging to a number of traders from
Santa Fe, captained by Solomon Houck of Boonville, Missouri, and moving eastbound across the uplands. Among the
merchants were Houck, James J. Webb of St. Louis, Cornelius
Davy of Independence, Christopher C. Branham of Platte
City, and Branham's brother from Columbia. There were
about seventy men in all, including twenty-three ex–Laclede
Rangers returning home. They were traveling along the Dry
Route (Ridge Road) of the Santa Fe Trail and had a large
number of extra mules. Seeing this, Lieutenant Love and
Fitzpatrick rode up from the valley below. They reported the

fight, the loss of the oxen, and the needs of Henry Miller, who faced bankruptcy if he could not move his two wagonloads of merchandise to Santa Fe. They hoped to arrange a sale or exchange for some of the extra mules. The traders turned off the trail and went into camp with Love and the others. Among their group was a merchant from Taos, Peter Joseph, who had escaped the uprising of the Pueblo Indians and was heading to the States. During the afternoon, Joseph and Miller began to bargain, and soon Joseph had purchased the wagons and goods owned by Miller. Then he worked out a trade for harness and mules in exchange for the ox yokes. By noon of the following day they had concluded their trade, and Miller prepared to return to his home in Missouri with Houck while Joseph accompanied the Fagan train to New Mexico.[19]

On July 2, with the wounded stabilized, Lieutenant Love ordered the trains to break camp and resume the march to Santa Fe. By thinning the number of oxen pulling the Fagan train, the teamsters had been able to make up enough yokes to pull thirteen of Hayden's wagons, using two or three yokes for each. They cached 180 ox yokes at the campsite on the Arkansas and left behind seventeen wagons. Then they moved slowly on to Fort Mann, making five to eight miles per day. They found the fort abandoned and derelict, but at least it offered some protection; they left Hayden, his men, and his wagons there. Love and his dragoons, Fitzpatrick, the paymaster and his party, Fagan's train, and Wethered and the other traders left Fort Mann by July 8 or 9, crossed the Arkansas on about July 11, and reached Santa Fe on August 6. Lieutenant Colonel Easton and his four companies of Missouri Volunteers reached Fort Mann on July 23. With them came the cattle that Major Dougherty had left at Council Grove; 360 head of these were yoked up to the remaining wagons of the Hayden train when the yokes cached at the battle site were brought in. Hayden finally got back on the trail, and by August 13 he and his train had reached the Middle Cimarron Spring.[20]

The march of Lieutenant Love and Company B, First Dragoons, demonstrated that the Indians of the plains, particularly the Comanches, were not afraid to attack American soldiers in fairly large units and could be formidable foes. Such fights would for the most part be hit-and-run raids, usually intended to drive away the livestock that pulled the hated trains and, if possible, to capture any of the contents that might be of use. The engagement that occurred on June 26, 1847, was later referred to by the newspapers as "Lieutenant Love's Defeat," despite the prudence that Love had exercised in protecting the paymaster and the respect and agreement expressed by Thomas Fitzpatrick and Love's own men. The point along the Arkansas where the fight occurred was for many years thereafter called "Love's Defeat." Though humiliating to a conscientious and competent officer, it was perhaps appropriate. It was not a victory.[21]

More Soldiers for Santa Fe

When the Army of the West was created, the government evidently had not anticipated a lengthy campaign. Or perhaps, in the haste to raise troops, no one had given studied consideration to the time frame for which volunteers were needed. As a result, Doniphan's First Regiment of Missouri Mounted Volunteers, Price's Second Regiment of Missouri Mounted Volunteers, Willock's "extra battalion," and the Mormon Battalion had all been enlisted for only one year. The terms of enlistment were to expire during June, July, and August 1847. Secretary of War William L. Marcy alerted Missouri's governor John C. Edwards of the need for additional troops in New Mexico by a letter written on March 25, 1847; on March 31, he made a specific requisition for manpower. This time he asked the governor to raise a regiment of ten companies of mounted volunteers who were to serve for the remainder of the war with Mexico. On April 19 the secretary directed Governor Edwards to raise an additional battalion of five companies of volunteer infantry. At the same time he asked the governor of Illinois, Augustus C. French, to provide a regiment of ten companies of volunteer infantry. In all cases, the term of enlistment was to be for the duration of the war. [1]

The requisitions for more troops were met with enthusiasm. The recruiting and organization of a new regiment of mounted volunteers was completed during July; by late July, all ten companies had arrived at Independence, Missouri, their place of rendezvous. They were sworn into the service of the United States, elected officers (as was the practice with volunteers), and were designated as the "Third Regiment of Missouri Mounted Volunteers." John Ralls was elected colonel, Richard H. Lane, lieutenant colonel, and William W. Reynolds, major. The infantry were raised even more rapidly. The five Missouri companies were recruited within a month, all from St. Louis, and chose Alton R. Easton, the former commander of the St. Louis Legion, as their lieutenant colonel. They left St. Louis by riverboat between May 15 and June 7 and were taken directly to Fort Leavenworth. They were to be known as the "Missouri Battalion of Infantry Volunteers." Illinois likewise had no difficulty in meeting its levy, and all ten companies had reached full strength and completed organization by June 8. The "First Regiment of Illinois Infantry Volunteers," as they were known, elected E. W. B. Newby their colonel, Henderson P. Boyakin, lieutenant colonel, and Israel B. Donalson, major. They left Alton, Illinois, their rendezvous point, by riverboat and reached Fort Leavenworth by the end of June. The mounted regiment joined the infantry at that post by mid-July and prepared for the march across the plains. All told, the three units numbered about 2,250 officers and men.[2]

The first of the new volunteer units to march were the men of Easton's infantry battalion, who left Fort Leavenworth in three detachments. On June 17 Company A, with eighty-five officers and men, started down the trail under orders to escort a government train of forty ox-drawn wagons that had left two days earlier. The slow-moving column reached the Council Grove on July 2 and Diamond Springs on the fifth. They were ultimately overtaken on the trail by the rest of the battalion and subsequently traveled behind them, arriving in Santa Fe on August 25. Beyond Council Grove they were accompanied by the trader B. F. "Frank" Coons and his wagons, seeking the security of travel with a company of armed men. Company B left the fort on June 19 and reached Council Grove on July 1. Here they found a number of traders waiting for the arrival of

military units with which to travel for safety. The reports of
heavy Indian attacks on trains from beyond the Little Arkansas to the Cimarron River had created much uneasiness
among all the traders, and most were anxious to travel with the
marching volunteers for protection. When B Company left the
grove on July 5, a number of well-known traders and forty
wagons of dry goods and provisions moved out with them.[3]

The rest of Easton's battalion left Fort Leavenworth on June
21, proceeding down the Fort Scott military road until striking the Santa Fe Trail. Included were Lieutenant-Colonel
Easton and his staff, Companies C, D, and E, and a large
government train they were to escort. They reached Council
Grove on the afternoon of July 2, one day after the arrival there
of B Company. In addition to Company B and the trading
caravan awaiting an escort, Easton also encountered Maj.
John Dougherty of Liberty, Missouri, whose 550 head of beef
cattle had stampeded and who had stayed behind to recover
his missing animals. By the time Easton's troops arrived,
nearly all the cattle had been found, but now Dougherty
needed an escort to protect the herd during the trip through
the dangerous middle stretches of the trail. Dougherty apparently made the necessary arrangements with Easton to take
the cattle on to Santa Fe, presumably with Dougherty's
herdsmen, then returned to Fort Leavenworth to attend to
other affairs.[4]

On July 3 Easton's command at Council Grove was enlarged by the arrival of Company A, Third Regiment of
Missouri Mounted Volunteers, which continued on with them.
Also arriving at the grove on the third was an express with the
news of the engagement between Lieutenant Love's dragoons
and the Comanches. Love's dispatch reported the critical need
for additional draft animals to pull the wagons of Hayden's
government train on to Santa Fe. With nearly six hundred
cattle in his herd, most of them Dougherty's, Easton knew he
had the means to provide the necessary help. To do so, he
decided to march for Fort Mann, where Love intended to take
Hayden's wagons, as soon as possible. The column left
Council Grove on the fifth with three infantry companies, one

of cavalry, thirty-three wagons and their teamsters, one hundred horses, two hundred mules, approximately six hundred head of cattle, and thirty armed and mounted herdsmen. Following close behind was B Company with its caravan of trader wagons under escort, which stayed with the others for the balance of the trip to Santa Fe.[5]

Easton and his men marched westward as rapidly as possible considering the slow pace at which ox-drawn wagons moved. En route, probably at Lost Springs or Cottonwood Crossing, they had their first Indian scare when an alarm, sounded just after retreat, indicated Indians were hard by. A cavalry patrol was sent out to reconnoiter, followed by sixty infantry, but no Indians were found. Continuing on, they reached the Little Arkansas on July 11 and Walnut Creek on the fourteenth. On the fifteenth, near Pawnee Rock, they met a wagon train bound for Independence under a Captain Grooms as wagonmaster; the train had lost one man, a wagon, and many head of cattle during an attack by Indians (probably Comanches) two nights earlier. The column crossed the Pawnee Fork on the sixteenth. Easton elected to take the Dry Route (Ridge Road), which split from the River Road about four miles south of the Pawnee Fork. Finding no water at all along the line of march, on July 19 he changed his course and struck off to the south for the trail along the river. Until this time no Indians had been seen, although Indian signs were plentiful beyond the Cottonwood. On the afternoon of July 20 Easton put his men into camp along the Arkansas some twenty-five miles downstream from Fort Mann, their immediate destination. He was then approximately two and a half miles east of the Black Pool* and six or seven miles east of the Lower Crossing.[6]

---

*The Black Pool is a spring at the bottom of an arroyo; extremely deep, it has an underlying strata of black shale that makes the water very dark. On the rock strata nearby are the incised words "Black Pool Disc. by E. Post 1843," surrounded by a rectangular border. Since the pool is so close to the trail, it must have been known to travelers on the Wet Route from the earliest days, despite the claim made by Post. Travelers often inscribed their names on surrounding rocks, and more recent visitors have continued doing likewise.

The men of Colonel Easton's infantry battalion were green city boys, all from the St. Louis area. They had been thrust onto the plains with only minimal training and, as recent civilians, had no grasp of the importance of discipline to the operations and safety of a military unit. Despite abundant Indian signs, word of troubles ahead from eastbound wagon trains, and frequent reprimands and warnings from their own officers, many of these volunteers had become careless in wandering away from camp, often without arms. Now, as they halted along the Arkansas, some twenty-five to fifty of these men decided to gather firewood from among the trees in a small grove of cottonwoods on the opposite bank. Wading across the river in groups of two or three, entirely unarmed, they began wandering around looking for fallen branches or just taking in the marvel of trees in the midst of the treeless plains. Suddenly, and without warning, a large number of Comanche warriors rose from the taller valley grasses at the edge of the sand dunes beyond the river and rushed the men with spears and lances. The soldiers panicked and ran for the river. In their flight, eight of the men were killed, one just as he reached the opposite bank, and four others were wounded. Four of the dead were scalped.[7]

When those in Easton's encampment heard the commotion, they seized their weapons and rushed to the riverbank. Most began firing at the Indians on the opposite side, but a few crossed to rescue soldiers running toward them. One warrior was believed killed and another wounded, both of whom were immediately carried off by their comrades. The engagement was over in a moment, since the Comanches had no intention of taking on several companies of soldiers. They quickly returned to their horses, doubtless left beyond the dunes, and disappeared. Before they left, one was heard to call out in understandable English, "Come on, if you will fight!" Meanwhile the dead and wounded soldiers were brought across the river, where the eight dead were buried and the injured tended to. One of the wounded, Benjamin Frost of E Company, was not found until the following morning when a search party discovered him on the riverbank where he had crawled.

Though badly injured and scalped, he miraculously responded to the crude treatment he received and eventually recovered.* Reports filtering back to St. Louis and reported in local papers gave different versions of his ordeal. A sensational story in the *St. Louis Daily Republican* said he was found by a relief party and told them he had been scalped by a white man. Allegedly he told this man he had a family dependent on him for support and begged for his life; the assailant replied that he "did not care a damn" and went about his work. But another, probably more reliable story, reported in the *St. Louis Weekly Reveille*, stated that Frost said he remembered nothing from the time he fell until the next morning, when he heard the sounds of firing from the soldiers' camp.[8]

The sudden attack on the careless soldiers from Easton's camp must have had a sobering effect on all of them. They were forcefully confronted with the fact that this was no lark, no mere adventure filled with fun and frolic. The trail to New Mexico was filled with hazards, and the dangers were real. An Indian enemy might strike at any moment, when least expected. With hearts heavy over the loss of their fallen comrades, the long cavalcade of infantry companies, cavalry, trading companies, government supply wagons, and livestock moved slowly along the Arkansas during the day of July 21, going back into camp about fourteen miles below Fort Mann, probably opposite Jackson's Grove. It was Colonel Easton's intention to move on to the little post and remain there for three days, giving his troops time for rest, and also to send a party back to the site of "Love's Defeat" to recover the ox yokes and chains cached there by Lieutenant Love. With these he would be able to outfit Hayden's train, permitting it to continue on to Santa Fe.[9]

Easton and his men camped within sight of and about two miles below Fort Mann on July 22. Already there was A

*The *Santa Fe Republican* reported in its October 23 and 24, 1847, issues that Frost was there "hardy and well," swearing vengeance against the Indians.

Company with the train under its escort, and now the entire battalion was reunited. Also there was the remaining portion of the Hayden train, which had lost most of its oxen. A party was dispatched to recover the ox yokes and chains, and when these arrived, Hayden was provided with sufficient cattle from Dougherty's herd to permit him to continue. Company A and its charge left on July 24, with B Company following the next day. The balance of Easton's command left Fort Mann on July 26 and reached the Middle Crossing on the twenty-seventh after a long and tiring day of travel. All five companies were reunited and in one caravan by the time they reached the Cimarron. They arrived in Santa Fe in a long strung-out column, having encountered no further difficulties, between August 22 and August 25.[10]

When Easton's battalion left Fort Leavenworth, the men of Ralls's Third Regiment of Missouri Mounted Volunteers were just arriving. Four companies reached the fort on June 19, and the last arrived on July 15 or 16. They began their departure for Santa Fe, as had the infantry volunteers before them, in detachments, most assigned to escort government supply trains or trader caravans. The first to leave was Captain McNair's A Company, which reached Council Grove on July 3 and there joined Easton's command for the rest of the trip. Leaving a few days later was Company B under Capt. Gabriel de Korponay, with most of the others following intermittently during early, mid, and late July. The last to leave were Companies C and J, which departed Fort Leavenworth on August 1 along with Colonel Ralls and the regimental staff.[11]

On July 5 the express from Lieutenant Love reached Fort Leavenworth, bringing word of the Comanche attack and the grim results. In addition to oxen for the wagons of the Hayden train, Love also wanted additional troops to ensure the safety of the paymaster and the two government trains in his charge. He feared the Comanches might return in overwhelming force while he and his men were burdened with the injured and Hayden's immobilized wagons. In response, Capt. Augustus Jones and part of Company D were dispatched to Love's relief. With them were two six-pounders intended for Easton's com-

mand and seven mule-drawn wagons. They left Fort Leavenworth on July 9, under orders to proceed by forced marches to
the aid of Love and his men. By the fifteenth they had reached
Council Grove, where they lay over for a day. When they
continued on the morning of July 17, they took with them,
under escort, the nine-wagon train of the Mexican firm of R.
Armijo and Co., with Emanuel Armijo in charge. The column
reached the Pawnee Fork on July 25 and on the twenty-ninth
arrived at Fort Mann. There they found that Lieutenant Love
and his command, with the Fagan train, Wethered, and the
other traders, had left for Santa Fe some two and a half weeks
earlier. Even Hayden and his train were gone, having moved
on after the arrival of Easton with the replacement oxen. Jones
and his men continued their march and reached Santa Fe on
August 23, one day behind Easton and the advance units of
his battalion.[12]

While Captain Jones and his troops were marching for Fort
Mann to relieve Lieutenant Love, Lt. Christopher ("Kit")
Carson, newly commissioned in the U.S. Mounted Riflemen
by President James K. Polk, was leaving Fort Leavenworth
bound for Santa Fe. Carson was bearing dispatches from
Washington, D.C., intended for delivery to the military com-
manders in New Mexico and California. As escort he had 2d
Lt. Stephen D. Mullowny and fifty men from Company D,
Third Regiment of Missouri Mounted Volunteers. They de-
parted the fort on July 17 and marched to the vicinity of
Pawnee Rock without incident. On the evening of July 31
Carson's party pitched their tents at the Ash Creek camp-
ground on the south side of that stream. Capt. Benjamin W.
Smithson's Company I, Third Regiment of Missouri Mounted
Volunteers, from Polk County, Missouri, and a very large
train of government wagons they were escorting were in camp
about three hundred yards away.[13]

The night of July 31 passed peacefully, and as the sun's
first rays were crossing the horizon on the morning of August
1, the men of Smithson's company began leading their horses
away from camp to be picketed in new grass. It was vital to
provide all livestock with sufficient grazing to maintain their

health and strength and to prevent their breaking down. As the inexperienced volunteers moved out from the campground, the calm was suddenly shattered by the shrieks and war cries of a large party of mounted Comanche warriors who appeared without warning from behind the cover of the scrub trees lining the banks of the stream. There were about four hundred of them, and they galloped directly at the horses and the herd of oxen and beef cattle. The animals panicked, and the cattle began to stampede. Fortunately the cattle turned directly to the camp of Carson and his men, who managed to ward off the Indians with their gunfire while regaining control of the cattle. Men from both camps brought heavy fire to bear on the Comanches. The latter, evidently concluding that the danger outweighed the benefits, quickly broke off the engagement. As they disappeared to the west, however, they took with them twenty-six horses from Smithson's company and two from Carson's camp. The latter were lost when two of Carson's men, anxious to fire at the Comanches, dropped the leads in their hands, and their horses joined in the stampede as the Indians swept by. Three of Smithson's men were wounded in the surprise attack. Carson and his men and the Smithson column left Ash Creek later that morning and completed their march to Santa Fe without further incident.[14]

Except for the Indian attack on Smithson's command, none of the other companies in Colonel Ralls's regiment encountered hostile action. The need to escort slow-moving supply trains pulled by oxen did cause all of the companies to move toward Santa Fe at a very slow pace. The greatest danger encountered by most was the disease and fatigue that plagued them through the blazing heat of high summer on the plains. Four men from Company G died during the march, and many were sick. By the time they reached the Cimarron, six horses had died, and the rest were in poor condition. Captain Simond's H Company lost their commander when he died shortly after arrival at Council Grove. Despite these difficulties, all of the companies marched steadily westward, and most reached Santa Fe during August and September, with the last arriving in early October.[15]

Though Newby's regiment of Illinois Infantry Volunteers
had arrived at Fort Leavenworth before Ralls's cavalry, they
did not leave the post until several of the cavalry companies
were well on their way west. They left in three detachments,
just as had Easton's battalion before them. The first to march
were Companies B, C, and E, under the command of Lieutenant Colonel Boyakin. They acted as escort for a thirty-wagon
government supply train in the charge of Captain Findlay of
Westport, Missouri. Boyakin led his men south on the military road to the Delaware (Grinter's) Crossing, where they
ferried the Kansas River, then continued to the Shawnee
campground on the Santa Fe Trail. They reached the Lone
Elm on the thirteenth, and there suffered the first casualty of
the march when Pvt. John W. Collins died. He was buried at
the side of the trail. A second man, Pvt. Aaron J. Campbell,
died and was buried at Pool Creek on the twentieth. The
column reached Council Grove on July 22, where it was
joined by a second government train with thirty wagons in the
charge of Captain Elliott. Continuing on, they reached the
Pawnee Fork on August 5 and there buried another of their
men, Pvt. Robert Easley. When they passed Fort Mann on the
twelfth it was derelict. On the thirteenth they reached the
Middle Crossing of the Arkansas and laid by a day of rest.
They crossed the river on the fifteenth and began the worri-
some passage of the Jornada. The column finally reached the
Lower Cimarron Spring on August 19; while they were encamped there, an express arrived from Colonel Newby, ordering them to wait at that point until he could join them. Newby
and his men reached the Lower Spring the next day.[16]

Departing Fort Leavenworth shortly after Boyakin and his
men were Companies A, H, I, and K, under command of
Major Donalson. Accompanying them was a government
wagon train and about four hundred head of beef cattle. Just
as with Boyakin's column, disease stalked the men of Donalson's command, and Capt. Franklin Niles of I Company died
and was buried at 110-Mile Creek. Because of the large herd
of cattle they were guarding, Donalson and his men moved
more slowly than the others and were soon passed by the

remaining companies under Colonel Newby. They reached the Middle Crossing on the nineteenth and by then were a little more than a day behind Newby. On July 29 they were at the Middle Cimarron Spring. Donalson's command experienced no significant difficulty for the rest of the march and arrived in Santa Fe during mid-September.[17]

Colonel Newby and Companies D, F, and G, along with a supply train, probably left Fort Leavenworth not more than a day behind Major Donalson and his men. Along the Santa Fe Trail they were joined by the traders Alexander Barclay and Louis Tharp, with seven wagons, who were looking for the security of travel in the company of soldiers. The trip was largely uneventful until they reached the Great Bend of the Arkansas. Then, as they were perhaps halfway across the floor of the valley en route to the river, they began to hear a rumbling noise like distant thunder. The wagonmaster told them that it was a huge herd of buffalo moving northward and that they should corral the train for the protection of all. This was quickly done, with the livestock placed inside. The men were told to make all of the noise they could in hopes of causing the herd to veer from the train; when the bison were close enough, they were to fire at the leaders in an effort to turn them away. Soon the great herd appeared from south of the river, moving in a densely packed column six to ten abreast and crossing the trail just ahead of the train. The men of the advance guard commenced firing and continued steadily until they were nearly out of cartridges. But the huge beasts paid no heed and moved on relentlessly, as if responding to some important summons. The guards, after firing at least forty cartridges each, had to restrict their fire for want of ammunition. Finally the herd split, and the last hundred or so bison passed to the rear of the train. Then they disappeared to the north, leaving behind a great cloud of dust and the lingering sound of distant thunder. A dozen or so dead buffalo lay near the trail, and before they moved on the soldiers butchered some of the younger ones, taking the choicest cuts and leaving the rest for the wolves and coyotes.[18]

The weather was extremely hot, and the life gone from the

In mid-July 1847, while marching to Santa Fe, Col. Edward W. B. Newby and companies D, F, and G of the First Regiment Of Illinois Infantry Volunteers approached the Great Bend of the Arkansas River. When halfway across the valley they heard a rumbling noise like thunder. Their wagonmaster said it was a huge herd of buffalo and corralled the train for protection until the animals passed. A firing party helped keep the great beasts from wrecking the train, but it was a close call for all concerned.

shortgrasses that carpeted the plains. With the exception of the stampeding buffalo at the Great Bend, little happened to break either the monotony of the march or the stifling heat and dust that made each day miserable for Newby and his men. Great numbers of rattlesnakes sunned themselves on or near the trail, adding one more disagreeable aspect to the experience. But every few miles they would encounter a huge prairie dog town, always good for a smile as the men watched the antics of the little creatures who scolded and chided the passing column. On the second day beyond the Great Bend they passed Pawnee Rock, and a short distance beyond received the first indication of hostile Indian activity ahead. There they encountered Col. Sterling Price and part of his regiment, en route to Fort Leavenworth. Their term of enlistment had expired, and they were returning to be mustered out of service. Price's men had just recaptured a number of horses that Indians had stampeded away from a westbound party of traders about six miles ahead of Newby. They recovered all but one of the horses, that one having followed the retreating Indians so closely the soldiers lost sight of it.[19]

A day or so after meeting Price and his troops, Newby's column camped along the Arkansas, probably near Coon Creek Crossing. During early evening a light rain began to fall, which ordinarily would have been a most welcome event. But it came as they were preparing their principal meal of the day, and the rain dampened the buffalo-chip fuel, causing much smoke but no heat. Hoping to find suitable firewood, several of the men decided to cross the shallow waters of the Arkansas to a small island where there were a few scrub trees. Only one of these men took a weapon, but he carelessly dropped it into the water, rendering it useless. When they reached the island they were immediately attacked by a party of Indians, probably Comanches or Arapahoes, concealed behind the brush. The startled volunteers dashed headlong for the river's northwest bank, but before they could reach it two had been killed and one injured; all three were scalped. The sounds of the fracas on the island brought a quick response from those in the camp, twenty-five of whom rounded up horses and set off in pursuit of the Indians. But by this time the Indians had mounted their own horses and were rapidly disappearing beyond the sand hills to the southeast. After a fruitless five-mile chase the Indians vanished, and the soldiers returned to camp. The injured man who had been scalped was placed in the ambulance for the rest of the journey to Santa Fe. Surprisingly, he eventually recovered and was discharged to return home.[20]

The day after the Indian attack, a white trapper appeared in Newby's evening camp. Because of his unconventional appearance, with buckskin clothing and Indian-style accoutrements, a number of the Illinois men concluded he must be an Indian spy and threatened to kill him. The officers intervened, interrogating the man and satisfying themselves that he was entirely innocent. But the volunteers would not believe it, and some had to be restrained from attacking him. He was placed under guard for his own protection, then conducted about a mile beyond the camp, whence it was believed he could safely continue his trip alone.[21]

For the next few days of the journey the marching column was constantly aware of the presence of Indians. Occasionally the soldiers saw a single mounted scout, watching them motionlessly from atop one of the dunes on the opposite side of the river; sometimes a small party rode parallel with them in the distance or followed a quarter mile or so behind. Often only the glint of the sun on a lance point beyond the dunes betrayed a warrior's presence. But always the Indians were there, waiting for a straggler to drop behind or to leave the column and move away from the road to get a better look at something that had aroused his curiosity. Their efforts to decoy the poorly disciplined and inexperienced volunteers away from the main body of troops were often clever and sometimes nearly successful. On one occasion, apparently near the south bend of the Arkansas, a number of seemingly riderless horses appeared on a rise about a mile north of the trail. Believing them to be wild, a large number of men started toward them, hoping to catch a few. There were many herds of wild horses on the plains, but experienced soldiers and plainsmen knew that they seldom allowed humans to approach them. They kept a great distance between themselves and trail traffic and were usually seen as no more than specks on the horizon. These horses remained motionless, as if curious about the two-legged creatures advancing on them. The volunteers had gone only a few hundred yards, however, when the wagonmaster, a man with previous experience on the plains, urgently called for them to come back. He told them that each of the horses carried an Indian, merely waiting for the soldiers to get close and beyond help from the column. The men reluctantly returned. No sooner were they back in camp than the Indians, perceiving that their ruse was detected, swung themselves up on the backs of their mounts and rode off. They had been hanging on the sides of the horses with one leg slung over their backs, the same method they used in fights with wagon trains and other armed white travelers.[22]

A day or so later the men of Newby's command had their last brush with the Plains Indians. Six men, including Charles Buercklin, had been dispatched onto the plains as a hunting party to procure fresh buffalo meat. Once beyond view of the marching column, these men were surprised by a band of about twenty-five mounted warriors galloping directly at them. Buercklin instructed the others to aim their weapons at the leader but not to shoot unless attacked. The Indian, seeing his danger, halted his party and made signs of friendship. Skeptical of the intentions of what appeared to be an Indian war party, the soldiers kept their weapons aimed at the leader. After a short time the Indians concluded nothing was to be accomplished and rode off. Not until the warriors were out of range did the soldiers lower their weapons.[23]

Somewhere during their march along the Arkansas, Newby's troops overtook the men of Major Donalson's command,

and by the time they reached the Middle Crossing they were a day's march ahead. On August 18, at "Battle Ground,"* about fifteen miles southwest of the Middle Crossing, the column encountered the famous trader and plainsman Francis X. Aubry, who was eastbound for Independence. By the twentieth they had joined with Lieutenant Colonel Boyakin's command at the Lower Cimarron Spring. Here Newby reorganized his troops for the remainder of the march to Santa Fe. Newby left with Boyakin, Companies B, C, and D, and eighteen wagons, reaching Santa Fe on September 11. All companies of the Illinois Volunteers were in the city by mid-September. With the arrival of the remaining companies of Ralls's cavalry regiment in October, the last of the major military movements along the Santa Fe Trail during 1847 was complete.[24]

*On June 20, 1843, "Battle Ground" was the site of the fight between a party of Texas freebooters, led by "Colonel" Charles A. Warfield, and approximately one hundred poorly armed Mexican soldiers, acting as advance guard for the force Gov. Manuel Armijo was bringing up the trail to escort the Mexican caravan back to Santa Fe. Eighteen Mexicans were killed in the fight, about another eighteen wounded, and all but one of the remainder captured.

Fort Osage, a few miles northeast of present Independence, Missouri, was the western terminus of the Osage Trace, a road that followed Lewis and Clark's trail west from Franklin, Missouri, itself at the end of the Boonslick Road from St. Charles, Missouri. Founded by William Clark, the fort was both a military garrison and a government trading post doing business with the Indian tribes of the lower Missouri River. It was from Fort Osage that the 1825 government survey of the Santa Fe Trail began, and even now such eastern Kansas streams as 110-Mile Creek and 140-Mile Creek record the fact that the trail crossed them 110 or 140 miles from Fort Osage. Shown above is the fort as reconstructed by the Jackson County, Missouri, Parks and Recreation Department. *Photo by author.*

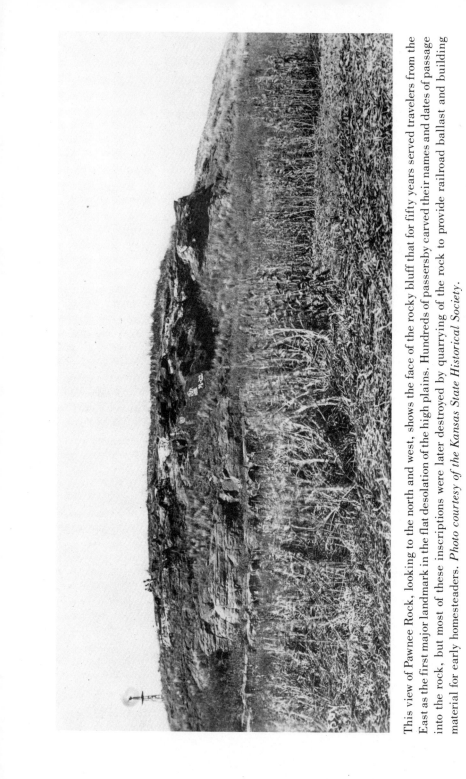

This view of Pawnee Rock, looking to the north and west, shows the face of the rocky bluff that for fifty years served travelers from the East as the first major landmark in the flat desolation of the high plains. Hundreds of passersby carved their names and dates of passage into the rock, but most of these inscriptions were later destroyed by quarrying of the rock to provide railroad ballast and building material for early homesteaders. *Photo courtesy of the Kansas State Historical Society.*

This photograph shows the tracks of the Santa Fe Trail in what is now western Kansas before its occupation by European whites and the introduction of agriculture. It was a treeless and barren wilderness inhabited by vast herds of bison and other forms of wildlife and also by the warlike Plains Indians. *Photo courtesy of the Kansas State Historical Society.*

Shown above is the dry bed of the Arkansas River in western Kansas, looking south. Little has changed since the Mexican War in this particular locale, except for a vastly increased growth of trees in the river valley. This view is probably essentially as it was seen by early passersby, with sand sage, yucca, and cactus providing the only relief to the otherwise bleached brown hues of the shortgrass plains in high summer. *Photo by author.*

The southwestern edge of Indian Mound, a famous marker along the trail to Bent's Fort, is shown above. Immediately below is the former site of Chouteau's Island, now part of the north bank of the river by virtue of the changing channel. The trail crossed the Arkansas at the Upper Crossing a few miles below Chouteau's Island, then tracked along the south bank until it reached the mouth of Bear Creek across from Chouteau's Island. It passed through the sand hills on the dry bed of the creek, then crossed the dreaded Jornada to the Lower Cimarron Spring, the first water south of the Arkansas. Indian Mound was reputedly used by Plains Indians as a vantage point from which to see, preparatory to an attack, wagon trains and trading caravans moving along the Santa Fe Trail. *Photo by author.*

Henry Worrall painted this picture of a herd of bison grazing near the Santa Fe Trail in 1871; the view would not have changed appreciably from the time of the Mexican War. The shortgrass, the passing wagon train, and the buffalo wallow in the left foreground were typical of the country the trail traversed on the high plains. *Courtesy of the Kansas State Historical Society.*

Approaching the Point of Rocks on the Cimarron River (in present Morton County, Kansas), westbound travelers on the Santa Fe Trail saw the landmark in the distance as little more than a thin pencil-like break in the arid plains. *Photo courtesy of the Kansas State Historical Society.*

Arrival at the Point of Rocks on the Cimarron brought the formation into focus as an impressive and important trail marker in the midst of the vast ocean of grass. Water was found by digging in the sandy bed of the Cimarron or at the nearby Middle Cimarron Spring, which became an important campground along the trail. *Photo courtesy of the Kansas State Historical Society.*

The Point of Rocks in New Mexico is a substantial stone protrusion that served early travelers as a trail marker. That it does not stand out in its own environment as does the Point of Rocks in present Kansas, even though it is considerably larger, is solely because the landmark in New Mexico is surrounded by the foothills of the Rocky Mountains, with the great bulk of the Sangre de Cristo Mountains due west and the Sierra Grande twenty-five miles north. *Photo courtesy of the Kansas State Historical Society.*

Wagon Mound is one of the most impressive sites along the Santa Fe Trail, for it looks from the distance like a covered wagon and a team of oxen. It was an important trail marker, with the trail itself passing on the west side through the gap between Wagon Mound and the adjacent Pilot Knobs. These early photographs were taken before construction of the highways that crossed the same gap, the latest being I-25. *Photo courtesy of the Kansas State Historical Society.*

Bent's Fort, referred to as Bent's Old Fort after construction of its successor some thirty-five miles east in the Big Timbers, was the most important and famous trading post on the southern plains. Built by Bent, St. Vrain, and Co. in approximately 1833, it was originally known as Fort William for its resident manager, William Bent. It served as the rendezvous point and supply depot for the Army of the West before the invasion of New Mexico. It was abandoned and partially destroyed in 1849. Today it has been beautifully restored by the National Park Service, as shown above. *Photo by author.*

Mora, New Mexico, is a small town on the Mora River twenty-four or twenty-five miles
west of the Santa Fe Trail. William Gilpin led his Indian Battalion troops into camp
nearby to obtain additional livestock and supplies before his abortive campaign east
along the Canadian River. This sketch shows the town circa 1858, very much as it was
at the time of Gilpin's visit. *Courtesy of the Museum of New Mexico, Neg. No. 14761.*

San Miguel del Vado was the third town the Army of the West passed through en route to Santa Fe. Here Gen. Stephen W. Kearny administered the oath of allegiance to the citizens, just as he had in Las Vegas and Tecolote. The sketch above, drawn in 1848, shows the town as it appeared to the invading Americans two years earlier. *Courtesy of the Museum of New Mexico, Neg. No. 9777.*

This photograph shows San Miguel del Vado in 1912 and indicates that little had changed since 1846. *Photo by Jesse L. Nusbaum, courtesy of the Museum of New Mexico, Neg. No. 13873.*

Santa Fe is shown above in a sketch, from the 1848 report of Lt. James W. Abert, depicting the city as it appeared circa 1846–47. The view is to the northeast, with the bastion of Fort Marcy on the hill above the city. *Courtesy of the Museum of New Mexico, Neg. No. 10118.*

Richard H. Kern sketched this view of Santa Fe in 1849. The city itself, seen from the east, is essentially as it was, though the topography was distorted by artistic license. *Courtesy of the Museum of New Mexico, Neg. No. 136509.*

This early photograph of Santa Fe, circa 1871, indicates there had been relatively little change in the city since 1846. *Photo courtesy of the Museum of New Mexico, Neg. No. 10205.*

The Army of the West crossed the Great Plains during the summer of 1846, first following the Santa Fe Trail to the Upper Crossing, then the Bent's Fort Trail to Bent's Old Fort, the assembly point and supply depot for the invasion of New Mexico. During its passage of the plains, the army endured heat, dust, serious shortages of food and water, and enormous discomfort. *Illustration from The History of the Military Occupation of the Territory of New Mexico from 1846 to 1851, by Ralph Emerson Twitchell.*

This sketch shows the Army of the West crossing the Rio Sapello near La Junta de los Rios en route to Las Vegas and beyond to Santa Fe. Gov. Manuel Armijo had suggested that Kearny halt his army at the Sapello while the two negotiated. Kearny ignored the request. *Illustration from The History of the Military Occupation of the Territory of New Mexico from 1846 to 1851, by Ralph Emerson Twitchell.*

At 8:00 A. M. on August 15, 1846, the Army of the West reached Las Vegas, and General Kearny and his staff galloped into the plaza. There he met the alcalde, Don Juan de Dios Maes, and many of the citizens. Kearny suggested that he (Kearny), his staff, and the alcalde climb to the top of a one-story adobe building on the north side of the plaza, where they could be seen by the citizens. There Kearny addressed the populace and administered the oath of allegiance. The scene above shows Kearny making his speech, with the alcalde on his right. *Illustration from The History of the Military Occupation of the Territory of New Mexico from 1846 to 1851, by Ralph Emerson Twitchell.*

This drawing depicts General Kearny's dragoons leaving the plaza at Las Vegas with guidons unfurled, continuing their march to Santa Fe. *Illustration from The History of the Military Occupation of the Territory of New Mexico from 1846 to 1851, by Ralph Emerson Twitchell.*

After leaving Las Vegas, the Army of the West continued westward along the Santa Fe Trail toward Santa Fe. As they reached the Mexican communities of Tecolote and San Miguel del Vado in turn, they repeated the citizenship ceremony first administered in Las Vegas. Then they crossed Glorieta Pass and descended into Apache Canyon, the place where Armijo and his force of two thousand men reputedly awaited them. That force had dissolved before the Americans arrived, with Armijo, his dragoons and artillery fleeing to the south. Shown above is the Army of the West as it passed through Apache Canyon. *Illustration from The History of the Military Occupation of the Territory of New Mexico from 1846 to 1851, by Ralph Emerson Twitchell.*

The Army of the West entered Santa Fe without resistance on August 18, 1846. The American flag was raised over the governor's palace near sundown, followed by a thirteen-gun salute. The ceremony is shown above. *Illustration from The History of the Military Occupation of the Territory of New Mexico from 1846 to 1851, by Ralph Emerson Twitchell.*

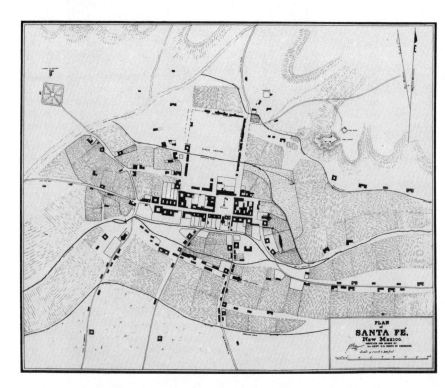

The city plan of Santa Fe shown above was drawn by 1st Lt. J. F. Gilmore, U.S. Corps of Engineers, in 1846–47. The plaza is in the center of the town, marked by the flag. The governor's palace is on the north side of the plaza; the bastion of Fort Marcy is on the hill overlooking the city from the northeast. The Santa Fe Trail entered the city from the south and is the easternmost of the three roads shown. Its terminus was in the plaza, and today a stone monument commemorates this fact. *Reproduction from the Cartographic Bureau of the National Archives.*

Brig. Gen. Stephen Watts Kearny, shown above, was the commander and organizer of the Army of the West. A stern but capable officer, he led his troops in occupying Santa Fe and the rest of New Mexico without firing a shot. Thereafter the Army of the West assisted in the conquest of California, thus expanding the United States from Atlantic to Pacific. This engraving is from the original daguerreotype made circa 1847. *Courtesy of the Museum of New Mexico, Neg. No. 7605.*

Col. Alexander W. Doniphan was a frontier lawyer when he was elected
colonel of the First Regiment of Missouri Mounted Volunteers. He led his
undisciplined troops, who styled themselves the "Ring-Tailed Roarers,"
on a remarkable one-year campaign in which they participated in the
bloodless conquest of New Mexico, then engaged in a series of successful
campaigns in Mexico south of the Rio Grande. *Courtesy of the Kansas
State Historical Society.*

Sterling Price was a congressman from Missouri when he resigned his seat to accept appointment as colonel of the Second Regiment of Missouri Mounted Volunteers. He led the garrison forces in New Mexico and put down the rebellion against the American government. *Photo courtesy of the Kansas State Historical Society.*

William Bent, one of the founders of Bent, St. Vrain, and Co. and the proprietor of Fort William (popularly known as Bent's Fort), was a powerful figure in the development of the southern plains. Married to Owl Woman, a Cheyenne, and after her death to her sister Yellow Woman, he wielded considerable influence over the Plains Indians and was a force for peace. *Photo courtesy of the Kansas State Historical Society.*

Ceran St. Vrain was a partner with Charles and William Bent in the operation of their famous trading empire. He was probably the source of the livestock and supplies that William Gilpin obtained from Mora, New Mexico, before leading the Indian Battalion troops eastward on an expedition against the Comanches and Plains Apaches. *Courtesy of the Kansas State Historical Society.*

William Gilpin, major of the First Regiment of Missouri Mounted Volunteers and subsequently lieutenant colonel and commander of the Indian Battalion, had an exceptionally distinguished career, eventually becoming the first governor of Colorado Territory. *Photo courtesy of the Museum of New Mexico, Neg. No. 50393.*

Thomas Fitzpatrick, a veteran mountain man and plainsman, became the first agent for the Plains Indians inhabiting the region roughly bounded by the foothills of the Rocky Mountains on the west and the ninety-seventh meridian on the east, and lying along and on either side of the Platte River on the north and the Arkansas River on the south. He became one of the few Indian agents genuinely liked and respected by his charges, who called him "Broken Hand." *Courtesy of the Colorado Historical Society.*

The French-Canadian Francis X. Aubry, whose real name was Francois Xavier Aubry, was one of the most remarkable men to travel the Santa Fe Trail. An eminently successful trader, he was especially noted for his crossings of the trail in record time and under difficult conditions. *Courtesy of the Kansas State Historical Society.*

The plainsman, mountain man, and pathfinder Christopher (Kit) Carson had vast experience along the trail to Santa Fe. He eventually became one of the most renowned and admired men of the western frontier. He is shown above in his later years. *Photo courtesy of the Kansas State Historical Society.*

8

1847: A Time of Trouble

The year 1846 saw the Santa Fe Trail become a road of military conquest, with the peaceful pursuits of commerce making way for those of war. In 1847, the continuing needs of the conflict with Mexico generated a constant stream of men and supplies bound for Santa Fe. At the same time the violent reaction of the Comanches and other Plains Indians was creating a new war along the trail's course through their homelands. Though Indians had neither wanted nor consented to the "temporary" presence in their country of Americans and New Mexicans passing through, their previous efforts to expel the invaders had largely been confined to raids on small trading caravans. They hoped these attacks would deter further traffic while providing economic benefits useful to their people. But the massive increase in the numbers of men and livestock moving across the trail in response to the needs of the Mexican War dramatically altered the environment in which the Indians lived. The streams they camped by were now usurped by whites, aliens who feared them and would not tolerate their presence. Americans seeking firewood destroyed the scattered groves of cottonwoods that shaded their villages. Grass the Indians needed to graze their horse herds was gone, consumed by the unending flow of the intruders' animals along the trail. And the game they depended on for food and clothing thinned in number and moved away from the river. Starvation and disease stalked their

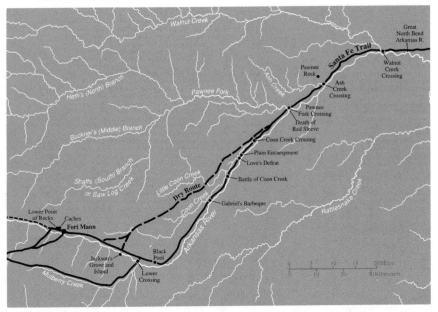

Santa Fe Trail from the Great Bend to Fort Mann showing important actions occurring in 1847 and 1848

camps, and a fearful desperation set in. The raids on commerce became raids to kill whites, the beginning of the long and futile effort by the natives to stem the invasion and save their land. In small villages scattered across the plains the chiefs of the many bands of Comanches, Kiowas, Cheyennes, Arapahoes, and Plains Apaches gathered in council to plan the war they could not win.

During 1847, resistance to the growing traffic along the trail brought attacks early and often on trading caravans, government supply trains, and military units alike. The first of the traders to start for Santa Fe in the spring of that year was a man named Brown,* who left Independence in April with a

*This was probably James Brown, who had brought the mail express from Santa Fe and picked up three members of Lieutenant Abert's party at the Pawnee Fork in mid-February. Or possibly it was Judge or Col. James Brown from Pettis County, Missouri. See Louise Barry, *Beginning of the West*, 674.

"few wagons." This was unusually early, since the new spring grass was unlikely to have grown enough to provide sustained grazing. Concern arose for Brown's safety during mid-May when travelers arriving from Santa Fe reported they had seen neither him nor his men. Rumors finally began to surface that he had been robbed along the Arkansas by Comanches who had taken his oxen and trade goods and killed two of his men. Another story reported that an eastbound party encountered Brown at the Pawnee Fork and was told he had been robbed by Pawnees farther to the east. He said the Indians had whipped him and threatened to kill him but were deterred from doing so by their chiefs. Whatever happened, Brown evidently detoured to Bent's Fort as the closest safe haven.[1]

Near the end of April a number of other traders left Missouri bound for Santa Fe. Included were James C. Bean, Thomas G. Clarkson, and a man named Reynolds, all from Jackson County, Missouri, Dr. G. W. Hereford from St. Louis, the wagons of McCauly and Shaw of St. Louis, and those of Bullard, Hooke and Co. of Lexington, Missouri. Their caravan reached the Pawnee Fork by mid-May, where it was held up for a time by high water caused by spring rains upstream. While they were in camp near the crossing, Indians made several attempts to steal their livestock. When the water subsided, the party continued, camping at the crossing of Big Coon Creek the following afternoon. The next morning, as dawn broke and the camp was stirring itself into life, the dim morning light revealed that the caravan was surrounded by nearly seven hundred Comanche and Arapaho warriors. The Indians were well mounted, and more than four hundred carried the formidable Comanche war lance. There were only thirty of the traders, and their situation seemed desperate, if not hopeless. But Capt. Tom Clarkson had experience with Indians, and when the attack on the corralled wagons came, the first three warriors to penetrate the enclosure were knocked down, disarmed, and taken prisoner. The teamsters were instructed to shoot the first one who tried to escape, and shortly thereafter (according to their story) they did kill one who attempted to flee. The perplexed war party besieging the train could probably have easily overwhelmed the traders had it chosen to do so. Captain Clarkson's bold action in taking prisoners so unsettled the Indians, however, that they contented themselves with harassing the train, running off livestock, and making forays at the traders whenever the opportunity presented itself.[2]

On May 28 the caravan camped overnight next to Fort Mann. A short distance upstream was the Arapaho village whose warriors had been in league with the Comanches during the attacks, and this generated considerable fear and ill will among the traders. When their train resumed its journey the following morning, the attacks began again and continued until they reached the Middle Crossing. There the war party finally withdrew after the train crossed the Arkansas and headed southwest across the Jornada. The Indians had mounted raids on their wagons and livestock at least every other day from Coon Creek to the crossing. Unfortunately, the troubles of the traders did not end, for in the Jornada they encountered some 270 Mexican renegades and had to remain on the defensive until they reached the Cimarron. Happily they suffered no more attacks after this and arrived in Santa Fe on June 25, having lost fifty-one head of oxen to the Comanches at Coon Creek and another twenty from lack of grass.[3]

Even as the first rumblings of trouble were reverberating along the trail at the beginning of the 1847 travel season, another step was being taken to advance white power and control to the very edge of the Plains Indians country. On January 14, 1846, Superintendent of Indian Affairs Thomas H. Harvey had negotiated a new treaty with the Kansa Indians near the mouth of Mission Creek in present-day Shawnee County, Kansas. By its terms the Kansa tribe ceded to the government their two-million-acre reserve north of the Kansas River in exchange for $202,000 and the promise of a smaller reservation to be selected later. The Kansas had been beaten into submission, ravaged by disease and war, and were on the verge of starvation. Seth M. Hays, then the operator of the Kansa trading post owned by the Chouteau

brothers, was a witness to this treaty. He was thus aware of the
coming move and may have had a fair idea about where the
new reservation would be located. Armed with this knowledge, in April 1847 Hays opened a trading post and store at
the Council Grove for his new employers, the traders Albert G.
Boone and James G. Hamilton of Westport, Missouri. It was
no more than a log cabin, but along with the government-
operated blacksmith shop, it constituted the farthest western
outpost of white civilization along the eastern reaches of the
trail—the seed from which the later town would spring. On
June 8 the agent for the Kansas, Richard W. Cummins, began
his search for a proper site for their new reservation. After
rejecting two other possibilities farther west because of the
hostility of the Plains Indians and the lack of timber, Cummins finally selected a tract, twenty miles square, centered
on the Council Grove. At its center was the Boone and
Hamilton store operated by Hays. Not surprisingly, the firm
already had a license to trade with the Kansa tribe.[4]

The spring of 1847 proved to be a time of great danger for
travelers on the Santa Fe Trail. At Fort Mann the men of the
garrison, fearful for their own survival, nervously struggled to
complete its construction. Nearly all of the trains and trading
caravans passing the forlorn post had endured their own
Indian attacks somewhere between Walnut Creek and the
Middle Crossing. Even the military suffered their share of
surprise attacks and losses. As the year progressed there
would be many more, as if the ghost of the slain Red Sleeve
had provoked his followers into raids of revenge.

On April 30 the remarkable Francis X. Aubry departed
from Missouri bound for Santa Fe with mail from the east. He
had sent his trading party ahead three days earlier but
quickly caught up with them down the trail. Somewhere
beyond Walnut Creek, probably near the Coon creeks, he and
his train encountered a war party of Comanches or Arapahoes. One of his men was killed and scalped within a few
rods of the train during a surprise ambush. This was their
only loss, and after the Indians moved on Aubry and his men
continued their journey. At the newly abandoned Fort Mann

they found two terrified men who had taken refuge there after being chased by Indians. The two joined the Aubry party, thankful to find a way out of their dilemma. During the last days of June, Aubry and his men met the eastbound train of Solomon Houck in the Jornada and warned them of the hostile war parties ahead. They did the same for every eastbound party they met. For Aubry's party, fortunately, the worst was over. They encountered no Indians beyond the Cimarron, and the rest of their trip was uneventful.[5]

Because of the urgent need for logistical support of the troops in New Mexico, the army maintained a continuing flow of supplies carried in the large government trains. On May 17 and 18 three of these trains, with thirty wagons each, left Fort Leavenworth bound for Santa Fe via the Cimarron Route. Two more followed on May 22. On June 17 one of the trains was attacked by a combined Comanche and Arapaho war party, probably in the area of the Coon creeks. It reached Fort Mann on June 21 and went into camp near the Caches. In the interim the train had been harassed by Indians for four straight days and had suffered two outright attacks. In the first attack the teamsters believed they had wounded one warrior, and in the second, which took place on the morning of the twenty-first, they claimed to have killed four Indians and wounded six or eight others. One of the following trains lost six mules to the raiders. At Fort Mann they found the seven surviving members of the garrison in desperate condition, hoping for the arrival of a strong train they could attach themselves to for safety, no matter whether it was bound east or west. The commander of the fort, Thomas Sloan, related their plight, including the recent attacks by more than four hundred Comanche warriors and the loss of three men. Sloan and the others had decided to abandon the post as the only means of saving their own lives. When the trains left the following morning, Sloan and his men went with them, the fort's cannon at the head of the column.[6]

During the spring and summer of 1847, Walnut Creek was frequently the scene of attacks on passing trains by Comanches, Arapahoes, and others. It provided the next major

campground beyond the Great Bend for westbound travelers
and beyond Pawnee Rock for those moving east. Though only
a shallow stream, the Walnut had steep banks that required
time and effort for a safe crossing. Scrub timber along these
banks provided fuel for fires, and nearby grazing was ample
for the overnight needs of most travelers. But the very qualities that made Walnut Creek a desirable stopping point for
traffic along the trail also made it hazardous. Located in the
heart of the buffalo plains, its winding course had provided
prized camping grounds for Plains Indians for untold genera-
tions, particularly the Comanches, Kiowas, Cheyennes, and
Arapahoes. The proximity of the trail's crossing to the mouth
of the stream meant it was easily reached from the Indian
villages, just as was the case with Ash Creek, the Pawnee
Fork, and other small streams feeding the Arkansas. The
timber screened the Indians during an approach, making it
an excellent ambush point, and the steep banks slowed the
crossing by wagons, leaving them especially vulnerable to
attack. From Walnut Creek Crossing to the Cimarron, the
danger of Indian attack for those traveling the Santa Fe Trail
was at its peak.

The eastbound train of Bent, St. Vrain and Co., which had
passed Fort Mann on May 24, crossed Walnut Creek on the
evening of May 27 and went into camp. Early the next morning
the mules and oxen were turned out to graze. As they were
doing so, a few of the men, including Frank DeLisle, the
commander of the train, and William Tharp, the young trader
who was accompanying them, set out on a buffalo hunt.
Without warning, a large party of mounted warriors—Comanches, Arapahoes, or both—struck the circled wagons,
the grazing livestock, and the hunting party simultaneously.
The raiders ran off sixty of the mules belonging to Tharp,
about forty mules and oxen belonging to Bent, St. Vrain and
Co., the seven horses and mules belonging to John S. Smith
(the former commander at Fort Mann), and two mules owned
by Lewis Garrard and entrusted to Smith. The most grievous
loss, however, was that of William Tharp, who had been cut
off from the others, killed, and terribly mutilated.[7]

On May 15 Alexander Barclay left Bent's Fort for Independence with wagons filled with skins and robes. As Barclay and his men moved eastward along the trail on the north bank of the Arkansas, they encountered a series of Indian encampments. First were Arapahoes and Cheyennes at a sacred village with a Medicine Lodge a few miles downstream from Pretty Encampment. Farther east, at the Pawnee Forts and upper Point of Rocks, were members of Yellow Wolf's Hair Rope band of Cheyennes. On the whole the Cheyennes were still friendly to whites, although 1847 brought the beginnings of a change in attitude. These Indians confirmed what Barclay had been hearing about the hostility of the Comanches and bade him use great caution in the miles to come. Those in the camp at the Pawnee Forts told him of a government train ahead that had fired on and killed one of their best and wisest chiefs, a man named Tsinimo (Tobacco). Tsinimo had ridden to the train's evening camp near the Middle Crossing in an effort to warn the teamsters of hostile Comanches. The inexperienced and frightened men in the camp shot and mortally wounded the chief without attempting to learn the reason for his appearance. Tsinimo was able to return to his village, where he died five days later. As he lay dying in his lodge he begged his family and relatives to refrain from taking vengeance on the white men, as was the Cheyenne tradition, because "his friends had killed him without knowing who he was." The death of Tsinimo nonetheless created deep resentment and was the first of many similar actions that would one day bring war with the Cheyennes.[8]

Barclay and his men caught up with the government wagon train, under the command of Captain Fowler, at Fort Mann. An Arapaho village located along the river about a half mile above the fort appeared suspicious to Barclay's party, making them apprehensive as they passed. They circled their wagons near those of the government train, a few yards from the gate, then spent the rest of the day visiting with members of the tiny garrison and exchanging news and information. About mid-afternoon, the westbound trading caravan of James C. Bean, Thomas G. Clarkson, and the others in their party, including the wagons of Bullard, Hooke and Co., arrived and made camp above the fort. Their party was greatly agitated by the presence of the nearby Arapaho village, since warriors from that band had participated in the harassment and attacks on them during the previous four days. The government train left Fort Mann the next morning, accompanied by Barclay and his wagons. Beyond Jackson's Grove, particularly near the Coon creeks, everyone in the column was tense, expecting an Indian attack at any time. But nothing happened, and when they reached the Pawnee Fork they went into camp on the north bank, then dispersed in search of buffalo. Ceran St. Vrain and his party caught up with them at Big Coon Creek, but the next morning, June 3, St. Vrain and the others left early in an effort to make a fast passage to Independence. Near noon the government train, including Barclay and his men, reached Ash Creek. As they were crossing this stream they were stunned with a sudden attack by a Comanche war party that appeared without warning from the creek bed. The Indians wounded and scalped both an American named McGuire and a young sixteen-year-old Mexican herdsman caught at the rear of the train. Captain Fowler took the injured men on, but McGuire died at Walnut Creek. He was buried near the grave of William Tharp, who had been killed the previous week. The Mexican boy was taken to Fort Leavenworth, where he lived for about a month before succumbing to his injuries.[9]

Sometime during mid-June, an entire government train, consisting of thirty wagons drawn by mule teams and accompanied only by the teamsters and eight or ten horsemen, was destroyed. This party had left Fort Leavenworth two weeks earlier bound for Santa Fe with military supplies. As they approached Walnut Creek a large mounted war party of Comanches and Arapahoes unexpectedly appeared, probably coming from the screen of trees along the nearby stream. The train was soon surrounded by the Indians who, satisfying themselves as to the weakness of its defense, made a sudden charge. The riders were knocked from their saddles and killed, and in a short time the teamsters were also dead. The

Indians took all of the horses and mules and those of the supplies that were of use to them, then disappeared. The story of what happened was carried to Westport by the young son of Nacomo, a principal chief of the Delaware tribe. He had been homeward bound from Taos, where he had been a prisoner of the Mexicans until freed by Colonel Price. Along the Arkansas he found himself in the company of the war party, members of which threatened to kill him if he did not join with them against the whites. The day after the destruction of the wagon train, he was given a fine large government mule and permitted to leave.[10]

Even large trains accompanied by military units were not immune from sudden ambushes and raids, and individuals leaving the immediate shelter of the evening corrals or the moving wagons were at risk. On June 13 or 14, on the banks of the Pawnee Fork, the camp of a returning government train under a Captain Craven from Buchanan County, Missouri, was struck after dark by a raiding party of unknown size. One man was killed, another was scalped, and many oxen and one wagon were taken. Accompanying this train was Capt. William Z. Angney's company of Cole County, Missouri, infantry volunteers, returning to Fort Leavenworth for discharge after expiration of their one-year term of enlistment. Their presence clearly did not deter the raiders. One night later, another eastbound train also lost a man near the crossing of the Pawnee. Either there were more than one large raiding party in the area between Walnut Creek and Fort Mann, or perhaps the raiders were shifting from one stream to another every few days to maintain the element of surprise.[11]

The trading caravan of Francis X. Aubry, which had suffered an attack by hostile Indians along the Arkansas in June, reached Santa Fe in early July. Aubry disposed of his goods within a week, then prepared to depart for Missouri. He left on July 28 with Captain McKinney's company of Monroe County, Missouri, volunteers (en route to Fort Leavenworth for discharge), a train of sixty-five government wagons, and a trader named James H. Barney. Probably because of the size of the party, they experienced no troubles with

Indians. At or near the Pawnee Fork, Aubry left the train and struck out on his own with the mail, in what was to be his first attempt at record speed. He made three hundred miles in the last four days, arriving in Independence on August 31. He immediately left for St. Louis by riverboat and reached that city on September 6.[12]

During the summer, even as new volunteers and their supply trains were moving west, a continuing stream of men from Price's Second Regiment of Missouri Mounted Volunteers and Willock's "extra battalion" moved east along the trail, bound for Fort Leavenworth and discharge. Because of casualties, reenlistments, and desertions, the returning companies were said to average less than forty men each. Although most marched as military units, some of the men simply straggled in small groups. Despite a year of military experience, the hard-learned lessons of the westward march were forgotten by some. On September 3 a Marion County, Missouri, volunteer was killed, presumably by Indians, while hunting buffalo near the Middle Crossing. In mid-September a party of sixteen men, including Lt. Col. David Willock, Dr. G. W. Hereford, Elliott Lee, and James C. Bean, reached the Missouri border. Hereford and Bean had been among the traders under attack by the Comanches and Arapahoes during their westbound trip but apparently felt secure enough in the company of only fourteen others on their return. This small party met no Indians but came close to losing all of their horses during a buffalo stampede near Pawnee Rock.[13]

As long as the weather held and they were not forced into their winter camps, Indians continued to harass the traffic along the Santa Fe Trail. On October 8 the trader James Wethered had left Santa Fe eastbound for Independence with nineteen men and several wagons, carrying the "express mail." At the Middle Crossing of the Arkansas the Wethered party was overtaken by B. F. Coons of St. Louis, who had left Santa Fe ten days later carrying dispatches. On October 25 the train was attacked near Fort Mann by a raiding party thought to be Pawnees but most likely made up of Comanches, Arapahoes, or both. The raiders were attempting to run off the livestock but, in the course of doing so, lost one warrior. The next night the Indians struck again, this time for revenge. The train suffered no losses and continued on its way without further attacks. When they were beyond Walnut Creek and the area in which the war parties were operating, Coons left the others and made a dash for Independence. He arrived there on November 4 after a trip of only seventeen days, a new record. Wethered and his men reached Independence a few days later.[14]

On September 25, only nineteen days after his arrival in St. Louis, the intrepid Francis X. Aubry left Independence, Missouri, with two partners, fifteen wagons, and about forty thousand dollars of merchandise for sale in Santa Fe. Following a generally uneventful trip, Aubry and three companions reached the New Mexican capital on October 29, with the wagons arriving the next day. This time his goods were all sold within two weeks, after which Aubry announced his intention to return to Missouri between December 20 and 25 and solicited mail for the States. He left Santa Fe on the morning of December 22, planning a trip of eighteen days. He was accompanied by four of his employees and his black servant. The pace he set in his effort to establish a record was so fast that each of the others tired and dropped back in succession, including his servant, who gave up sixty miles west of Council Grove. During the last three days Aubry averaged one hundred miles per day and reached Independence on January 5, 1848. En route he and his party had been attacked by Mexican bandits and robbed of ten mules, suffered four days of exceptionally severe cold weather, lost half a day in a snowstorm, and been delayed a half day by hostile Indians. Unfortunately, Aubry killed three mules by hard riding. Yet he traveled from Santa Fe to Independence in only fourteen days, breaking the record set by Norris Colburn in August 1846 by ten and a half days and that set by B. F. Coons by three days.[15]

If, along the Santa Fe Trail, the close of 1847 would be remembered for new travel records, the story of the preceding days was one written in blood. A long parade of soldiers had marched west to Santa Fe, and others had returned east at the end of their enlistment. An endless flow of government trains had carried supplies to New Mexico, and empty trains had returned to Fort Leavenworth. The number of traders on the trail had scarcely been reduced. These were the ingredients for war that aroused the wrath of the Indians of the plains, and they struck often and hard. The dream of forcing whites from the Indian country drove their actions, but the economics of survival and the need for livestock and supplies were perhaps equally strong inducements to raid. The efforts of the Indians were costly to the United States but in the end were like the bite of a gnat to a buffalo—they could not halt the inexorable advance of the white society closing in around them. When he made his report for 1847, Agent Fitzpatrick referred to the conflict as the "skirmishing, and 'scrapes' on the Santa Fe road last summer and spring." By his calculations, in that year's fighting with Indians, not more than twenty-seven white men had been killed, though the Comanches and Kiowas alone claimed sixty. Writing from Fort Mann on August 1, 1848, Lt. Col. William Gilpin estimated that in addition to the men killed, which he thought to be forty-seven, 330 wagons had been destroyed and sixty-five hundred head of livestock taken. In terms of the lives lost in white men's battles, this was a trifle, but the monetary loss to government and traders alike was significant. Teamsters were afraid to enter the lands of the warrior tribes, and the movement of supplies was to some degree impaired. It was a problem in need of a firm solution.[16]

9

Fort Mann and the Indian Battalion

The incessant attacks on both military and civilian traffic along the Santa Fe Trail demanded strong action. The previous policy of having the supply trains defend themselves was clearly a failure. In his annual report for 1847 Q.M. Gen. T. S. Jesup stated: "The Indians of the plains have committed many depredations on the trains; they have driven off all the cattle of some of them, and have killed many of the drivers. Unless an imposing mounted force be employed against them, and they be severely chastised, it will be impossible to send supplies on that route." Unfortunately there were no mounted troops in garrison at Fort Leavenworth to deal with the problem, all of the dragoons being in the field in Mexico or California and all the volunteers having gone to New Mexico or other theaters of operation. Those in New Mexico were preoccupied with keeping the peace or pursuing Navaho and Apache raiders. Pending operations in Chihuahua would divert any extra troops that might otherwise be available to patrol the trail. Adding to the government's problem, the Mexicans were rumored to have promised a bounty to the Comanches, Kiowas, and Plains Apaches for attacking and disrupting movement of Americans and their supplies along the road to Santa Fe. These and other factors forced President Polk and his military advisors to conclude that a new military force would be required, a force devoted solely to patrolling the trail and seeking out and attacking marauding bands of Indians.[1]

On July 24, 1847, Secretary of War William L. Marcy implemented the president's decision by requisitioning an additional five companies of Missouri volunteers to serve for one year. This new battalion would consist of two companies of cavalry, two of infantry, and one of artillery. Their task was to protect those traveling the Santa Fe Trail from attack and "to chastise the offenders, and procure, as far as practicable, the restoration of the plundered property." John Edwards, the governor of Missouri, quickly responded and created the "Separate Battalion of Missouri Volunteers." They had no official name and during their days in the field were variously referred to as the Indian Battalion, Gilpin's Battalion, the Santa Fe Trace Battalion, and the Battalion for the Plains, as well as other titles. The First Regiment of Missouri Mounted Volunteers, the "Ring-Tailed Roarers" who had gained fame in the conquest of New Mexico and subsequent fighting in Chihuahua and northern Mexico, had just completed their one year of service and returned home. Governor Edwards expected that many of the veterans of that regiment could be induced to reenlist for another year, this time to fight Indians. He approached the regiment's former commander, Col. Alexander W. Doniphan, in the hope he would accept command of the new unit. But Doniphan had left Mexico at the end of his term rather than continue with the military because he was "for going home to Sarah and the children." His statement became the watchword for the Ring-Tailed Roarers, and few could be induced to remain in service. Nor could Governor Edwards persuade Doniphan to return and lead another unit of volunteers. Though he personally declined, Doniphan warmly recommended the appointment of William Gilpin, the former major of his regiment, to the new command.[2]

It was, by Gilpin's own recollection, on a day in late August 1847 that Governor Edwards went to his home to urge him to accept command of the new volunteer battalion. Gilpin was sick in bed and under a physician's care, apparently because of the malaria he had contracted in Mexico. Still he was a sound choice for the position. From a distinguished

Philadelphia family, Gilpin had been appointed to and briefly attended West Point, from which he resigned to go west. He fought in the Seminole War in Florida, leaving the service as a first lieutenant, edited the St. Louis newspaper the *Missouri Argus*, and traveled to Oregon with Frémont in 1843. He was a friend of Andrew Jackson and Missouri's Senator Thomas Hart Benton. When war came with Mexico, he was among the first to volunteer his services, becoming the major of Doniphan's volunteer regiment. He marched to Santa Fe with the Army of the West and then south to Chihuahua. Gilpin's principal accomplishment had been the campaign to subdue the Navahoes before his regiment moved on to face Mexican troops to the south. He was the most experienced of the choices available to lead the battalion, but for health and other reasons he hesitated when Governor Edwards offered him the job. Edwards finally persuaded him by stating, "If you do not accept this mission, some inexperienced person will be put in, with no knowledge of what it has taken you twenty years to learn." Gilpin was sworn back into the service on September 18 with the rank of lieutenant colonel. He was later confirmed in that rank by the popular vote of his volunteers.[3]

The idea of sending out another five hundred Missouri volunteers to fight Indians was not popular in all quarters of the state. The *St. Louis Weekly Reveille* had editorialized in its August 30 issue that the state that had provided so many patriotic volunteers should not have its energies overtaxed and that its young men should not be exposed to the chances of a campaign that, from the outset, promised to be a failure. The fact that the state's troops had proven their powers of endurance, skill, and bravery in New Mexico, reasoned the editorial writer, did not mean that a badly organized handful could check the numerous hostile Indians of the plains. The infantry troops and artillery, he observed, would likely never be close to the Indians, and the two hundred mounted troops could hardly be expected to face the six or seven thousand warriors of the fiercest and most warlike Indians on the continent commonly believed to infest the Santa Fe Trail. The editorial suggested that a mounted force of not less than two thousand picked men would be required to do the job.[4]

The complaints of the newspaper men fell on deaf ears, and recruitment of the new force progressed rapidly. In one matter, however, Gilpin was to be sadly disappointed. Only a few of the Ring-Tailed Roarers could be induced to sign up for another year of service with the army. What emerged was a force largely made up of green city boys, misfits, and foreigners, mostly Germans newly arrived in Missouri. Nearly all of these men were lured into the service by the promise of a soldier's bounty lands, the result of a February 11, 1847, law that provided volunteers with 160 acres of land in exchange for at least one year of military service. Dallas County and Grundy County each raised a company of mounted troops, while St. Louis provided two of infantry and one of artillery. The cavalry force consisted of Companies A and B, the former having a full complement of 110 men commanded by Capt. John C. Griffin and the latter 113 men commanded by Capt. Thomas Jones. Company C, under the command of Capt. William Pelzer, was artillery and included 104 men, all Germans, with four heavy six-pounder howitzers. The infantry was made up of Companies D and E, the former being predominantly German and having 80 men under the command of Capt. Paul Holtzscheiter. Company E was made up of Capt. Napoleon Koscialowski's "Kosciusko Guards" with 86 men, a unit originally raised to be a part of Ralls's Third Regiment but not accepted in it. In all, there were more than 450 men in the five companies, including field and staff officers.[5]

After organization and the election of officers, the five new companies left for Fort Leavenworth. The cavalry companies marched to the fort, Company A arriving on September 1 and Company B on September 8. The three companies of foot were carried to their destination by riverboat, Company C arriving on September 8 on the *Bertrand*, D on September 17 on the *St. Joseph*, and E on September 17 on the *Amelia*. Each was mustered into the service a day or two following arrival and provided with uniforms, weapons, and basic supplies. Unfortunately, the equipment was of very poor quality, and neither sabers, officers' arms, books of military regulations and instructions, nor forage were provided. Only minimal medical supplies were available, and arms and camp equipment were defective, worn and decayed. What was supplied was insufficient in quantity, including wagons and teams, food, arms, and ammunition. The men lacked adequate clothing to face a winter on the high plains, and they were dispatched to their stations along the trail without the training or discipline necessary to make soldiers of them. That the battalion suffered greatly during its term of service is entirely understandable; that it enjoyed some measure of success is little short of a miracle.[6]

It is said that when William Gilpin accepted command of the new unit from Governor Edwards, he did so with four conditions, first that his health improve, second, that he be permitted to determine his own tactics, third, that he have priority for supplies, and finally, that he be allowed to do his own recruiting. History does not reveal whether that was true or, if so, whether the conditions were agreed to. But at least his health remained sufficiently stable to permit him to perform his duties, and he certainly did determine his own tactics in the field. Indeed, the orders creating the battalion were so general and vague in character that they left Gilpin and his men without a clear chain of command. Nothing was specified with certainly, not a department or headquarters, nor even their name. As a result, Gilpin became accustomed to dealing directly with the army's adjutant general, the secretary of war, and even the president when his needs were pressing. He seemed answerable to no one short of Washington, but there was also no one who was responsible to aid or direct him or to whom he could turn for help.[7]

The absence of a defined chain of command, the lack of proper equipment, supplies, arms, clothing, and ammunition, and nothing but the most rudimentary kind of training were only some of the problems faced by Gilpin from the beginning of his new command. The nature of the battalion's duties required dispersal of the various companies to the most troublesome locations within the area of danger. This meant that effective command was necessarily delegated to company officers during the times of their independent operations. That would have worked well enough with trained professionals, but all of Gilpin's men, including officers, were volunteers almost totally lacking in military training and experience. This problem was magnified by the fact that the officers were elected from the ranks after a spirited campaign in which promises and concessions were made. Their authority was derived from the popular vote of their fellows, substantially weakening their control and subjecting their decisions to debate and argumentation. There was no discipline, and orders were obeyed when the majority approved of them. Further compounding these difficulties was the ethnic make-up of the force. Two companies were comprised almost entirely of German immigrants, new to the country and certainly new to the West. The native-born volunteers resented the Germans, many of whom spoke little or no English, and mutual suspicion and distrust quickly developed. Rumors abounded, and the Germans soon concluded that the other companies would as likely fight them as the Indians. This irritation continued throughout the battalion's time in the field.[8]

Of all the problems faced by Lieutenant Colonel Gilpin in shaping a capable military unit, none grated more harshly than those he perceived to be caused by Lt. Col. Clifton Wharton. Wharton, a thirty-year veteran of the army, was the commanding officer of Fort Leavenworth and therefore in charge of supply for all troops in the greater southwest, from the Missouri River to New Mexico and south to Chihuahua. Though under orders to supply the new battalion of volunteers, he had little enthusiasm for the task. He held all volunteer troops in low esteem and in particular appeared to have little respect for Gilpin's men or their ability to perform the job. Gilpin always believed that Wharton deliberately shorted his troops of supplies and intentionally provided them with inadequate and worn equipment. In fairness to Wharton, he was responsible for supplying nearly all of the troops in the southwestern quadrant of the country on an ongoing basis and likely had nothing better to give. The ill will between the two men exacerbated the problem and to some degree was probably the result of the serious health problems of each. Wharton would in fact succumb to his sickness within a few months, while Gilpin and his men were still in the field.[9]

Although the orders given to Wharton were to supply the new battalion and nothing more, he took it upon himself to assume authority over the unit by issuing operational orders for the fall and winter. He probably thought Gilpin and his staff incapable of devising a reasonable plan of action. This greatly angered Gilpin, further inflaming relations between the two. The orders, issued on September 20, directed Captains Griffin and Jones to take rations for sixty days and leave with their companies, A and B (the cavalry companies), on September 22, then march down the trail to the vicinity of the Middle Crossing. There they were to reconnoiter and patrol the trail, provide protection for travelers, attack and disperse any Indian war parties they might encounter, and recover all American property found in their possession. The two companies were to go into winter quarters at Fort Scott, close to the Missouri border and the Permanent Indian Frontier along the ninety-fifth meridian. That post was one of a chain extending from Minnesota south to Louisiana, originally intended to defend the Indian country from white expansionism and exploitation and to protect whites from the incursions of Indian raiders. Fort Scott was well to the south of the Santa Fe Trail and far removed from the trail's danger zone and the intended site of the battalion's operations. The artillery and two companies of infantry were directed to take rations sufficient for about an eight-month stay in the field, or until May 31, and to leave for the Arkansas River as soon as equipped and supplied. Once there, they were to either reoccupy the abandoned Fort Mann or select another suitable site along the river for the erection of temporary defenses, quarters, storehouses, and hospitals for the three companies. Whatever location was selected, they were to remain in garrison for the defense and protection of persons and property traveling the trail.[10]

The orders promulgated by Wharton angered Gilpin for two reasons, namely that Wharton was attempting to assert a command authority he had not been given and that he would be keeping the battalion confined to the immediate proximity of the trail, without freedom to pursue and strike the raiders wherever they could be found. Wharton's concept of the unit's purpose was a static one, limited to patrols and protecting travelers from attack. Gilpin viewed his duties broadly, maintaining that he and his men could, within the scope of the order creating the battalion, actively and aggressively seek out and punish hostile war parties as the most effective means of protecting the trail. Certainly his ideas contained the greater strategic insight and were much more likely to have a lasting effect for the safety of travelers than mere defensive actions. Gilpin's angry response to Wharton's orders, in effect refusing to abide by them, brought a sharp reaction whereby he was commanded to retract what he had said or face arrest. Gilpin refused and was arrested but later recanted and was released.[11]

Gilpin must have been disillusioned as he prepared his troops for departure. They were green and inexperienced, almost entirely untrained, furnished with aged and defective equipment, undersupplied, without proper means to face the oncoming winter, and with scant provisions. Nearly two-fifths of them spoke little or no English, and none were disciplined. Gilpin later wrote that the battalion was sent into the field "in a most naked condition" and was "rushed upon the wilderness in a raw and crippled condition." Although their muster rolls carried 493 men for the five companies, losses to disease, desertion, discipline, and other causes had reduced the battalion's manpower to 436 officers and men by the time they were ready to march. Added to the other concerns were Gilpin's ongoing health problems as his malaria continued to plague him throughout his time in the field.[12]

In compliance with the orders issued by Lieutenant Colonel Wharton on September 20, Companies A and B, the cavalry, began their westward march on September 22. At some point beyond Council Grove, probably west of the

Cottonwood Crossing or the Little Arkansas, the troopers discovered that Indians had burned the grass along the trail to discourage traffic during the fall and winter when they would be in their winter camps and relatively immobile. Captain Jones and his Company B returned to Council Grove to warn the foot units that would be following, since with them would be the supply train, a cattle herd, and extra horses, mules, and oxen. With no available grazing, Jones feared that the livestock could not survive a march to Fort Mann. Captain Griffin and Company A apparently made camp either at Walnut Creek or just short of the burned area to await Gilpin's decision as to whether to continue west or return to Fort Leavenworth for the winter. Meanwhile the artillery and the infantry companies left the fort between October 4 and October 6, accompanied by Gilpin and his staff. The column included the three companies, a supply train of seventy wagons, a herd of 500 cattle, and a remuda of 350 horses and mules. They reached Council Grove on October 17 and met Captain Jones and his men. Gilpin called an officers' council to consider the problem posed by the lack of grazing ahead. They decided to proceed, reasoning that their supply train and cattle herd together gave them provisions sufficient for one hundred days and that, even if the cattle died from lack of grazing, the men would be in the buffalo range and able to replace their meat supply. After a layover of no more than a day, they continued the march to Fort Mann. [13]

The westward movement of Gilpin's command was uneventful except for the hardship and suffering of the animals resulting from the lack of grass. Dissension did flare up between the German and the non-German soldiers during the march. Based on the later court-martial charges lodged against 1st Lt. Amandus V. Schnabel of Company D, it appears he was guilty of, among other things, circulating rumors that the non-German companies were going to surround and attack the German companies. Although the rumor apparently had no real basis, it caused a mutinous spirit among the Germans and serious breaches of discipline. Captain Pelzer of Company C also played a destructive role, making seditious speeches that incited his men to mutiny and to resist lawful authority. Moreover, he distributed ammunition to the Germans and ordered them to load their weapons, presumably to ward off an imminent attack by the others, all of which violated the express orders of Gilpin. The potential mutiny was successfully dealt with by threatening death to anyone who did not submit to lawful orders. This they did, but it was an ill omen for the days to follow. On October 25 Pelzer was noted to be drunk, the first of what would be many such occasions. Altogether these incidents were ample evidence of the low state of training and discipline among the volunteers and augured poorly for the battalion's capacity to fulfill its mission along the trail.[14]

By November 1 all five companies of Gilpin's command were concentrated at Walnut Creek, in the area of greatest hazard. From that point they marched to Fort Mann in detachments, probably company sized or smaller, to accommodate the lack of grazing. The trader B. F. Coons, on a return trip to St. Louis, passed some of Gilpin's troops at the Pawnee Fork and found their animals in "deplorable condition" due to the want of grass. As his men marched west, Gilpin had been inquiring of eastbound trains from Santa Fe about conditions across the plains, particularly with respect to the Indian danger. Based on what he was told, he concluded that from the time the trail reached the Arkansas until it left the Cimarron, the threat of attack was primarily from Comanches, Kiowas, Cheyennes, Arapahoes, Osages, and Pawnees. Most hostile actions by the Plains Apaches reportedly occurred between the crossing of the upper Canadian River and the Pecos. The most destructive attacks, so he was told, were those perpetrated by the Comanches, Kiowas, Plains Apaches, and Pawnees. Why the Arapahoes were omitted is not clear, for the southern bands of that tribe were certainly allied with the Comanches in attacks along the trail. Likewise the Pawnees were credited with far more of the raiding than was reasonably possible, considering the great distance between the trail and their homes to the northeast, the presence near the trail of their bitter enemies, the southern Plains tribes, and their own desperate situation with the continuing Sioux attacks against them. In truth, few of the whites traveling the trail were sufficiently experienced to know one tribe from another, and they tended to lump all Indians together under the name with which they were most familiar. Accurate or not, Gilpin believed these tribes to be the ones against which he must campaign, and he began to formulate his operational plan accordingly. Also brought to his attention was a rumor that the Comanches and Plains Apaches were trying to influence the Cheyennes and Arapahoes to form an alliance with them in an effort to close the trail to traffic during 1848. It was this rumor that determined Gilpin's selection of a winter station for his cavalry troops.[15]

The first of Gilpin's companies reached Fort Mann on November 6 and the last by November 9. 1st Lt. Henry L. Rouett, adjutant of the battalion, later stated that they had marched for thirty days and reached what was "certainly the most desolate and uninteresting place on the face of the earth." Since the abandonment of Fort Mann in June, the Comanches had made it "a perfect wreck," leaving it, by one description, "a miserable dog hole, surrounded by desolation, destitute of shelter and fuel." Gilpin had by now decided on his course of action. In the belief that Cheyennes and Arapahoes would likely join with Comanches, Kiowas, and Plains Apaches in a general war against whites along the Santa Fe Trail if not dissuaded, he determined to leave his three companies of foot at Fort Mann and take his cavalry companies west into winter camp at or near the Big Timbers. The Big Timbers was a favorite winter camping ground for several of the southern bands of Cheyennes and Arapahoes, although usually no more than one or two bands would be encamped there at any one time because of the requirements of sufficient grazing for horse herds and available game to sustain the people. There were ten principal bands of Cheyennes alone, two of which ranged to the north between the North and South Platte rivers. The remaining bands roamed and wintered over a broad territory between the Platte and the Arkansas, extending from about the ninety-eighth meridian to the foot-

hills of the Rocky Mountains. Two of the four bands of
Arapahoes shared this same territory with the southern bands
of Cheyennes. Gilpin believed that camping in or near the Big
Timbers would so intimidate the Cheyennes and Arapahoes
that they would refrain from uniting with the Comanches or
any other tribe in a war against whites. If they had intended to
join the Comanches, however, it seems unlikely that either
tribe would have been greatly influenced by the presence of
two inexperienced cavalry companies in winter camp near
one or two of their bands. There also appears to have been no
credible evidence that the Cheyennes ever seriously considered joining such an alliance. They had, in fact, told a
skeptical Thomas Fitzpatrick they would aid the Great Father
in punishing the "bad people, the Comanches" if he asked.
But Gilpin knew neither the Indians he was dealing with nor
their ways.[16]

When all of his companies reached Fort Mann, Gilpin
issued orders that the artillery and infantry companies were to
remain there and repair and enlarge the post to accommodate
its new garrison. Once restored, it would provide a safe haven
and assistance for travelers along the trail and would serve as
a supply depot and base of operations against the Indians
during the next spring and summer. Captain Pelzer, the senior
captain of the three foot companies, was installed as commanding officer, a selection dictated solely by seniority and
one that Gilpin would soon regret. Gilpin then turned his
attention to plans for his march to the Big Timbers. Before he
could complete that task, however, he and his men received
their first guests at the reactivated fort. On November 10 a
small military party of seven officers and fifteen privates,
commanded by Capt. Gabriel de Korponay, arrived and went
into camp, remaining for two days. Included were Korponay
and Lieutenants Dillon and John K. Hawkins, all from Ralls's
Third Regiment of Missouri Mounted Volunteers, Capt. George
W. Hook and Lt. Relly Madeson of Newby's Illinois volunteer
infantry, Lt. Abram Allen of Easton's Missouri volunteer
infantry, and 1st Lt. William B. Royall, adjutant of the
"Santa Fe Battalion," a volunteer battalion organized in Santa

Fe and composed largely of reenlisted Missourians. All of these men had been detached from their units and ordered back to their respective states for recruiting service. They had endured many hardships: a severe snowstorm in the mountains two days out of Santa Fe, the loss of nearly twenty of their pack animals from starvation and freezing near the Middle Crossing, and almost constant severe weather. They left Fort Mann and continued their eastward journey on the morning of November 12, probably at about the same time that Gilpin and the two cavalry companies began their march to the Big Timbers.[17]

The passage to the Big Timbers was uneventful for Gilpin and his men. They went into camp "in the midst of the winter residences of the Cheyennes and Arapahoes," probably at the western end of the famous grove, about thirty-seven miles below Bent's Fort. Or perhaps they camped near Bent's Fort itself. The winter was long and harsh, and the combination of a lack of grain and forage, lack of grass for grazing, and severe temperatures resulted in the loss of most of their horses. Even the troops lived marginally, depending on what they could purchase from the Indians, Bent's Fort, the American settlement at the Pueblo, or the New Mexican settlements of Hardscrabble and Greenhorn.* In mid-December a small train arrived from Fort Mann bringing supplies recently delivered from Fort Leavenworth. They proved inadequate to support the troopers for more than a small part of the difficult

---

*The Pueblo, located on the north bank of the Arkansas west of the mouth of Fountain Creek, had been planned and built in 1842 by George S. Simpson, Robert Fisher, Mathew Kinkead, Francisco Conn, and Joseph Mantz. Primarily intended as a trading post, it was also a center of early farming in the Arkansas Valley. Hardscrabble and Greenhorn, settlements in the Mexican territory south of the Arkansas, had been established by American trappers and traders without either the knowledge or the authority of the Mexican government. Hardscrabble was founded by George S. Simpson, Alexander Barclay, and Joseph Doyle in the early part of 1844 and was, from its beginning, intended to be a farming and cattle-raising center, trading its surplus produce to others. Greenhorn was a small trading center, with some farming, begun in the valley of Greenhorn Creek by John Brown in 1845. see Janet Lacompte, *Pueblo, Hardscrabble, Greenhorn*, 45–59, 107–26, 136–46.

winter. The now dismounted cavalry companies spent the winter huddled in their tents for warmth, unable to move or do anything more than wait out the season. The monotony was broken by occasional visits to Bent's Fort, where they could converse and share the monotony with others. The new Indian agent, Thomas Fitzpatrick, was then in temporary residence while he visited and familiarized himself with some of his charges, making these occasions especially stimulating for Gilpin, who was well acquainted with him. The two men had served together with Frémont's 1843 expedition to Oregon and had traveled together to New Mexico with the Army of the West. Though they now had the common goal of pacification of the Plains Indians and many shared ideas as to how that should be accomplished (more forts and mounted troops), strain soon developed between them. Fitzpatrick thought Gilpin's idea of turning Arapahoes and Cheyennes into farmers near the crossing of the Arkansas, both to supply and defend travelers, to be naïve and "visionary." He also suggested that Gilpin was conducting a "sit-down" campaign against the hostile tribes, in reference to the camp-bound cavalry force he led. In his December 18, 1847, report to the Office of Indian Affairs, Fitzpatrick strongly suggested that the War Department withdraw Gilpin's battalion because he was certain it would "only excite ridicule and be instrumental of doing more mischief to the cause than can be remedied perhaps in five years to come." Gilpin, by the same token, refused Fitzpatrick an escort to the South Platte to arrest a notorious whiskey peddler from Taos and a suspected murderer from the Pueblo,* asserting it was beyond the scope of his battalion's duties. He also reported Fitzpatrick as uncooperative with his battalion and its mission. Despite these irritations, each man had considerable respect for the judgment and ability of the other.[18]

While Gilpin and his cavalry were enduring a harsh and

---

*The murder suspect was Jim Waters, who had just killed Ed Tharp, younger brother of the dead William Tharp, in a fight over Waters's woman, Candelaria. Janet Lacompte, *Pueblo, Hardscrabble, Greenhorn*, 204–5.

monotonous winter in their tents at the Big Timbers, considerably more was occurring back at Fort Mann. Since nearly 260 men were now occupying the sparse accommodations of the post, surely one of their first priorities was to "repair and enlarge" it as directed by Gilpin's order. The fort became, in due course, an enclosure with eight buildings rather than the original four. Even as they were laboring to complete it, however, other matters were evolving which would, in time, shame men and officers alike, seriously impairing their capacity to perform their duty. Their first contact with Indians was a complete disaster, ending in the unnecessary death of a number of warriors and sharp criticism of the battalion by journalists. "Broken Hand" Fitzpatrick had correctly noted that in the entire command, there was not "a single officer" who "possessed the slightest knowledge of Indians, or their character." Such men were fated to make serious mistakes, and they did. The principal culprit was the senior captain, William Pelzer, who had been left in command of the post. A man with neither military experience nor ability, and no knowledge of either the Indians or their country, he was incompetent to command and held his rank only because of the popular vote by his company. He lacked courage and in times of stress sought refuge in drink.[19]

The unfortunate consequences of Captain Pelzer's ineptness manifested themselves within less than a week after the departure of Lieutenant Colonel Gilpin and the two cavalry companies. On November 16 a wandering band of Pawnees, probably on their way north to their homes on the Platte River after a horse-stealing expedition, approached Fort Mann from the south side of the Arkansas. About midafternoon a sentry observed a party of some sixty-five Indians "coming down the heights opposite the fort" on the far side of the river. They crossed the stream below the post, then stopped while four of their number detached themselves and, bearing a white flag, advanced to the gate. Captain Pelzer, having called the garrison to arms, left the fort with 1st Lt. Caleb S. Tuttle and a six-man guard to greet the Indians and find out the purpose of their call. In response the four warriors, one of whom was a leader of the party, presented several letters to the officers. These letters stated that the Indians were friendly Pawnees and could be trusted. The Indians shook hands with Pelzer and Tuttle, and Pelzer invited them into the fort. There they had a smoke of peace and friendship, after which Pelzer showed them his artillery pieces and fired a howitzer to impress them. From what little he could learn from them, Captain Pelzer evidently concluded that the Pawnees either were scouting the fort and the strength of its garrison preparatory to an attack or were planning to steal its livestock.[20]

Pelzer, fearing the worst, ordered a number of volunteers to their quarters to secure and load their weapons, then to stand by pending further directions from him. Based solely on his suspicion of their intentions, he had apparently devised a plan to disarm and capture the entire band and hold them until word was received from Gilpin about their proper disposition. The battalion's adjutant, First Lieutenant Rouett, was opposed to the plan, pointing out that there were insufficient provisions to feed that many prisoners. But Pelzer ignored the advice and sent a detail to invite the rest of the Indians into the fort precincts and at the same time alerted the guard they were not to be allowed to leave. The Pawnees, doubtless expecting a fine meal, filed into the enclosure and seated themselves in a circle around the flagpole, with the exception of three or four warriors who chose to remain outside. At the same time sentries inside the post observed a larger body of Indians, estimated at three or four hundred, on the opposite side of the river.* Perhaps apprehensive that this band was preparing to rescue those in the fort, Pelzer ordered the guard to bring in the three or four warriors who had remained outside the gates. While they were doing so, Pelzer asked the leader of the Pawnees whether the newcomers were members of his party. He denied it, and Pelzer, by signs, accused him of lying. Realizing the dangerous position he and his men were now in, the Indian became agitated. Pelzer and Lieuten-

---

*These may have been members of a war party from one of the southern Plains tribes, looking for the Pawnee raiders.

ant Rouett had another hurried conference to determine the best course of action. In response to Rouett's suggestion that the Indians be released, Pelzer angrily retorted that before he did so, he would "butcher" them all.[21]

Whether or not the Indian leader understood Pelzer is unknown, but he gave a signal to his men, and they made a dash for freedom just as the guard was escorting into the fort the three or four warriors who had remained outside its walls. There was a great melee, and Captain Pelzer shouted his orders to open fire. At the first volley one Pawnee was killed and two others wounded. Except for three who took refuge in Pelzer's quarters, the rest of the Indians escaped after a chase of about two miles. The soldiers remaining in the fort then turned their attention to those hiding in the commanding officer's quarters. One of these Indians suddenly dashed out and was killed by a firing party outside the walls of the fort. The other two refused to surrender, or at least made no response to shouted demands, most likely because they understood neither English nor German. On orders from Captain Pelzer, the guards began firing through the door and window of the room. To provide cover for themselves, the two Indians inside started throwing anything combustible, including officer's cloaks, coats, uniforms, and similar materials, into the fireplace to produce a heavy smoke. It was to no avail. The soldiers poured a withering fire into the room, riddling the bodies of the two warriors and killing them instantly. The affair was soon over, leaving four Pawnees dead and fifteen to twenty-five wounded, two of whom were held prisoner at the fort. Three of the volunteers, including Captain Holtzscheiter, were slightly wounded.[22]

The attack on the defenseless Pawnees and their subsequent escape left all of the troops at Fort Mann, including Pelzer, nervous that they would return to exact revenge. But the Pawnees had disappeared, probably as anxious to be away from the territory of the southern tribes as from the military. If they had any other thoughts, the arrival on November 18 of Gen. Sterling Price and more Missouri volunteers bound for New Mexico probably deterred them. Not only did the presence of a large body of troops bring temporary added security, but they also brought with them the welcome news that a large government supply train with winter provisions for the battalion was en route and only about two weeks behind them on the trail. Price and his men left the following day, bearing with them Pelzer's report of the fight for delivery to Gilpin. Price also made a full report of the incident to Thomas Fitzpatrick at Bent's Fort. Meanwhile, back at Fort Mann the men remained apprehensive that the Pawnees would return, seeking vengeance.[23]

Trouble was not long in once again finding the garrison at Fort Mann, though this time it came in a most unusual form. Before the departure of Company D from Fort Leavenworth, First Lieutenant Amandus V. Schnabel, the same man who had spread false rumors and incited his German company to a state of near mutiny during the westward march, had met an "abandoned" woman (a prostitute), with whom he was much taken. Most likely she had followed him to that point from St. Louis, which appears to have been her home. Rather than take her along in the guise of a laundress, on September 18, the day after Company D's arrival at Fort Leavenworth, Schnabel enlisted her as a private soldier. Her real name was Caroline Newcome, but she was entered on the muster rolls as Pvt. Bill Newcome and was provided with male clothing and uniforms. Others in the company likely knew of the ruse, probably friends of Schnabels who would have helped him perpetuate the deception. By various artifices, "Bill" Newcome was usually kept on some kind of special duty away from the rest of the company, although some men said that "he" stood guard duty and performed other soldierly tasks. All during this period Schnabel, as his court-martial charges stated, was "tenting, sleeping, and cohabiting with the said female." But all good things come to an end, and so it was for Caroline and Amandus. Not surprisingly she became pregnant, and after the arrival of the supply train from Fort Leavenworth on December 1, plans were made for her hasty departure. When the empty train began its return trip a few days later, Pvt. "Bill" Newcome turned up missing. The train had made it only a few miles downstream the first day, and when the absence of Private Newcome was discovered, a party was sent to bring him back. The train, of course, offered the only means of escape for a lone deserter far from the States in the middle of the barren plains and surrounded by hostile Indians. "Bill" was soon found and returned to Fort Mann. There she frankly acknowledged being a female, and a pregnant female at that.[24]

Caroline Newcome was held at Fort Mann until another train arrived that could take her back to Fort Leavenworth. This occurred on May 15, 1848, when a thirty-two-wagon supply train began its return trip. Traveling with the company were seven men returning from Santa Fe, including George Rutledge Gibson, who had first gone to New Mexico as an officer with Doniphan's First Regiment. Gibson observed that en route, Caroline behaved like any teamster and smoked, chewed, and acted like a man. The train reached Fort Leavenworth in mid-June, at which time Caroline was interviewed by Col. John Garland and Lieutenant Colonel Wharton about her recent activities. Satisfied concerning the fraud perpetrated on the government, the officers released her to return to St. Louis. History does not record what became of the child Caroline must have borne for Amandus or if Amandus ever returned to find her and the baby and assume his parental duties. Apparently Caroline was not expecting any such display of loyalty. The St. Louis Weekly Reveille carried an article in its June 30, 1848, issue noting the arrival at Fort Leavenworth of "the far famed Bill Newcomb [sic]," still in uniform but soon reduced to petticoats. It said that she was placed aboard a riverboat for St. Louis but left the boat at the mouth of the Kansas River, probably at Westport Landing, and there fell in love again. She was, the writer said, "ordered to be drummed out of camp next morning!" The love Caroline bore for Amandus Schnabel was seemingly as fickle as that which he bore for her.[25]

The case of Caroline Newcome had introduced both scandal and humor into the usually monotonous routine and hardship of life at Fort Mann. Not so humorous was an

incident marking the close of the year at the post. When the
supply train had arrived on December 1, some of the supplies
and provisions were immediately prepared for reshipment to
the cavalry companies. These would be carried in the battalion's own train, brought with it during the march west. When
it was readied, Captain Pelzer assigned a number of men as a
detail to escort the train to Gilpin's camp upriver, all under
the command of a young second lieutenant named William
O'Hara, an Irish-American officer in Company D, a unit
composed mostly of Germans. O'Hara had recently promoted
another Irish volunteer in the same company to the noncommissioned rank of corporal, earning the enmity of most of
the German enlisted men. Included in the escort detail were
two German privates named Auguste Fahlbush and William
Goldbeck, both of whom were angered by the appointment.
The train apparently left for Gilpin's camp on December 15,
1847. Before departure, however, Pelzer gave orders to Sergeant Franz, the senior noncommissioned officer of the detail,
and to others, instructing that they seize and carry away the
baggage wagon of the train while on the march and also
inciting them to mutiny and disobedience of any orders given
by Lieutenant O'Hara. Pelzer's motives are not clear. He
heartily disliked Gilpin and frequently gave speeches against
him to the men at Fort Mann. It is possible he wanted to cause
hardship and failure for his commander out of either spite or
jealousy. He was also later accused by his officers and many
of the men of stealing government property and appropriating
it for his own benefit, perhaps by selling it to passing
travelers. Whatever his motive, when the detail began its
march as escort for the supply train, Lieutenant O'Hara soon
experienced difficulties.[26]

Only a few days beyond Fort Mann the German troops in
the escort detail began to refuse to obey O'Hara's orders.
When he ordered night travel, these men became insolent,
cursing him, threatening him, and finally refusing to camp at
the site he selected or to march with the train. Then Fahlbush
and Goldbeck, who seemed to be the ringleaders of the
troublemakers, deserted the train and took the baggage wagon

with them. They remained at a distance from the others for the rest of the trip, then rejoined them as they arrived at Gilpin's camp. Gilpin, on hearing what had happened, promptly convened a court-martial to try Fahlbush and Goldbeck for disobedience of orders and disorderly conduct. They were found guilty and sentenced to one month of hard labor without pay. The two offenders were apparently unimpressed, for on the return trip they once again refused to obey Lieutenant O'Hara. This time they shot at him, pursued him, and forced him to leave his command to save his life. When the train finally reached Fort Mann, the events of the trip were made known, and after an investigation, charges were prepared for an eventual court-martial. Unfortunately for O'Hara, charges were also placed against him for failure to control his men, allowing himself to be driven from his command, and desertion. Rather than be tried, he submitted his resignation effective July 10, 1848.[27]

The year 1847 had clearly not been a promising one for the Indian Battalion. It was composed largely of green and undisciplined troops who were too often a mutinous rabble, and many of those at Fort Mann were poorly led and out of control at the company level. It was ill equipped and supplied and seemed to be slowly disintegrating at its separate winter quarters. There had been no glory, no successful fights or accomplishments. Its record to date was little more than a shameful display of jealousy and infighting between men and officers, of sloth and drunkenness, and of disobedience to orders. William Gilpin fumed in his winter quarters and planned his next move to regain control and form a fighting unit. Fortunately for him, better days were ahead.

10

The Spring of 1848:
War, Peace, and Frustration

The winter of 1847–48 was hard. At Fort Mann the men were surviving well enough, though there were a few cases of scurvy. For the animals it was a different matter. Of the 75 horses belonging to the garrison, 63 died, and the remaining dozen were barely able to stand. Of 144 mules brought with them the previous November, only 6 or 8 were alive in mid-January, and fewer than 200 of their oxen had survived. The wolves were said to be devouring the carcasses of the dead each day. At Gilpin's camp near Bent's Fort, the situation was no better. The horses quickly perished, the result of the lack of grain and forage, the absence of sufficient grazing, and the harsh cold weather. The cavalry companies degenerated into dismounted units, immobilized and confined to the area of their camp. They were hardly the impressive military force, capable of overawing the Plains Indians, that Gilpin intended. Worse, they were now so weakened it would be impossible for them to mount an effective spring campaign against the Comanches and Plains Apaches. They were in desperate need of remounts and supplies, as well as reinforcements, in order to perform their assigned task. Meantime they lived on what they could buy or trade from William Bent, the settlements to the west and southwest, and the very Indians they were supposed to be keeping "in awe."[1]

As the difficult winter dragged on, Gilpin formulated plans for his anticipated spring campaign and for the season

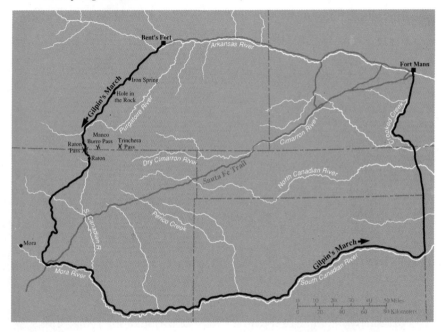

Route of Gilpin's spring 1848 campaign against the Comanches and Plains Apaches

beyond. Even assuming he could acquire replacements for the dead horses and mules and adequate supplies for an expedition, he believed his two companies of cavalry insufficient in number to track down and engage large parties of Comanches or Apaches. To do the job properly, he needed additional troops, preferably mounted, plus artillery. This would be even more important when summer came and traffic along the trail would require protection. His difficulties with the two German companies, almost always in a near mutinous state and seemingly more dangerous than helpful, convinced him they should be discharged and replaced with additional mounted units. Fortunately, on January 8 an express from Santa Fe arrived at Bent's Fort en route to Fort Leavenworth. It was made up of several men with their pack animals, and they would be passing Fort Mann on their way east. When they left

the cavalry camp on the morning of January 9, Gilpin sent
with them at least two letters, one for delivery at Fort Mann
and the other intended for Secretary of War Marcy in Washington. The first ordered Capt. Napoleon Koscialowski and
his Company E, along with a detachment of artillery, to
prepare for departure as soon as possible and then march to
Gilpin's camp near Bent's Fort to serve as part of the forthcom-
ing expedition. The second letter urged the secretary of war to
discharge the two unreliable German companies, convert E
Company from infantry to cavalry, and provide three additional cavalry companies as soon as possible. In its present form,
Gilpin stated, his battalion was "too small to cover the Santa
Fe Trail." The express reached Fort Mann on January 15 with
Gilpin's orders, left the following morning, and reached Fort
Leavenworth at the end of the month.[2]

Preparations for the march of Company E and the artillery
detachment began as soon as the orders were received. It was
a difficult task, in part because of the shortage of supplies but
primarily because of the miserable condition of the remaining
livestock. The best the soldiers could do was assemble
fourteen wagons to be pulled by only five yokes of oxen each,
with a total of 140 oxen. They were finally able to leave on
January 21. In addition to Company E there was a small
detachment of artillerymen from Company C under the command of 1st Lt. Phillip Stremmel, with one six-pounder
howitzer. The road from Fort Mann to the Big Timbers was not
difficult, running entirely along the north side of the Arkansas and crossing no major streams. But because of the poor
condition of the animals, it took the column a startling thirty-
five days to make the trip to Gilpin's camp. He had hoped to
have them there by February 12; instead they arrived on
February 24. Of the original 140 oxen, only 70 survived the
journey, and three of the fourteen wagons had been abandoned en route for lack of oxen to pull them. It was a blow to
Gilpin, since now he had to find mounts for all three companies and the artillerymen, as well as draft animals for his
train. William Bent had promised to find at least some mules
for Gilpin to make it possible for his expedition to leave camp

by March 10. Then they would march to Mora, New Mexico, seeking additional mules and supplies sufficient to keep them in the field during the spring. But before preparations for departure were complete, further troubles at Fort Mann interfered with Gilpin's plans.[3]

Even as Gilpin struggled with the difficulties facing him, in Mexico and California other events took place that would in time have a dramatic effect on the Santa Fe Trail, the Indians of the plains, and the country as a whole. On January 2, 1848, far to the south in Mexico City, Nicholas P. Trist, the principal negotiator for the U.S. State Department, began secret peace negotiations with representatives of the Mexican government. The most critical issues were the new national boundaries and the amount the United States would pay Mexico for the vast territory the U.S. would acquire. After considerable haggling and a final ultimatum from Trist, the Mexican commissioners accepted a draft treaty and forwarded it for approval on January 31. The irresolute Mexican president, Manuel de la Pena y Pena, vacillated for a moment and then, following encouragement from Gen. Winfield Scott and advice from the British that the terms were as favorable as could be obtained, authorized the commissioners to sign the treaty. This occurred at the provincial town of Guadalupe Hidalgo, ten miles north of Mexico City, on February 2, 1848. After intense debate, the treaty was approved by the U.S. Senate on March 10, 1848. The Mexican government ratified it on May 30, and President Polk issued a proclamation terminating the state of war with Mexico on July 4. So ended the conflict by which Mexico lost more than half its territory and the United States gained New Mexico and California, which then included all or portions of present Arizona, Nevada, Utah, and Colorado. The Rio Grande was recognized as the southwestern border of Texas, and Mexico's claims to its former province were surrendered. Except for a small strip of land which would be acquired by the Gadsden Purchase in 1853, the boundaries of the contiguous continental United States were finally established. In return for all of this, the United States was to pay Mexico $15 million in cash and assume $3.25 million of claims against Mexico held by American citizens. "Manifest Destiny" had now expanded the country from coast to coast, and the time for the westward growth of the population was at hand. But along the Santa Fe Trail and across the West, the original owners of the land, its inhabitants from time immemorial, were consulted by neither the former nor the new sovereign. The claims of ownership and the rights of the indigenous Indian population were simply ignored. As if to accelerate the process of stripping the natives of their country and their way of life, gold was discovered at Sutter's Mill in California on January 24.[4]

In Gilpin's camp east of Bent's Fort, the momentous events occurring in Mexico and California were as yet unknown, and other serious matters were occupying the minds of the men. William Bent had managed to acquire enough mules to mount the two cavalry companies plus the infantry and artillery battery and also to pull the wagons of Gilpin's small train. Preparations for the projected March 10 departure were well under way when the simmering difficulties at Fort Mann once again came to a boil. On February 20 three of the officers stationed at Fort Mann—Capt. Paul Holtzscheiter and Lts. Edward Colston and Albert F. Schnabel (probably the brother of Amandus Schnabel)—wrote a letter to Gilpin complaining of the lack of discipline at the post and making specific charges against Captain Pelzer. Among other things, they alleged that Pelzer had been intoxicated and totally unfit for duty during a time when there was the threat of Indian attack, that he had disobeyed Gilpin's orders to carry out the court-marital punishment of Pvts. Fahlbush and Goldbeck, and that he had misused government property and abused the battalion quartermaster. Further, he had ordered Captain Holtzscheiter's men to disobey their commander's orders, and had been guilty of "ungentlemanly and unofficer-like conduct during the entire period of his command." On February 22 a petition was signed by 112 of the men of Companies C and D, most of those still at Fort Mann, requesting removal of Captain Pelzer as commander of the post because he no longer had the confidence of his men and was "not capable to sustain

military order & discipline." These documents were immediately forwarded to Gilpin at the cavalry camp and arrived a
few days before his intended departure date. Lieutenant
Stremmel, commander of Gilpin's artillery detachment, added
further charges in a letter dated March 9. In it he called Pelzer
"a coward, swindler and a thief" and charged him with being
intoxicated on a number of occasions while in command,
selling government property under his control to others and
appropriating the money, and swindling his men of money
owed them as military pay, which he had received from the
paymaster at Fort Leavenworth.[5]

Receipt of the various charges against Pelzer probably
came as no surprise to Gilpin, given Pelzer's previous history.
But the problem raised itself at a difficult time for the
battalion commander. He was some distance from Fort Mann
and, considering the eminent departure of his expedition
against the Comanches and Plains Apaches, could not return
to take care of the matter either promptly or in person. Instead
he wrote a letter to Secretary of War Marcy outlining the
complaints and his quandary in dealing with them expe-
ditiously. He again requested that the two companies of
German volunteers be discharged in the best interest of the
service and the country and asked that he be authorized to
constitute courts-martial with sufficient authority to deal
with the battalion problems, including officers, as the only
means of maintaining a "high state of discipline." The
adjutant general of the army, Brig. Gen. Roger Jones, sup-
ported Gilpin's request that the two German companies be
discharged. He also suggested that because the Indian
Battalion was scattered and could not come together for
courts-martial, Bvt. Col. John Garland, commander of the
Third Military District headquartered at Jefferson Barracks
near St. Louis, be sent to Fort Leavenworth and thence, in the
company of Lt. Col. Clifton Wharton, to Fort Mann to conduct
an investigation of the various charges and to discharge guilty
parties. The president approved the plan for an investigation,
and orders to proceed were forwarded to Garland and Wharton. But the wheels of military justice moved slowly in an era

of poor communications. Jones did not receive Gilpin's request until late April, and the orders to conduct the investigation did not leave Washington until May 9. Before any investigation occurred, Gilpin had completed his expedition and was back at Fort Mann. Meanwhile dissension and lack of discipline continued to haunt the post, for Pelzer remained in command until higher authority arrived. On March 6, before Gilpin's departure for Mora, New Mexico, mutinous demonstrations against Pelzer broke out at the fort that were of such magnitude it was necessary to "order out the Battalion" to quell the disturbance. Fort Mann was a troubled island located in a sea of danger.[6]

While mutiny seethed at Fort Mann, and Gilpin's command prepared to break camp, others were attending to matters of peace and to the commerce of the trail. During the latter part of February, before he left for the Pueblo and the South Platte to visit other Indians within his agency, Thomas Fitzpatrick had counciled with a number of chiefs and other leaders of the Kiowa tribe somewhere along the Arkansas. Following their discussions, the Kiowa chiefs promised to sever their relations with the hostile northern Comanche bands and join the Cheyennes and Arapahoes on the Arkansas. In large part they kept their word and did not participate significantly in raiding along the trail in 1848. So successful were Fitzpatrick's efforts that on November 17 the explorer John C. Frémont wrote from Bent's Fort of a meeting he had had with Fitzpatrick at the Big Timbers, praised Fitzpatrick's abilities, and commented that he had "succeeded in drawing out from among the Cumanches the whole Kiowa nation, with the exception of six lodges." It was a major accomplishment for the new agent, who would, in time, become the only Indian agent outside of Texas that the Indians of the southern plains ever really trusted or respected. When he wrote his report on August 1, 1848, however, Gilpin claimed it was the presence of his cavalry companies near the Big Timbers that had so "overawed" the bands in winter residence there that they had broken off relations with the Comanches and Apaches and had persuaded the Kiowas to do the same. None of the tribes involved—Cheyennes, Arapahoes, and Kiowas—had ever had any real conflict with the American military until that time, and each thought of themselves as easily the superior fighting force, able to outride, outfight, and outshoot any white man on the plains. Although Gilpin probably believed his small force to be "awe inspiring" in the eyes of Indians, it seems much more reasonable to believe the Kiowas withdrew from their alliance with the Comanches because of the persuasive efforts of the experienced plainsman and mountain man Thomas Fitzpatrick.[7]

In early March a number of traders, both Americans and Mexicans, began to arrive in Missouri from Santa Fe. They had left the New Mexican capital on February 1 and made the trip in approximately thirty-two days. The first trader to leave from Missouri westbound for Santa Fe was the adventurous Francis X. Aubry. He knew that the earliest to arrive was the most likely to make profitable sales. He left Independence in mid-March with about fifteen wagons laden with merchandise. Realizing there would be insufficient growth of the native grasses to provide sustained grazing, Aubry had corn hauled out in advance of his train as far as Diamond Springs. It was enough to feed his animals until they reached Fort Mann, where he intended to buy more. Aubry reached Santa Fe on April 21 and sold his goods at wholesale before the train even reached the city.[8]

On March 11, 1848, as activity was once more beginning to stir along the length of the Santa Fe Trail, William Gilpin led his command of approximately three hundred officers and men away from their winter camp on the first leg of the expedition in search of Comanches. Behind him he left the troublesome problem of the mutinous garrison at Fort Mann; the solution for that would have to await his return. The winter had been long, cold, and for the most part dry, and it was good to have it over. Even with the mules and supplies provided by William Bent, Gilpin and his men were still lacking nearly everything, including mounts. Therefore he intended to go first to the closest of the more substantial New Mexican settlements, the town of Santa Gertrudis de lo de Mora (usually called Mora), where, Bent assured him, he could purchase additional livestock and supplies. It was in the valleys near Mora that Bent, St. Vrain and Co. maintained its grazing grounds and raised grain, vegetables, and forage for use at Bent's Fort.

Gilpin's command marched west to the intersection with the trail leading southwest to Raton Pass and beyond, crossed the mountains, and moved south following General Kearny's route until they reached the Mora River. Then they moved west along the river on the road to the town of Mora, going into camp about five and a half miles northwest of the confluence of the Mora and Sapello rivers, nineteen or twenty miles below the town. The trip probably took two weeks, considering the leisurely pace of mules and the presence of a slow-moving supply train. They would have arrived in their new camp about March 25, and Alexander Barclay visited them there on March 31 while he was returning to Bent's Fort from Santa Fe. In camp Barclay found William Bent, who had come south with Gilpin and his men to assist in acquiring supplies. Barclay and Bent remained at Gilpin's camp through April 7, awaiting the arrival of a Bent wagon train from Santa Fe, then left for Taos on April 8. While in camp on the Mora River, Gilpin's men allowed their mounts to rest and enjoy undisturbed grazing. Meanwhile the wagon train was sent to Mora to secure additional supplies and mules. The expedition was ready to embark on the search for Comanches or Plains Apaches by the time Barclay and Bent left for Taos.[9]

The intelligence received by Gilpin indicated that at least some of the Comanches or Plains Apaches might be found in winter camps along the main or south fork of the Canadian River. He intended to thoroughly scour this region and, if the Indians could be found, to deal a severe blow against them while their horses were still weak from lack of grazing. The expedition left its camp on the Mora River sometime during the second week of April. In addition to the troops there were twenty-six mule-drawn supply wagons, plus seven Indians and three mountain men employed as guides. Their route is not clear, but because the Mora was a tributary of the

Canadian, they likely followed its banks eastward to the junction of the two streams. If they wanted to examine the extreme upper reaches of the river, they would have marched northeast along the Santa Fe Trail to the Rock Crossing of the Canadian, then followed it downstream.[10]

Whatever route Gilpin and his men took, the river would have led them onto the plains and into the country of the Kwahadi Comanches, the band that primarily roamed the Llano Estacado, the Staked Plains of Texas and New Mexico. As they moved farther east they passed from the range of the Kwahadis into that of the Nokonis to the south and the Kotsotekas to the north of the Canadian. But though they plunged deep into Comanche country, neither Comanches nor Plains Apaches were to be found. What they did find was that the Indians had been warned of the approach of the military expedition by a band of renegade Mexicans, possibly Comancharos,* and had set fire to the grass on both sides of the river in an effort to halt the advancing soldiers. American horses and mules were large and grain-fed, requiring substantial grazing to retain their health and avoid breaking down while on long marches. Although the burning did not stop Gilpin and his men, it undoubtedly slowed them. Scouting the country on either side of the south fork of the Canadian would have taken considerable time at best, but it took Gilpin and his troopers approximately forty days to reach the Antelope Hills, more time than some of the plodding ox trains took to travel from Independence to Santa Fe. During their entire trip they saw no Indians other than their own scouts. What they did not know was that in mid-May, even as they were approaching the Antelope Hills, to the north—along the Arkansas near the crossing of the Pawnee Fork—about twenty-five well-mounted Comanches had attacked the eastbound

---

*"Comancharos" was the Spanish term for those non-Indians trading with the Comanches—usually Mexicans. Some were legitimate traders, but there were those who preferred to trade for goods stolen from whites. In time, the term had the connotation of renegades who promoted Comanche raiding of white commerce or communities to obtain goods for trade, sometimes in exchange for firearms and ammunition.

train of a trader named Fink. One of the Mexican traders in
Fink's party was wounded by a lance. It was the first reported
Comanche attack on the commerce of the trail for the new
year. [11]

The absence of hostile Indians puzzled Gilpin. Later,
based on what he learned from captives, he became convinced that the coming of American soldiers had so frightened
the bands inhabiting the region that they had abandoned their
own country, the Plains Apaches going south to the White
Mountains, near El Paso, and the Comanches farther south
into Texas. This seems unlikely. All of them could have
avoided Gilpin's small expedition with ease without moving
any great distance. Both their horses and their people had the
stamina and endurance to stay ahead of or even circle behind
Gilpin if they desired. Once aware of his coming, the Indians
would have had scouts watching the slow progress of the
column and would have simply stayed beyond his reach. The
country was big, and they knew it well; Gilpin knew it not at
all, and even his scouts were probably seeing much of it for
the first time. The Kwahadi Comanches had done little if any
of the raiding along the Santa Fe Trail; those bands that had
were likely already leaving their winter encampments and
moving to the Arkansas. The Penetaka Comanches of west-
central Texas were quiet, the result of nine new companies of
Texas Rangers raised specifically to protect the frontier while
the army was preoccupied with the war in Mexico. Of nearly
equal importance in keeping peace in Texas was the new
Indian agent, Maj. Robert S. Neighbors, one of the few honest
and capable men to hold the position and also gain the respect
and confidence of his charges. No significant Comanche raids
were reported in Texas during 1848, whether by members of
southern or northern bands; all of the serious fighting and
raiding took place along the Arkansas. Although Gilpin took
credit for and sincerely believed he had "overawed" the
Indians, most likely his expedition along the Canadian was a
fool's errand, destined for failure from its first day. Far from
being "overawed," the Comanches were probably contemptu-
ous and perhaps somewhat amused. [12]

While Gilpin was moving slowly eastward along the south fork of the Canadian River, activity was picking up along the Santa Fe Trail. In mid-April a party of thirty traders reached the Missouri border after a twenty-seven-day trip from Santa Fe. But westbound traffic was delayed. Reports from eastbound traders indicated there was little grass and the season had been remarkably dry, with the first rain of the year not occurring until the evening of April 27. Prolonged cool weather had also contributed to delayed growth in the grasses of the plains. By the end of April, meanwhile, approximately 670 new volunteers had arrived at Fort Leavenworth; men recruited during the winter from Missouri and Illinois to replace those whose terms of service had expired or who were discharged for health, disciplinary, or other reasons. Of these, about 300 from Missouri had been enlisted by Capt. Gabriel de Korponay and Lt. John K. Hawkins and were intended for Ralls's Third Regiment of Missouri Mounted Volunteers. Seventy-one others were enlisted for the Santa Fe Battalion by 1st Lt. William B. Royall, its adjutant. Another 300 volunteers from Illinois arrived at the fort by the month's end under command of Capt. Vantrump Turner of Newby's First Regiment of Illinois Infantry Volunteers. All of these men were being issued uniforms and equipment and given a brief period of training before departure for Santa Fe.[13]

By the middle of May, westbound traffic along the trail was growing rapidly, with the road between Independence and the Council Grove carrying as many as two hundred heavy freight wagons containing a wide variety of trade goods. The country along the trail was covered with encampments of traders, and at least one hundred wagons were reported to have already passed the Grove and to be on the high plains. It was predicted that the amount of goods in transit would far exceed the volume of exports in any previous year. Between May 15 and 20 the approximately 300 Illinois volunteer infantry recruits under command of Captain Turner, along with the 71 recruits for the volunteer cavalry of the Santa Fe Battalion under First Lieutenant Royall, marched from Fort Leavenworth en route to Santa Fe. They probably reached Council

Grove at about the end of May and went into camp to rest and to allow their livestock to graze. They remained there for several days awaiting the formation of caravans of traders or the arrival of government supply trains in need of escort through the most dangerous part of the Indian country.[14]

At approximately the same time Turner's command was leaving Fort Leavenworth, Francis X. Aubry left Santa Fe on the night of May 19, bound for Independence. There were seven men in the party, including Aubry, but the other six gave out after about three hundred miles of trying to keep up with him. He was robbed by Indians (probably Comanches) near the Pawnee Fork and lost his baggage, provisions, packages of mail, and other items, as well as more than a day of travel time. En route he killed three horses and two mules by hard riding, walked more than thirty miles to Fort Mann for a remount, went three days without food, and slept only four or five hours. He arrived in Independence an hour before sunrise on May 28, having made the entire journey in an incredible eight days and ten hours, thereby breaking his own record by five and a half days. Had he not been detained by Indians, he would have completed the trip in only seven days.[15]

On May 13, while Gilpin and his troops were still examining the country along the south fork of the Canadian River, and Captain Turner and his volunteer recruits remained at Fort Leavenworth, Maj. William Singer, a paymaster with the volunteers stationed in New Mexico, lost his mules and the contents of his wagon to Indians near the Middle Crossing. What was otherwise a trifling incident soon became a prime example of Capt. William Pelzer's incompetence to command. Singer, with his servant and a teamster to drive his mule-drawn wagon, had left Santa Fe on May 1 and reached Las Vegas on May 3. There he joined a party of four who were carrying the mail to Independence, including George R. Gibson, formerly a lieutenant in Doniphan's regiment, Capt. Anson Smith, lately of Willock's battalion, William Raymond, and a man named Swift. The combined party of seven left Las Vegas on May 4 and experienced little difficulty, except for the usual discomforts of travel across the plains, until they approached the Arkansas. On May 10, twenty-one or twenty-two miles northeast of Willow Bar, they encountered the first traders en route to Santa Fe, a thirty-wagon train belonging to the firm of Lightner, Herd, and Shaw. From the traders they learned that a large band of Kiowas had moved south from the Arkansas to Sand Arroyo Creek or the north fork of the Cimarron a few days earlier and also that nothing had been heard from Gilpin and his men. The train had an infantry escort of twenty men under a lieutenant from Fort Mann, all of whom were anxious to return to the fort. But Gibson's party had no wagons for them to ride in, and they proceeded west in hopes of meeting an eastbound train with which to return.[16]

Gibson and the others camped the night of May 10 near the Point of Rocks, a short distance west of the Middle Spring, and the following morning met another train. This one belonged to Mr. Reid and was escorted by nineteen more soldiers from Fort Mann. After leaving camp the morning of May 12, the party crossed an Indian trail, no more than one day old, which was quite large and apparently represented a hunting party or a war party. From that point, all of the men worried about the possibility of a dangerous encounter with hostile Indians. On the morning of May 13 they reached Battle Ground, about fifteen miles southwest of the Middle Crossing of the Arkansas. The sounds of gunfire could be heard clearly in the distance, indicating that a party of Indians was nearby, probably hunting buffalo. Two or three miles northeast of Battle Ground, Gibson's party came upon a herd of about sixty Indian horses grazing at the side of the road, but their riders were not in sight. Major Singer, for whom Gibson and his three companions had developed a hearty dislike, had continued on without them the previous night, presumably anxious to reach the vicinity of Fort Mann before dawn revealed his presence to the Indians. The tracks of Singer's wagon could still be seen in the dust of the trail, but Gibson's party had gone only a short distance when they saw three men afoot on a sand hill waving at them. It proved to be Major Singer with his two men. They said they had been surrounded by a large party of Indians. They had abandoned their wagon, leaving it in a hollow between two ranges of sand hills in hopes the Indians would not find it, then fled through the hills to save their scalps.

As Gibson, Singer, and the others talked, they noticed a small party of warriors watching them from a sand hill nearer the Arkansas. The Indians soon rode down the hill and approached Gibson and the others, bearing a piece of old blanket as a flag of truce. There were three of them: athletic, robust, warlike in appearance, splendidly mounted, and armed only with bows and arrows. They communicated through sign language and a little Spanish, telling Gibson and the others they were from a large band of Kiowas camping along the river and presently hunting buffalo in the area south of it. They said that they were now friendly to Americans, having promised Thomas Fitzpatrick, their new agent, they would be. They also said a band of Comanches whose warriors were hostile to whites was camped nearby. It was the Comanches who had fired the guns they heard. The Kiowas shook hands and left, and the seven white men resumed their travel in haste, anxious to be away from the Indians. They soon found Major Singer's wagon, stripped of everything of value—his sword, uniforms, and valuables, his papers, and the mules. The men were so alarmed by their vulnerable state that they quickly continued on, crossed the river, and traveled through the night. They reached Fort Mann on the morning of May 14.[17]

The arrival of Gibson, Smith, Singer, and the other four in their party brought out the best Fort Mann had to offer. The unpredictable Captain Pelzer attended to their needs with food and drink and turned his quarters over to them to rest and recuperate. After a refreshing siesta, the seven spent the rest of the day preparing for departure to Fort Leavenworth. When they had reached Fort Mann, a large thirty-two-wagon government supply train, with several discharged soldiers, had been leaving en route back to Fort Leavenworth. They intended to catch up with the train the following day and accompany it on the homeward journey. Meanwhile, after receiving their report of hostile Comanches in camp near the Middle Crossing, Captain Pelzer decided to mount an expedition against them. He assembled sixty-five volunteers and fitted out five wagons and a howitzer, the latter disguised as a corn wagon. The men, so far as possible, were dressed as traders. Pelzer's plan was to tempt the Indians into an attack on a small and, from appearances, relatively defenseless party of traders, then open fire when they were well within range of the powerful weapons and kill as many as possible. The train had traveled only three miles from Fort Mann when it overtook the westbound caravan of the traders Eugene Leitensdorfer and James J. Webb, camped beside the river next to the trail. Pelzer sent the train ahead while he remained with the traders, spending the afternoon in conversation and boasting how he intended to give the hostile Indians a "sound thrashing" and exterminate them all. As evening came, Pelzer mounted his horse and started after his troops. He was back within an hour, claiming to have seen at least 150 Indians and declaring it to be unsafe to proceed farther. 1st Lt. Caleb Tuttle, who had delayed his departure from the fort to attend to other matters, arrived at that time and was advised of the threat of hostile Indians. Pelzer thought his men would reach the crossing at dawn but believed it too risky to follow them. Tuttle thought the officers should be with their troops and left without Pelzer. The captain remained with the traders and proceeded to drink himself into a stupor, his usual solution for dealing with danger or stress.[18]

Night had fallen as Lieutenant Tuttle moved along the Arkansas in search of the bogus train from Fort Mann. Making his task more difficult, a thunderstorm arose, bringing with it violent wind and stinging rain. Somehow the storm masked searcher and quarry from each other as they passed in the dark, Tuttle riding west and the soldiers returning eastward to the fort. Probably the train stayed along the well-defined ruts of the trail while Tuttle left it to take a shorter, faster route on his horse. When he reached the crossing and found neither the men nor their wagons and teams, he realized what had happened. Rather than return empty-handed, he

decided to scout north in search of the Indian camp. He
located it on the south fork of the Pawnee, later known as
"Shaff's Branch" or "Saw-Log Creek," about twelve miles
north of the Arkansas River. When he returned to the trail the
following morning he encountered the traders' caravan near
the crossing and told them what he had learned of the Indians.
Pelzer and the rest of his men had already returned to the fort,
so Tuttle followed them in. A few of the men in the trading
caravan, hoping to recover Singer's goods, rode over to the
Indian encampment. It proved to be a combined hunting
party of friendly Cheyennes, Arapahoes, and Kiowas. They
readily acknowledged having Major Singer's property and
returned it voluntarily, one of them even stating that they
would have taken it to the fort themselves except for the fear
they might receive the same treatment as had the Pawnees the
previous fall. Singer's wagon and goods were sent to him, and
the traders moved on. Back at Fort Mann, Major Singer had
secured new mules for his wagon and additional provisions,
and after the return of his property, he prepared to continue
the journey. William Raymond booked passage with the
departed wagon train for the rest of the men, and on the
morning of May 15 Gibson and the others hurried to catch up
with the train at its last camp a few miles downstream. One of
their traveling companions, it developed, would be the infamous "Bill" Newcome. They reached Fort Leavenworth on
May 28 and delivered the mail.[19]

Although Indians of at least four of the principal tribes of
the southern plains were much in evidence along the Santa Fe
Trail during April and May of 1848, along the south fork of the
Canadian William Gilpin and his men had endured a fruitless and frustrating search for Comanches. When they finally
reached the vicinity of the Antelope Hills on May 18, a point
near the one-hundredth meridian, Gilpin decided to end the
expedition and return to Fort Mann. He turned his column
north, crossed the Wolf, Beaver,* and Cimarron rivers,

*The Wolf and Beaver rivers are the two streams that join to form the north
fork of the Canadian.

probably followed Crooked Creek northward, and finally reached the Arkansas near the fort on May 30. The men were tired, worn, and empty-handed, having traveled a great distance and suffered much hardship without achieving tangible results. As if to emphasize the difficulty in tracking down and "overawing" Plains Indians, shortly before or immediately after Gilpin and his men reached the fort, a large band of Comanches attacked the train of a Mr. Brown at Walnut Creek, running off livestock and killing one of the traders. The Indians were from a raiding party that had been operating in the area from Walnut Creek to the Coon Creeks for "some weeks past" and had successfully attacked and robbed several trains, wounding a number of people. The foot soldiers at the fort had been powerless to stop them, and Gilpin and his mounted troops were then far from the scene of action.[20]

Arrival at Fort Mann enabled Gilpin to turn his focus to other pressing problems. In camp nearby he found a number of chiefs of the Cheyenne, Arapaho, and Kiowa tribes, all of whom professed a desire to enter into treaties of peace with the Great Father. Except for the Kiowas in 1837, these tribes had signed no treaties with the United States, and there was no treaty authorizing the establishment of roads such as the Santa Fe and Oregon trails across their lands. They had, however, heard of such treaties from others and particularly of the fine presents the Great Father sent to secure their goodwill. In their innocence they were so delighted with the pots and pans, blankets, guns and ammunition for hunting, and other cheap baubles the government sent as a reward for "touching the pen" that few stopped to reflect on what they gave in return, if indeed any of them understood. But Gilpin was an honest servant of his country, and he had no authority to enter into treaties with Indians on its behalf. In the absence of the Indian agent, or anyone else who could bind the government, he ordered these chiefs to take their bands away from the Santa Fe road and move north to the upper Platte to await the arrival of some proper authority empowered to make treaties. Gilpin believed that they did as he directed and that they spent the rest of the year waiting in vain for the arrival of the treaty maker. Perhaps this was so, but Gilpin had no way of knowing. There seems to be no evidence of large gatherings of southern bands of Cheyennes and Arapahoes along the upper Platte or the Arkansas for any extended period in 1848 and certainly none of Kiowas. Most likely they simply went about the usual routine of their lives, holding their sacred ceremonies, hunting bison across the plains, and doing the many other things that made life dear to them. They probably assumed that when the Great Father was ready to make a treaty, he would find them wherever they were. Gilpin did note in his August 1 report that the three tribes were "awaiting peace" near Bent's Fort on the Arkansas, which probably meant that at least one band of each was camping nearby, perhaps to trade, perhaps to receive presents. Wherever the bulk of these tribes were, in 1848 they made no war on whites.[21]

The other important problem facing Gilpin was dealing with the troublemakers at Fort Mann. Immediately on his return, Gilpin relieved Captain Pelzer of his command authority and placed him under arrest. What that meant is difficult to say, but it probably did not include confinement. The eight buildings available in the fort had to house a garrison, quartermaster and commissary supplies, weapons and ordinance, and all of the other gear necessary to sustain operations of the battalion. There was no room for a guard-house. Merely being at the fort, in the middle of the desolation of the plains, far from civilization, and surrounded by hostile Indians, was doubtless a sufficient form of confinement. Gilpin's next move was to prepare the charges and specifications against the officers and enlisted men accused. For Pelzer and Amandus Schnabel this was essentially a rephrasing of the various complaints and petitions made against them, with the addition of Pelzer's latest bout with intoxication and Schnabel's involvement with Caroline Newcome. Charges were also prepared against Lts. John Stephens, William Crudington, and William O'Hara. Then there were the cases of the two enlisted troublemakers, Fahlbush and Goldbeck.

On June 10 Gilpin wrote a letter to the secretary of war forwarding the resignations of Captain Pelzer and Lieutenant O'Hara. In the letter he referred to the charges reported in his February letter and to the demand he had made for courts-martial. He repeated his complaints about the two German companies and referred to harmful correspondence written by officers in those companies and published in the St. Louis newspapers. He also could not resist taking a swipe at Lieutenant Colonel Wharton, whom he claimed was guilty of "injurious scribbling." Gilpin concluded by stating, "A general court martial is *absolutely* necessary to purge the command of men whose [sic] disgrace their country & the service by their crimes." What Gilpin did not know was that Bvt. Col. John Garland had left Jefferson Barracks on or about June 1 under orders to proceed to Fort Mann and conduct an investigation. He had gone straight to Fort Leavenworth by riverboat and was at that post when Caroline Newcome arrived there in mid-June. He participated with Lieutenant Colonel Wharton in interviewing her. Garland and Wharton then started out for Fort Mann together, but poor health forced Wharton to return to Fort Leavenworth, where he died on July 13. Garland continued on alone and reached Fort Mann on June 30. The matter of discipline for the recalcitrant garrison would soon be addressed.[22]

The return to Fort Mann of Companies A, B, E, and the artillery detachment brought all of Gilpin's command together for the first time since November 1847. During the first six months they were in Indian country, they had suffered much but accomplished little. The two German companies that garrisoned the fort were discontented and mutinous. It must have seemed to William Gilpin that fate had dealt him an unkind hand in placing him in command of this undisciplined rabble. Yet many of his men, particularly the cavalry, did have soldierly qualities and could perform well when given the tools and the opportunity. Opportunity was about to knock.

11

The Battle of Coon Creek

William Bedford Royall was a tall man, muscular and well built, with dark hair and piercing blue eyes. He was born in Virginia on April 15, 1825, but moved to Missouri with his family while still a child and there grew to manhood and completed his education. When the Mexican War began he enlisted in the Second Regiment of Missouri Mounted Volunteers during July 1846. He was quickly elected as first lieutenant of Company D and marched with his unit for Santa Fe. Though a nephew of Col. Sterling Price, commander of the regiment, Royall's own natural leadership abilities won him the post and launched him on a distinguished military career. In New Mexico he participated in the battle at La Cañada, the fight at Embudo, and the recapture of Taos, where he led the charge against the fortifications at the pueblo. When his one-year term of enlistment expired in 1847, he and others from his regiment who desired to remain in service consolidated the remnants of their units and reorganized as the Santa Fe Battalion. On August 14, 1847, Royall received his commission in the new battalion as first lieutenant and adjutant and in October was dispatched to Missouri on recruiting duty. He was able to enlist seventy-one new recruits, mostly young backwoods Missourians, and following the issuance of uniforms and a brief period of training, was conducting them to Santa Fe. Royall and his enlistees left Fort Leavenworth on May 18, 1848, marching under the overall command of Capt.

Vantrump Turner of Newby's First Regiment of Illinois Infantry Volunteers, who was leading some three hundred Illinois recruits westward. They reached Council Grove by the end of May and waited there for the arrival of government supply trains or the formation of trading caravans needing escort along the trail.[1]

Call for the services of Royall and his men was not long in coming. On June 5 Captain Turner placed Royall in charge of two government trains totaling sixty wagons and led by Messrs. Burnham and Fulton as wagonmasters, along with 425 government beef cattle in the charge of Mr. Fagan. At the same time Turner directed him to act as escort for Maj. Thomas S. Bryant, an army paymaster who was proceeding to Fort Mann to pay the men of Gilpin's battalion. With Bryant was his nephew, John Y. B. Dietz, apparently along to act as his uncle's clerk and for the adventure of entering Indian country. So now, at age twenty-three, 1st Lt. William B. Royall found himself charged with the imposing responsibility of protecting a very large quantity of government supplies, beef cattle intended to feed the army in New Mexico, a paymaster with his specie, and a youthful adventurer, along with the lives of his seventy-one young recruits. He felt equal to the task, and his men and their charges probably started slowly down the trail the same day, June 5. They proceeded without incident until the evening of June 13, when they crossed and camped next to Walnut Creek. Since the banks of this stream were quite steep, they attached ropes to the wagons in order to let them down to the ford below. They spent most of the afternoon at this task, and when dusk came they were exhausted.[2]

As Royall and his long column were working their way west, a new patrol was leaving from Fort Mann to reconnoiter to the east. Under command of 1st Lt. Phillip Stremmel, it consisted of sixty-five officers and men from C Company of the Indian Battalion with two six-pounder howitzers. Stremmel, who had been in charge of the artillery during Gilpin's abortive expedition against the Comanches and Plains Apaches, was under orders to scout east to Walnut Creek and there to

meet and escort back to Fort Mann the paymaster, Major
Bryant. Stremmel's command left the fort on June 3 and
marched east along the Wet Route. They encountered no
trouble until June 7, when they went into camp on the south
bank of the Pawnee Fork. It was late afternoon when they
arrived, and they selected a campsite west of the trail next to
a bend of the creek where the banks were steep. A trader was
just crossing the stream as they arrived, and he told them his
party had encountered no hostile Indians to that point. The
trader and his small caravan continued on, and the soldiers
spent the remainder of the afternoon erecting their tents and
organizing their camp.[3]

Toward evening, when the air was cooler and the men were
preparing and eating their supper, one of them began climb-
ing down the steep bank of the stream, probably to replenish
his water supply. As he did he heard the whizzing of an arrow
near his ear. He looked up and saw two Comanches moving
along the bank toward him. He scrambled back up the slope
and ran to 2d Lt. William Khulow with the news. Almost at
the same moment Khulow saw Indians coming within a few
yards of the tents and sounded the alarm. Large numbers of
warriors suddenly appeared from the cover of the trees along
the stream to the west and began moving rapidly toward the
soldiers' camp. Some were mounted, others were on foot, and
they seemed intent in running off the company's horses and
mules, either to secure the animals or to prevent escape by
the soldiers. When the warriors were within about fifty yards
from the camp they began to fire the eight or ten guns they
had, but without effect. Then another large band of warriors
was spotted coming from the vicinity of the trail to the east.
Most of the Comanches were armed only with lances or bows
and arrows, but they were masters at using them. In a short
time Stremmel and his men were completely surrounded; their
situation looked grim.[4]

Although Indians were on all sides, Stremmel's troops still
held a singular advantage. They had weapons far superior to
those of the Comanches and the know-how and discipline with
which to use them effectively. The soldiers commenced a

steady fire, which not only kept the warriors from reaching the livestock but killed or wounded several of them. For the Comanches, the danger was greater than the rewards to be had, and they began a hurried retreat beyond the reach of the military carbines. When he saw them moving out of range of small arms, Lieutenant Stremmel had one of his howitzers unlimbered and fired a six-pound ball. Although it probably frightened the Indians, its principal effect was on the military livestock. The result was immediate and disastrous, for the horses and mules began a stampede away from the camp and toward the Indians. Seeing this, the Comanches released a white horse, which galloped to the stampeding animals and led them away toward the main body of warriors. Stremmel ordered Lieutenant Khulow to take thirty men and pursue, which he did with great skill and daring, managing to recover five of the mules. Still, the Indians succeeded in capturing twenty-two mules and two horses, the latter belonging to Stremmel and a Sergeant Semmes.[5]

The Comanches now began to regroup at the Pawnee Fork Crossing, apparently intent on making another attack. Lieutenant Stremmel fired a howitzer at the main body of the enemy. Though it did not kill any Indians, it succeeded in intimidating them: they now abandoned further plans for a fight and moved off to the south along the trail. The whole engagement lasted about ten minutes. Stremmel believed that of about two hundred warriors in the Comanche war party, at least five had been killed and ten wounded. None of the soldiers were killed or wounded, but their losses in livestock were crippling. Stremmel immediately sent an express to Colonel Gilpin informing him of the action and requesting replacement animals. Then he and his men settled down to wait for the new mounts.[6]

The wait of Lieutenant Stremmel and his men was largely uneventful. There was occasional traffic on the trail, and on June 10 a number of mounted Indians were seen near dusk silhouetted against the sky on the ridge of a hill north of the Pawnee. They sat motionless on their horses, watching the soldiers below but carefully remaining out of reach of the guns. They were probably members of a Comanche scouting party, well aware of the power of Stremmel's howitzers. After a time they disappeared. Meanwhile, the express dispatched by Stremmel had reached Fort Mann with the report of the Indian fight and the loss of mules and horses. On June 10 Gilpin sent replacement animals to Stremmel under escort of 2d Lt. Ashley Gulley and fifty men from Company B. They had orders to deliver the remounts to the artillery camp, then scout the surrounding country in an effort to locate the Comanche force responsible for the attack. They were accompanied on their eastward march by an express en route from Santa Fe to Fort Leavenworth. Gulley and his men reached Stremmel's camp sometime during the morning of the thirteenth, delivered the replacement horses and mules, then proceeded on their scout. Stremmel and his troops, along with the express, immediately started for Walnut Creek to keep their rendezvous with Major Bryant, the paymaster. On June 14 they met Bryant, Lieutenant Royall, and the others a short distance west of Walnut Creek, their last evening's camp.[7]

The long column of government wagons and livestock under escort by Lieutenant Royall and his men, accompanied by Major Bryant, had experienced no difficulties with hostile Indians before reaching Walnut Creek. Beyond the Little Arkansas, however, and particularly after striking the Great Bend of the Arkansas west of the Plum Buttes, they were aware of Indian scouts on their trail. Sometimes a lone rider watched them from the opposite side of the river, or a lance point glinted beyond the sand hills paralleling the opposite bank of the stream. Sometimes two or three riders followed a half mile or more behind. But always the Indians were there, seen or unseen, watching, perhaps planning. When Royall's column was joined by Lieutenant Stremmel and his troops and learned of the attack on the artillerymen, Royall decided they should take extra precautions to avoid a surprise attack. He was the senior officer of the line and, as such, assumed overall command of both military units. Thereafter Royall's cavalry recruits and Stremmel's men alternated each day as the advance and rear guards. Including civilians, more than two hundred men marched with the column.[8]

A government wagon train was a slow-moving affair at best, and Royall found himself with two of these plus a large cattle herd—not the ingredients for speed. Nevertheless he had averaged fifteen to sixteen miles per day en route from Council Grove to Walnut Creek, a very respectable pace considering the nature of the caravan. To do this, they probably left at dawn and traveled through the better part of the daylight hours each day. It may have been Royall's intention to move as far as possible across the plains before the intense heat of summer fell on them and grazing was depleted, or perhaps he was simply anxious to clear the most dangerous part of the Indian country. Major Bryant also wanted to reach Fort Mann as soon as he could, since he had to return to Fort Leavenworth and pay troops there and at other points in his district as well. On the fourteenth they traveled as far as the famed trail marker Pawnee Rock, a distance of about sixteen miles, and went into camp nearby next to the Arkansas. Royall's young recruits spent at least a part of the evening trying to find an unused place on the rock where they could etch their names, but it was so covered with those of previous travelers that few had any luck.[9]

The following day, June 15, the column probably moved to the Pawnee Fork and camped on the north bank. The distance from Pawnee Rock was only about twelve miles, but they had to ford Ash Creek, which would have taken considerable time. More than sixty wagons and two artillery pieces had to be taken across, as well as men and livestock, so it is unlikely they would have attempted a passage of the Pawnee until the following day, when they would be fresh and have sufficient light. Just as at Walnut Creek, it was necessary to lower the wagons to the ford below by using ropes. The crossing would have begun early on the sixteenth and used much of the day. When all were across, they continued their march and apparently made camp about four or five miles beyond the Pawnee. Late in the afternoon some of Royall's men crossed the river to collect wood from a grove of trees on the southeast bank. As

they did they saw a small party of mounted Indians watching
them from the sand hills beyond, obviously reconnoitering the
camp. Large numbers of buffalo had been crossing their trail
beyond the Pawnee Fork, and the guide, Tandy Giddings,
advised the officers that it was a sure sign Indians were
nearby. Extra precautions were taken, and the men slept with
a wary eye that night.[10]

The column resumed its march on the morning of June 17.
After traveling about five miles they crossed Coon Creek, a
small stream draining the country to the southwest. When
within a mile or so of the Arkansas, the creek turned
northeast and ran parallel with the river for perhaps twenty-
five miles or more before finally emptying into the greater
stream. The country through which it ran was usually arid,
and Coon Creek seldom carried running water. The Comanches had long used its bed as a place of concealment from
which to ambush travelers along the trail. The Coon Creek
Bottoms, as the low-lying land about its course was known,
was a good place to camp and graze livestock but was also a
place of danger from Indian attack. Five miles beyond Coon
Creek Crossing, Royall's column reached the camping ground
known as Plain Encampment, or Plain Camp. It was at or near
this campground that Lt. John Love and his men had their
crippling fight with the Comanches the previous year, and the
place was now commonly referred to as "Love's Defeat."
Passing it by, Royall put his men into camp about five miles
beyond.* They had traveled more than fifteen miles during

*This camp would have been along the Arkansas River approximately two
miles northeast of present Kinsley, Kansas. Lieutenant Royall in his report
stated only that it was about five miles from the site of Love's Defeat and gave no
direction. However, a location five miles north of Love's Defeat would have
been at or near the mouth of Coon Creek, and surely Royall would have so described it. Moreover, that location would have been approximately sixty miles
northeast of Fort Mann. Royall and his men traveled only ten miles on June 18.
A Coon Creek campsite would thus have left them with fifty miles to travel in
two days, since they reached Fort Mann on the twentieth. As it was, they had to
travel forty miles, averaging twenty miles per day, a difficult task for such a
caravan. James H. Birch, who was one of Royall's recruits, later wrote that the
camp was near the present townsite of Kinsley, and in this he appears to be right.

the day, and it was time to graze and rest the livestock and look to the needs of the men. The day had been hot and the march dusty, with the omnipresent south wind carrying the dust of those in the lead back over the moving column. It was a weary band of men that made camp along the Arkansas late in the afternoon of the seventeenth.[11]

The process of making camp was usually time-consuming. Most of the moving column of men and animals would still have been at some distance from the site selected when the lead elements reached it. The commander had hard decisions to make concerning security arrangements and location of the military units, artillery pieces, picket lines for horses and mules, wagon corrals for both the military and the government supply trains, and the beef cattle, as well as adequate grass for the livestock. As they were arriving at the new campground Major Bryant told Lieutenant Royall that he wanted to leave early the following morning and move on to Fort Mann ahead of the others. The fort was thought to be no more than thirty-five miles away, and the delay imposed by travel with the slow-moving government trains and the beef herd was hurting his time schedule.* He requested a mounted guard of twenty-five men, which Royall readily agreed to. Because Bryant intended to depart well ahead of the others, Royall had the recruits assigned as his guard establish themselves in a separate line of tents at the south end of the campsite. Standard military practice was for a unit to halt in line parallel with the water source it would camp next to, in this case the Arkansas, then when the company wagons arrived, pitch their tents in a line where they had halted, facing away from the water. Horses and mules were picketed in front of the tents to permit grazing where they could be observed. A guard was customarily established beyond the picket line. Wagon trains were corralled in a circle, with their animals placed inside for protection during the night, while

---

*Bryant's conjecture as to the distance to Fort Mann was wrong. It was at least fifty miles from their new campsite.

beef cattle were herded to a secure area inside the perimeter established by the rear guard.[12]

Lieutenant Royall was young, but he had more than a year's experience with the military and was quite familiar with good camping and security practices. After placing Major Bryant and his guard detail at the lead, or southern, edge of the camp, Royall corralled one of the government trains immediately north of Bryant. Next in line were the rest of the Santa Fe Battalion recruits under Royall's command, followed by the corral of the second government train, the beef herd with its several wagons, and last, on the extreme north end of the line, Lieutenant Stremmel and his artillerymen. One of the howitzers was placed at the south end, to be manned if necessary by members of Bryant's guard, and the other at the north end, manned by personnel from the artillery unit. Horses and mules belonging to the three separate military camps, along with the rest of the livestock, were grazed during the afternoon and evening. When all elements of the column reached their assigned locations, the camp would have been strung out along the Arkansas in a compact version of their marching formation, except for the guard. By evening, each unit was in its place, and cooking fires were lit, using such wood as could be found along the river, supplemented by an abundant supply of buffalo chips. After the meal was finished and the livestock returned from their grazing grounds, the animals were corralled or picketed, and the camp was made secure. The guard was doubled on the recommendation of Giddings, who was uneasy because all of the signs suggested the presence of Indians at a place notorious for frequent ambushes of wagon trains. Most of the green recruits laughed at his warnings. Though young, these backwoods boys had ridden horses since childhood and were expert riflemen and hunters both afoot and on horseback. They had seen no more than a handful of Indians so far and doubted they would be so foolish as to attack such a large and well-protected column. Stremmel's artillerymen were probably less certain, but the fatigued men of each of the military units and the trains likely went to sleep when the sun went down, too tired to worry about Indians.[13]

The night of June 17 passed uneventfully. The wolves and coyotes gave their usual serenade, and there were other strange sounds unfamiliar to young men from the wooded hills east of the Missouri River. The more apprehensive probably slept with one eye open, fearful that some of the sounds were made by Indians preparing their attack. But nothing happened. Finally the night sky began to brighten in the east, and the stars faded as the first rays of the rising sun crept across the horizon. Major Bryant's men were already awake and preparing their breakfast over a few small fires. Some of the men fed grain to their horses and mules, then led them to good grass nearby to allow a brief period of grazing before departure. Elsewhere the rest of the camp was also coming to life, with fires being lit and coffee put on to boil. A rosy hue began to color the sky, shadows retreated, and dark objects took on form. Songbirds began their morning salute, while the livestock answered with nickers, snuffles, and bellows. As if to bemoan the coming of day, a wolf howled on the southeast side of the river and was immediately answered by others up- and downstream. Old Tandy Giddings, the guide, listened intently, then cautioned the men: "Lookout, boys, I have heard them wolves many a time. It is Indians howling." But few believed him, and the preparation of meals continued unabated. The new dawn of June 18 was soon upon them, and the pace of camp activity quickened. At 5:20 A.M., while Major Bryant's men were packing their gear and preparing to strike their tents, a single shout suddenly rang out from Lieutenant Stremmel's artillery camp on the north end: "Injuns!"[14]

The sounding of the alarm brought some of the men spilling from their tents, while others stopped whatever tasks they were performing. They unstacked their weapons and broke out their ammunition. As they did, all eyes were focused on the southeast bank of the river where two Comanche warriors had unexpectedly appeared from beyond the sand hills. They were now riding along the river's edge

During the evening of June 17, 1848, 1st Lt. William B. Royall and seventy-one recruits from the Santa Fe Battalion, a detachment of artillery from the Indian Battalion, an army paymaster, and two government supply trains, with a herd of beef cattle, camped along the Arkansas River about two miles northeast of present Kinsley, Kansas. At dawn the next morning, this camp was suddenly attacked by between two and three hundred Comanche warriors, with another four hundred observing the attack from the north and south. It was the beginning of the Battle of Coon Creek, the first important fight in which breech-loading carbines were used against the Plains Indians.

shaking their spears and giving their war cries. Then, as the men watched, they became conscious of another noise that sounded like distant drumming behind them. They turned and looked to the west, and what they saw made many a good man blanch. Coming directly at them at a gallop were between two and three hundred warriors, their faces and horses painted for war, brandishing their war lances and shields. The two Indians across the river had likely been sent to distract the soldiers until it was too late. To the north another two hundred or so warriors were spread across the plain, sitting motionless on their horses and watching the action unfold. To the south about the same number also held off and observed the charge. Almost simultaneously Royall and Stremmel yelled commands at their men, directing them to get beyond the picket lines of horses and mules and commence firing. The picket lines, of course, obstructed their field of fire; beyond they had clear shots. The element of surprise had first favored the Comanches, but now it was they who were about to be surprised.[15]

Fortune was with Lieutenant Royall's young recruits, for before their departure from Fort Leavenworth, a consignment of breech-loading carbines had arrived. Manufactured in Germany, they could be loaded and fired five times in a minute. They used a one-ounce ball, which emerged as a slug and held its force for about four hundred yards. Royall's backwoodsmen were armed with these carbines, a fearful weapon in their hands. Unitl this time the Comanches had made it a practice to draw the fire of their white enemy, protecting themselves with their thick war shields, which were usually effective in deflecting or stopping the bullets of that day. Then, after the whites had fired and were reloading their muzzle-loaders, the Comanche warriors would dash in and lance them to death. To avoid such a disaster, experienced leaders never let all of the their men fire at once, but even so they were often at risk. Now Royall and his men had in their hands a weapon that could be reloaded almost immediately and fired again.[16]

On came the charging Comanches, doubtless believing they would easily survive the initial volley, then overrun the entire column. When they were within about four hundred yards, the soldiers opened up, firing the first round. The shots seemed to have little effect but made a great racket as they hit the war shields and bounced off. The Comanches kept coming, expecting to quickly close the gap and be among the Americans, where they could fight hand to hand with lances and war clubs. At three hundred yards the soldiers fired their second round, surprising the charging warriors but doing no great damage. The Comanches kept coming. At two hundred yards Royall's men fired again, then at one hundred yards. Some of the Indians now collapsed, either killed or seriously wounded by the hail of bullets. Because they were tied to their saddles, these men were swiftly carried from the battlefield on their horses, which were led by a comrade. If they fell to the ground, they were lassoed and pulled out of range, then carried off. The warriors kept coming, and at about forty yards someone yelled, "Shoot their horses!" Up and down the line, men dropped their sights to the horses' chests and fired. The animals screamed their agony, and some dropped. The effect was immediate: and the whole Indian line wavered, veered, and retreated. As they did, another volley was fired from Royall's line, and more Indians fell. Cries of anguish and rage could be heard from the retreating warriors.[17]

After a brief respite the war cries were heard again, and a swarm of warriors emerged from the dry bed of Coon Creek, charging Major Bryant's side of the camp and through his line of tents. The soldiers' carbines fired again and again, and more Comanches fell. One was killed so close to the firing line that several of the men dashed out and dragged his body into their camp along with his weapons. The Comanches made several attempts to retrieve their fallen comrade but were beaten back each time. Having been thwarted at the south end of the camp with severe casualties, the Indians now charged farther north, through Royall's line of tents. They were greeted with a heavy sustained fire from the soldiers and suffered more losses. But their incredible bravery propelled them on through the camp; they were even so bold as to cut two horses loose while their riders held them by the lariats used to fasten them to their picket pins. When the firing from this quarter proved too intense, the warriors continued to the north, attacking the corral of the second government train and the nearby beef herd. But a corralled train was difficult to penetrate, and some of these teamsters were armed and good shots. A heavy fire greeted the Indians, causing them to retreat. One of them was shot and killed by Mr. Burnham, the wagonmaster, and dragged into camp. The frustrated Comanches could only howl with rage at their failure to recover the body.[18]

When the fight began, neither of the howitzers was able to be fired because the horses and mules on the picket lines screened the charging enemy. Meanwhile, both Royall's and Stremmel's men were so anxious to fire at the oncoming Indians that they soon moved well beyond the picket line, making it impossible to fire the artillery pieces without endangering the lives of their own men. On the south end of the camp the six-pounder, loaded with canister, was forced to remain silent while the action there was fought with carbines and officers' pistols. On the north end Lieutenant Stremmel had at the onset of the action ordered some of his men and the howitzer to move to the left of their line of tents to thwart an attack by a large body of warriors. Then the Indians began to charge into Stremmel's picket line, shaking their shields and lances in an effort to start a stampede. Stremmel ordered Lieutenant Khulow to take the best of the men and try to save their animals. The daring Khulow led his troops on a dash to the picket line, firing their weapons and forcing back the Comanches, and brought back all of the horses and mules unharmed. These were immediately sent to the rear and placed in herd. With the animals out of the way, Stremmel's howitzer opened fire and the Indians quickly retreated to the west and south.[19]

When the Comanches finally fell back from the south end of the camp, retreating before the deadly fire of Royall's carbines, Major Bryant seized the opportunity to use the howitzer. He ordered it pushed forward beyond the picket line and the corral of the lead wagon train and prepared for action. He personally took charge of it, sighted it, and directed its firing. The piece was fired several times, one of the shots killing two warriors and their horses. The boom of the artillery and the scream of the shot, together with the rapid and long-range fire of the carbines used by Royall's men, finally took the heart out of the Comanches' will to fight. They

fell back, then began a precipitate withdrawal from the battle
field, passing to both the north and the south of Royall's camp
and crossing the Arkansas. Once on the far side, the Indians
disappeared through the sand hills. Seeing this, Lieutenant
Stremmel had the howitzer in Major Bryant's camp moved so
as to command the river to the east and south and the country
to the southwest, enabling it to interdict the Indians fleeing
the battle. Major Bryant continued in its command. The piece
at the north end of camp was kept in position to control the
territory to the north and west, thus protecting the column
against further attacks from those quarters. Before all of the
Indians had disappeared into the sand hills, Major Bryant
killed two more with a shot from his howitzer, and one of
Royall's sharpshooters killed a third with a long-distance shot
from a carbine. The action then subsided almost as suddenly
as it had begun. [20]

As the guns fell silent between Coon Creek and the
Arkansas, the officers called for a report of casualties among
the men and of damage or loss to livestock and property. What
they heard was both surprising and gratifying. Not one man in
any of the camps or corrals had been killed or wounded.
Royall's men had lost fifteen of their horses to the Comanches,
and the government trains had lost five horses and four mules.
Two of the mules were later found lanced to death, probably
because of their stubborn refusal to go where the Indians
wanted them to go. Thanks to the gallant and fearless Lieutenant Khulow, no animals had been lost at Stremmel's
artillery camp. No other loss or damage was indicated, and
when the survey was complete, Lieutenant Royall turned his
attention to the line of some two hundred Comanches remaining to the north, who had held back from the fight. Those to
the south had already disappeared, apparently crossing the
river and joining the attack party beyond the sand hills. Major
Bryant thought the more important problem was the war party
that had attacked the camp and made off with the livestock.
After some discussion, the officers decided that Lieutenant
Royall should take as many of his men as could be spared and
pursue the fleeing Indians. He hoped to catch up with them,

inflict further punishment, and if possible, recover the stolen animals. The camp, meanwhile, would reorganize itself to continue the march to Fort Mann, at the same time staying alert for any reappearance of the Comanches.[21]

The detachment that Royall organized to follow the Comanches consisted of thirty-eight men, including John Dietz, Major Bryant's nephew. Dietz had performed well in the recent fight and seemed eager to see more action. When mounted, they set off at a gallop to overtake the Comanche war party. They first moved north parallel to the river, then crossed it about two miles below their camp after discovering a party of one hundred warriors apparently retreating before them, leaving several wounded horses behind. The two hundred or more other warriors remaining to the north of the battle site had in the meantime left the field and were nowhere to be seen. When Royall and his men reached the far side of the river they resumed their pursuit at a full gallop, moving to the southeast, until they reached the sand hills. Once there, they were forced to sharply reduce their gait as the horses struggled against the deep sand.[22]

Lieutenant Royall and his men had reached a point about two miles from the river and were laboring against the shifting dunes of fine sand when, without warning, they found themselves entirely surrounded by an estimated five to seven hundred Indians. The warriors began flourishing their war lances and shouting war cries preparatory to a charge. Anticipating their intentions, Royall looked around and spotted a considerably higher sand dune to their right (south). He shouted an order to charge, then he and his detachment bolted straight for the dune, completely surprising the Indians and killing four, possibly five of them, and wounding others as they drove past. Once on the high ground, Royall's men formed a perimeter to protect themselves from all sides. It was a wise move, for in a short time the warriors had surrounded the soldiers again and were preparing to charge.[23]

During the dash for the high dune, Royall himself had a close call. One of his men, Smith P. Carter, dropped his carbine, and as he tried to retrieve it his horse threw him,

After the Battle of Coon Creek, Lieutenant Royall led thirty-eight men across the Arkansas in an effort to recover stolen livestock. In the sand hills southeast of the river they were surprised and surrounded by more than five hundred Comanche warriors. While the troops were dashing for the highest dune to make a fighting stand, one of the warriors charged Pvt. James Roop with a lance, striking him in the abdomen. Incredibly, the lance struck the trooper's belt buckle and was held fast while Roop shot and killed the warrior.

then ran off with the others, leaving Carter behind in the sand. The young soldier knew his situation was desperate and began running after the rest of the men. One of the Comanches noticed his plight and started after him with a war club. Lieutenant Royall, seeing Carter's predicament, reined in his horse and fired his pistol at the pursuing warrior. His shot missed, and the Comanche turned on the officer, charging him with his lance. He made several passes, during one of which his lance pierced Royall's hat. Royall could not reload his pistol in time and probably would have been killed but for the timely intervention of Sergeant Northcutt. Seeing his commander's dilemma, Northcutt fired at the warrior with his carbine, killing him instantly. Carter, in the meantime, had also successfully avoided a lance attack. As a warrior charged him, he dropped to the ground, suffering only a bruise on his shoulder where it was struck by the hoof of the Indian's horse. Eventually Carter made his way safely to the dune and recovered his own mount. Meanwhile, Pvt. James Roop* was struck by a lance during the dash to the hill. While a Comanche was charging him with a lance, Roop attempted to shoot him with his carbine, but it misfired. On came the warrior, driving his lance into Roop's abdomen. By an incredible stroke of good fortune, the trooper was wearing a hunting belt with a large iron buckle; the lance struck the buckle squarely and was held fast by the tongue of the belt. Roop held the lance with one hand while he shot the Indian with the other. Though painfully injured, he quickly rode his horse up the sand dune and joined the rest of the command. [24]

Royall and his men had hardly reached the hill and formed their perimeter when the first Comanche attack came. But the German-made breechloaders performed their work well. Several Indians were killed or wounded in the first charge, causing the warriors to veer away and retreat behind the

---

*In his account written more than fifty years later, James H. Birch referred to this man as Dave Rupe, a hunter from Ray County, Missouri. Whether Royall or Birch had the correct name is unknown, but Royall probably used the name that appeared in the muster rolls.

surrounding dunes. There they would regroup and charge again, brandishing their lances and shouting their war cries at the beleaguered soldiers. Each time, several more of them were killed or wounded. After several of these failed charges, the Indians pulled back to positions just beyond the surrounding dunes and began firing arrows high in the air on an arc that would bring them raining down upon the soldiers and their mounts. These flights of arrows caused several injuries and were answered by rapid fire from the soldiers' carbines, inflicting more death and injury on the warriors. Eventually they moved back even farther from Royall's position, and the fighting began to subside.[25]

One of the most unusual events recorded in an Indian fight occurred during the course of the several Indian charges against Royall and his men. As they fired at the approaching Comanches, beyond them at a distance of about one hundred yards a woman mounted on a horse suddenly appeared. She wore a scarlet dress decorated with silver ornaments and was giving directions for the aid or removal of wounded warriors. She rode calmly and regally, and some of the soldiers thought she must be the Comanches' queen. Who she was and how she came to be there have remained a mystery, but of course she was not a queen. Neither the Comanches nor any of the other western tribes of Indians were ever ruled by hereditary monarchs or had royal ruling families. It is possible that the "scarlet lady" was a Mexican woman, captured and adopted into the tribe, one who had worn and was allowed to retain the colorful garb of her homeland. Or perhaps she was a prominent Comanche woman dressed in finery captured from some luckless wagon train. Whatever and whoever she was, she will no doubt remain one of the intriguing figures in the history of the American West.[26]

When the Indian attacks had subsided, Royall made a quick check of his men. Four had been wounded, including Private Roop. The other three had suffered arrow wounds. One of these, James Moody, had been struck by an arrow shot from beyond the dunes. It had penetrated the fleshy part of his thigh and imbedded itself in his saddle tree, holding him fast until the arrow could be cut off and he could be lifted down. The four wounded, though in considerable pain, did not appear to have serious injuries. With the Comanches having retired some distance, Royall decided to get his detachment back across the river and to their camp. He and his men began a slow and careful retreat, reached and crossed the Arkansas, and soon regained the security of their encampment. The Indians made no effort to interfere with their withdrawal.[27]

When they were safely back in camp, all of the men took time to rest briefly and to eat the breakfast that had been so violently interrupted. Stories were told, honed, and doubtless embellished as young men who had just survived a near disaster incorporated the stories into the memories of their great adventure. Some of the men recalled that one of the last shots fired during the initial battle had killed a splendid iron-gray Indian horse. The decoration of its saddle and bridle clearly showed that the horse had belonged to an important warrior.* The owner apparently held the animal's accouterments in high regard, for, having initially tried to get beyond the range of the soldiers' carbines, he stopped, then ran back and began removing them from the dead horse. This was a tragic mistake, for the soldiers shot him down as he worked to save the saddle. Then a boy, no more than twelve or fourteen years old, dropped out of the retreating party when he saw what had happened and dashed back to the fallen warrior. He brought his horse to a sudden halt and leaped over its head with lance in hand. He tied his lariat around the body of the dead man, remounted his horse and dragged him from the field. The men in the soldiers' camp so admired the boy's courage that not one raised his weapon against him.[28]

One of the more remarkable stories told was that of an Indian killed within twenty steps of the soldiers' line. The man had tied himself to his horse and was hanging over the

---

*James H. Birch believed the saddle had belonged to an Apache chief. It is improbable that, as a raw recruit unfamiliar with the Indians of the western plains, Birch could have identified the tribe by looking at the saddle. However, he might have heard this from Tandy Giddings, the guide.

animal's far side, firing arrows at the soldiers from under its neck while at a gallop. The frustrated soldiers shot the horse through the neck, killing it instantly. The shot that killed the horse passed through its neck and struck the Indian on his upper forehead, taking off the top of his skull. When the first soldiers reached the warrior, they untied him from the dead horse, and to their surprise he immediately sat up. He felt his head carefully with his hands. One lobe of his brain was uninjured, but the other was badly torn. He then felt to see if his scalp was gone. Satisfying himself as to his grave injuries, he looked at the surrounding soldiers with intense hatred on his face and said, "Kioombre, Kioombre." With that one of the men shot and killed him. Later, at Fort Mann, an experienced Indian fighter told Royall's men that the warrior's last words meant, "I'm a brave, I'm a brave." Whether true or not, it added color to the story.[29]

At 10:00 A.M. on June 18, with the men fed and given a short rest, Lieutenant Royall once again put his column into motion. They moved slowly along the Arkansas and after about ten miles went back into camp. During the night of the eighteenth a large body of Indians was heard crossing the Arkansas downriver from the soldiers' encampment, possibly those who had remained to the north during the fight. Later a sentry fired at four mounted Indians who had come to the riverbank near his post. The four vanished, but the nervous soldiers remained on the alert until dawn. From that point, Royall pressed his men and animals to move as far and fast each day as was possible and covered the remaining forty miles in a two-day march. They arrived at Fort Mann on the evening of June 20, and there they rested, replenished their supplies, and prepared to resume the journey to Santa Fe. Major Bryant paid the troops but evidently decided to delay his return to Fort Leavenworth, perhaps exhausted by the recent ordeal. He left on his return trip on July 1.[30]

On the morning of June 21 Lieutenant Royall sat down and composed a report of his engagement with the Comanches for Adj. Gen. Roger Jones. He recounted the events occurring after his departure from Council Grove and lauded the courage of his men—raw recruits but fine soldiers. Royall especially praised Lieutenants Stremmel and Khulow and their men, who, he said, "behaved bravely and gallantly." Likewise he noted the considerable help given to him by Major Bryant and his nephew, John Dietz. Of his four wounded men, he reported that J. L. Henry and John C. Slocum had suffered arrow wounds to the shoulder, James Moody the arrow wound to his thigh, and James Roop the injury to his abdomen. Royall reported that in the initial engagement, at least nine Indians were confirmed dead, with many more wounded and possibly killed, which of course could not be known with certainty. Those killed across the river were said to be fourteen, with at least twice that number wounded. Not less than ten Indian horses had been killed and a great number injured. He believed the attacking force to consist of Comanches and Osages. Here Royall may have been mistaken. The Comanches and Osages were trading partners, but the latter tribe seldom participated in attacks against whites. Due to previous hard experience, they usually confined their efforts to the theft of livestock. Most likely the attacking party consisted primarily of Comanches, with perhaps a few Kiowas and Plains Apaches. Royall's report was sent to Washington with the next express mail. The two wagon trains, the beef herd, and Royall's recruits rested a day or so longer, then once again took to the trail. Lieutenant Royall himself reached Santa Fe on July 17, three or four days ahead of his column. The eventful march of the Santa Fe Battalion's seventy-one recruits was now complete.[31]

12

Gabriel's Barbecue

June is a month of transition across the Great Plains. The rains of spring, such as they may be, greatly decrease in frequency; at the same time heat begins to build, foretelling the scorching temperatures of the summer that will follow. On June 9, 1848, Capt. George W. Hook and the 143 recruits he had enlisted for service with Newby's regiment of Illinois infantry volunteers left Fort Leavenworth bound for Santa Fe. With them went a fifty-three-wagon government train carrying supplies and specie to pay the troops in New Mexico, along with Maj. Noah Johnston, paymaster, Capt. George H. Kennerly, of the Quartermaster Department, and Orville C. Pratt, a lawyer en route to California. They reached the Council Grove on June 16 and camped there awaiting the arrival of Capt. Gabriel de Korponay's detachment of cavalry recruits, following a day or so behind. Together they would escort not only the supply train, a caravan of traders, the paymaster, and others but also Lt. Col. John Garland of the Fourth U.S. Infantry Regiment from Jefferson Barracks and Lt. Col. Clifton Wharton, commandant of Fort Leavenworth. The latter two had been ordered to Fort Mann to conduct an investigation into the allegations against Capt. William Pelzer and others at the post and had just concluded their interrogation of the notorious Caroline Newcome.[1]

Captain Korponay, who had been on recruiting duty for Ralls's Third Regiment of Missouri Mounted Volunteers, left

Fort Leavenworth on June 10 with his detachment of one hundred recruits, a number of supply wagons, and a small caravan of traders. They moved south on the Fort Leavenworth–Fort Scott Military Road and on June 11 camped eleven miles south of the Delaware Crossing of the Kansas River. They were to remain there pending the arrival of Colonels Garland and Wharton, then continue on to join Hook and his men at Council Grove. Garland and Wharton reached the cavalry camp late on June 13, and Korponay's men resumed their march the following morning. Before they reached Council Grove, however, Colonel Wharton's health deteriorated to the point that he was forced to return to Fort Leavenworth, where he died on July 13. Garland's orders had anticipated the problem of Wharton's poor health, and he was authorized, if necessary, to proceed to Fort Mann and conduct the investigation alone. He decided to do so, and the column continued on, reaching Council Grove on June 17, at about the same time that Lt. William Royall's column was going into camp along the banks of the Arkansas River in the Coon Creek Bottoms.[2]

Colonel Garland had intended to march immediately for Fort Mann, but a number of wagons had broken down, and it was necessary to lay over three days for repairs. These were completed on June 20, and the long column of troops, supply wagons, and traders resumed moving down the Santa Fe Trail on the morning of the twenty-first. In the meantime, Captain Kennerly received orders to return to St. Louis and left the same day. During the march west Garland rode with Korponay and his mounted volunteers and expected to reach Fort Mann in approximately twelve days. In fact they arrived there on June 30, having encountered no difficulties en route. As they were nearing the fort they overtook the slow-moving detachment of recruits commanded by Capt. Vantrump Turner, encumbered by a train of one hundred wagons and four hundred head of beef cattle. On reaching the post, the separate detachments of volunteers went into camp at intervals a few miles upstream in order to ensure sufficient grass for grazing their livestock. Meanwhile, Colonel Garland settled in at the commanding officer's quarters, eager to begin his investigation.[3]

With their duties for Colonel Garland completed, it was intended that the volunteer recruits immediately continue their trek to Santa Fe. To avoid problems with grazing, they were to leave at appropriate intervals but were to stay at reasonable distances, which would allow them to support one another. Turner and his men, with their large wagon train and herd of livestock under escort, left first, probably a day or so after arrival at Fort Mann. Captain Hook's troops, in camp twelve miles above the fort, left late on the afternoon of July 7. Turner seems to have followed the usual trail to the Cimarron and beyond, but for unexplained reasons Hook took his men along the Arkansas to Bent's Fort, then over the mountains on the Kearny route, making it impossible for him to lend support to Turner's column if the need arose. Hook and his men finally arrived in Santa Fe on July 31. Traveling with him were Major Johnston and the lawyer Pratt. Korponay and his men were expected to leave two or three days after Hook. But on the morning of July 4, just as the garrison and the encampments of recruits were preparing to celebrate the national day, a large number of horses and mules belonging to Korponay's command stampeded away from their grazing grounds. They disappeared to the east, going over the bluffs leading to the high plains. Though Indian raiders were suspected, that could not be proved because too few animals remained to let Korponay's men pursue with an adequate force. All they could do was report the loss to the headquarters at Fort Mann and request replacements.[4]

The disappearance of Korponay's livestock greatly irritated Colonel Garland, who probably thought it to be the result of the laxity and incompetence of volunteer troops. On July 6 he ordered Korponay and his men (now provided with replacement mounts) to conduct a vigorous search for the missing animals. If they were found in the possession of Indians (the Comanches or the Pawnees were prime suspects), Garland directed that they be recovered, using force if necessary. Korponay organized a search party

consisting of fifty men from his command, twenty-one foot
soldiers from Company D of the Indian Battalion led by Capt.
Paul Holtzscheiter, and one six-pounder howitzer manned
by a few of Korponay's men. He also took the guide Micheau
Duvall, a plainsman employed at Fort Mann. They left their
camp on the morning of July 7, moving slowly eastward along
the Santa Fe Trail while mounted patrols continually scoured
the plains north of the river. Shortly after their departure,
an express arrived from Fort Leavenworth bringing Colonel
Garland a copy of the preparatory order for withdrawing
troops from Mexico, indicating that a peace had been concluded. At noon the same day Capt. John C. Griffin also left
the fort in command of a cavalry detachment from Companies
A and B, one six-pounder howitzer and a crew to man it and
five infantrymen. Griffin was under orders from Colonel
Gilpin to march south in search of a Comanche village
believed to be located along the Cimarron, the suspected
source of at least some of the raiders then harassing the
commerce of the trail. It seemed that at last there was to be
some action.[5]

Captain Korponay and his men searched diligently, but
without success. The horses and mules had disappeared into
the immensity of the plains. Worse, summer had now come in
full force, and each day's march was filled with the misery of
searing temperatures propelled by the incessant south wind.
On the evening of July 9 the weary and discouraged searchers
camped on the banks of the Arkansas about thirty-five miles
below Fort Mann. The campfires were lit, and coffee was put
on to boil. As the sun made its evening slide below the
horizon, the heat of day began to abate. The animals were
turned out to graze, and the men ate their supper. Shadows of
a nearby grove of cottonwoods lengthened, then merged into
the dark as twilight came. The night noises of a strange land
began: the yipping of coyotes, the mournful howling of
wolves, the grunts and bellows of buffalo coming to the river to
drink, the cries of the night birds, and a myriad of other
unknown and unfamiliar sounds. While the men sat staring
into the dying embers of their campfires, exhausted from

their long day's ride, one of them noticed a light in the distance. Captain Korponay immediately gave it careful scrutiny. It was clearly a campfire along the river and seemed to him to be about five miles northeast of their own camp. The guide Duvall, asked to study it and ascertain if it was from an Indian or a white encampment, reported that it appeared to be the campfire of a Comanche war party. Korponay promptly reinforced the guard, anticipating a night attack.[6]

Although Korponay and his men probably got scant sleep that night, the expected Comanche assault never came. At 2:30 A.M., in the hope that he and his men could sieze the initiative by making a surprise attack on the Comanches, Korponay had reveille sounded, and the troops prepared for a march to battle. They moved out as quietly as possible and by 3:30 A.M. had reached the area of the presumed Indian encampment. Just as they thought they were about to engage their enemy, word came back from the guide that it was not a camp of Indians but of a patrol from Gilpin's battalion. Not wanting to alarm the sleeping soldiers with the sudden appearance of a large body of mounted men from out of the darkness, Korponay had his bugler sound the ordinance march. In an instant the startled men from the patrol arose in great confusion, hardly knowing what had happened. Just as suddenly a new discovery shocked them all: the opposite bank of the Arkansas was alive with Comanche warriors, who had also heard the bugle call.[7]

For Korponay and his men, thinking they had found a friendly military encampment and not an enemy, this rapid turn of events must have been astounding. But Captain Korponay was a man of steady nerves, and he ordered his men into company line and marched them to the river's edge. The first glow of light for the new day was by now beginning to illuminate the mass of men and horses on the other side of the river, revealing an estimated five to six hundred warriors. Their camp was nearby in a grove of trees, and Duvall may well have accurately assessed the source of the campfire seen earlier without detecting the presence of a military patrol nearby.* Either the patrol and the Indians were unaware of each other's presence until Korponay and his detachment came, or the Indians were preparing to attack the sleeping patrol when Korponay arrived.[8]

When the soldiers were in line facing the Comanche warriors on the opposite bank, Duvall called out to them and asked if they wanted to fight. The Indians answered by firing eight or nine shots at the soldiers from a handful of carbines. Korponay ordered his men to open fire, but the distance was too great to use small arms with accuracy, and the Indians had the advantage of the grove of trees and underbrush along the river in which to take cover. Finding his first volley ineffectual, Korponay ordered up the six-pounder howitzer and fired at the enemy using grapeshot. Again, the distance was too far, and the shot had no effect. He then had the piece loaded with six-pound balls. Captain Holtzscheiter directed the aiming and firing with great precision, and the result was a direct hit, killing two warriors. A second round killed another Indian and probably injured others, including their horses.[9]

The hits by the artillery piece demoralized the Comanches, and many started to fall back, anxious to move beyond the range of the fearsome weapon. As they began to retreat, Korponay ordered his men to cross the river in pursuit. This proved difficult. The river was high, the result of the June rise caused by melting snow in the mountains. Indian snipers on the southeast bank greatly increased the hazard. Nevertheless, Ordinance Sergeant Clarkson jumped into the river with Duvall, and the two swam over with ropes to assist in crossing the howitzer, a very dangerous feat performed while under fire from the Indians. Once the detachment had reached the

---

*Assuming the accuracy of the mileages given in the official report, the site of the Comanche village and the river fight would have been along the Arkansas approximately six to seven miles southwest of present Kinsley, Kansas. It also seems probable that Korponay and his men had gone into camp at or near the campsite along the Santa Fe Trail known as "Little Pond Camp." However, this is based on approximate mileages supplied in Charles J. Folsom's 1842 book *Mexico*, mileages that are of dubious accuracy.

opposite side of the river, Korponay reorganized his troops
and began the pursuit. They passed the Comanche camp
(where the cooking fires were still burning) and moved onto
the plains. Soon they encountered the sand hills, running
parallel with the river along its southeast bank, which at that
point were three or four miles in depth. Once beyond them
they found that the Comanches had reformed and were preparing to fight. Korponay had the howitzer unlimbered and fired
a few shots, again causing the Indians to retreat. The pursuit
continued in a southeastern direction, and twice more the
Comanches reformed in an effort to carry the fight to the
soldiers. Each time, the howitzer did its deadly work and
forced them to retreat beyond range. Whenever a warrior was
killed or severely wounded, several of his fellows would rush
in and carry him beyond the scene of battle. After following
the Indians for about fifteen miles, probably to the upper
reaches of Rattlesnake Creek and rougher country, Korponay
decided that they could not overtake their foe, and he called a
halt to the pursuit. His detachment retraced their route from
the river and returned to the Comanche camp. There they
found the Indian equipment abandoned and a morning meal of
buffalo meat still cooking over the campfires. The men had
eaten nothing except a little hardtack, and now they "partook
sumptuously" of the ready-made breakfast. Afterwards they
referred to the place and the fight as "Gabriel's Barbecue."[10]

When the men had finished their meal and rested, Captain
Korponay put them back on the road. They recrossed the river
and turned westward, moving steadily down the Santa Fe
Trail toward Fort Mann. They reached it on July 12, and
Korponay and his men went into camp at the cavalry encampment dubbed "Camp Gilpin." There Korponay wrote a report
of the engagement for both Colonel Garland and Adj. Gen.
Roger Jones. By his estimate they had killed seven Comanche
warriors, and from the blood seen in the pursuit he conjec-
tured they had severely wounded a number of others. He said
his men had performed their duties bravely and with discipline and order. A number of them were singled out for special
mention, either for extraordinary bravery or for the coolness

and efficiency with which they had performed their tasks. Especially noted were Captain Holtzscheiter, Ordinance Sergeant Clarkson, and the guide Micheau Duvall. They had not recovered the missing horses and mules, but "Gabriel's Barbecue" had been successful in forcing at least some of the Comanche raiders away from the Arkansas.[11]

Captain Korponay and his men remained at Fort Mann only a few days more. The end of the Mexican War removed the need for additional troops in New Mexico and also ended the term of their enlistment. Rather than continue on to Santa Fe, Korponay's volunteers simply waited for Colonel Garland to complete his investigation, so that they could escort him back to Missouri. They had not long to wait. By July 14 the investigation had been completed, the resignations of accused officers had been accepted, and court-martials for enlisted offenders had been concluded. Garland issued a final written order directed to the officers and men of the Indian Battalion. Colonel Garland, Captain Korponay, and the recruits probably marched for Fort Leavenworth on July 15. They reached it by the end of the month and embarked on steamboats for St. Louis. Garland and half of his escort reached St. Louis aboard the *Wyandotte* on August 2, and the rest (fifty-six men with twenty-four horses) arrived aboard the *Mandan* the following day. Korponay's recruits had never joined their units or met other members of their regiment; but the manner in which they performed their duties had been a credit to the Missouri Volunteers.[12]

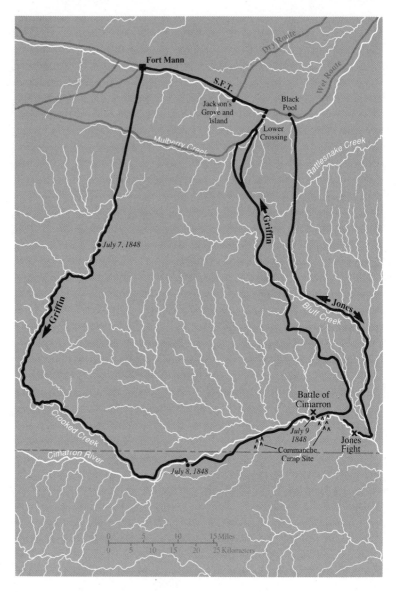

Routes of Captains Griffin and Jones to Cimarron River and return during
Comanche campaigns of 1848

13

The Last Campaigns

William Gilpin had found no Comanches during his spring
expedition. When he returned to Fort Mann, however, it was
clear that the Indians had not been "overawed" and were once
again active along the Arkansas. The stretch of the Santa Fe
Trail between Walnut Creek and the area of the Coon Creeks
had been experiencing recurring attacks on trail traffic by a
very large war party of Comanche warriors, perhaps by as
many as two or three such parties. Recently they had become
bold enough to attempt direct assaults on military units, such
as the fight with Lt. Phillip Stremmel's artillery detachment
on June 7 and the Battle of Coon Creek on June 18. During
those engagements, the Comanches had experienced serious
casualties for the first time, but their capacity to do substantial harm to travelers and their property remained unim-
paired. The daring action of Comanches was also suspected
when the horses and mules from Capt. Gabriel de Korponay's
cavalry detachment were stampeded on July 4. In response to
these attacks, Gilpin resolved to mount offensive operations
against the Indians as soon as possible, hoping to drive them
from the Arkansas and end the raids. On the morning of July 7
he issued orders to Capt. John C. Griffin of Company A,
Indian Battalion, to take a detachment of men and scout south
to the Cimarron in search of a Comanche village believed to
be the source of some of the raiding parties harassing traffic
on the Santa Fe Trail. After reaching the Cimarron, Griffin

was to move east, engage the enemy if found, then return to
the Arkansas near its south bend, whence his troops would
return directly to the cavalry camp across the river from Fort
Mann. Griffin and his men began their march at noon on July
7, a few hours after Captain Korponay and his men left on
their eventful scout eastward and a few hours before Capt.
George Hook's infantry recruits left for Santa Fe.[1]

The detachment led by Griffin included three sergeants,
three corporals, and fifty-two privates from A Company, under the command of Lieutenant Benson of Company B; one
sergeant, one corporal, and eighteen privates from B Company, commanded by Lieutenant Eldridge of Company B; two
sergeants and thirteen privates from C Company (artillery),
with one six-pounder howitzer; and five privates from D Company (infantry)—101 men in all, including officers. They left
the cavalry camp and marched a little west of south for twenty-five miles, following an established trail (probably an old
Indian trail) that led them to the upper reaches of Crooked
Creek. After a long and tiring march, Griffin finally put them
into camp along its banks at a place where they found a few
pools of water in the dry bed of the stream.* Griffin and his
men likely reached Crooked Creek about 7:00 P.M., having
averaged some three and a half miles per hour—a very credit-
able speed. The next morning, July 8, the men arose at day-
break and, after eating breakfast and grazing the animals,
should have been back on the trail not later than 6:00 A.M.
This day they followed Crooked Creek on its meandering movements south, then southeast to its junction with the Cimarron.
Crooked Creek usually had water in its bed, although in the upper reaches the flow tended to be subsurface during the dry, hot
days of summer. In the creek's lower reaches there was almost
always a surface flow of clear, sweet water. With good grass in
its valley, the stream was a favored camping ground for at least
two bands of Comanches—the Kotsotekas and the Yamparikas—as well as the Kiowas. But no Indians were seen during

*This camp would have been along the east bank of Crooked Creek in
present Meade County, Kansas, about five miles south of the Ford County line.

Griffin's march, and the men continued a steady course until reaching the mouth of Crooked Creek late in the afternoon.[2]

When Captain Griffin and his troops reached the Cimarron, they turned east and marched along its north bank. They continued eastward until near sundown, apparently traveling another seven or eight miles beyond the confluence of Crooked Creek and the river. Griffin then rode to a high point overlooking the Cimarron to observe the country ahead. From his vantage point, he could see to the east what appeared to be a large grove of trees on the south bank, extending south as far as he could see. He decided to examine the grove the next day and for that purpose led his men to the south bank of the river and made camp.* The night passed without incident, and as dawn broke on the morning of June 9 the column was already on the march. After traveling about twelve miles, Griffin and his men reached the grove he had observed, which turned out to be a few cottonwoods, a sprinkling of black willows, and a great number of Chickasaw plum bushes in the sandy bottoms where a small stream, Clark Creek, flowed into the Cimarron.† In the grove they found the remains of an abandoned Comanche camp, which Griffin estimated to have been large enough to hold thousands of Indians. They halted along the banks of the little stream to eat a delayed breakfast, probably hardtack, to refresh themselves, and to graze and water their horses. As they were eating and enjoying the peaceful solitude of this lonely place, Corporal Casstel of A Company suddenly called out that he had sighted a mounted Indian. Griffin immediately ordered Lieutenant Eldridge to take twenty men and reconnoiter the vicinity of the camp.[3]

*This camp would have been in present Harper County, Oklahoma, two or three miles east of the Beaver County line. Captain Griffin later reported that they had traveled "upwards of forty miles" that day. It was actually at least fifty miles, since their camp of June 7 was about forty-three miles north of the mouth of Crooked Creek.

†Griffin did not name the stream, but Clark Creek is the first stream flowing from the south into the Cimarron to the east of the mouth of Crooked Creek and is the correct mileage from the prior camp. This location would be in present Clark County, Kansas.

Eldridge and his men gathered their horses and mounted as quickly as possible, then started to the east. But the detachment had hardly cleared the grove when they met a young Mexican boy coming toward them, probably the person Corporal Casstel had seen and mistakenly identified as an Indian.* He was at once taken into custody and delivered to Captain Griffin for interrogation. From him they learned that the Comanche village was presently located about nine miles downstream. Griffin prepared his men for battle, and they started eastward. After a march of three hours they sighted a large party of Comanche warriors, ready for battle, occupying a well-chosen site on the north bank of the stream. Without delay the soldiers crossed to the opposite side of the river and marched against them. The Comanches were in a battle formation similar to a hook, or crochet, with their flanking wings thrown forward. Their left wing was on a ridge of low sand dunes at the edge of the river, shaded by cottonwood trees, and their right wing was on and behind a higher ridge to the north, with about half a mile separating the two wings. Griffin directed his men to the center of the Indian line, and they marched forward until striking a dry arroyo or ravine coming down from the high ground to the north, most probably the dry arroyo of Day Creek. At first this seemed a good place to make a stand and receive an Indian charge, so Griffin halted his men, surveyed the Indians' position, and estimated the size of the opposing force. During this time the warriors began firing a number of guns at the soldiers, some of the balls passing just above their heads.[4]

The survey of the Indians' position revealed that it was possible to cross the arroyo to their left. Griffin ordered Sergeant Kaedetz to unlimber the howitzer and fire a round shot at a group of warriors near the center of the Indian left

---

*Suspicious that he was a Comanche spy, Griffin took the boy captive. Later, at Fort Mann, the boy reported that his name was Stephen and that he had lived at the hacienda of a Colonel Quinto in Texas before being abducted by the Comanches. See Garland to Roger Jones, Aug. 2, 1848, enclosed with Garland to Roger Jones, Aug. 16, 1848, AGO, Letters Received, 368 G 1848, RG 94, N.A. (M567-R377).

wing while the cavalry prepared to charge. When weapons were loaded and ready, and the men prepared, Griffin deployed his troops to the left. In the meantime a party of warriors had entered the arroyo and taken position to the left of the soldiers. To counter them, Griffin ordered Lieutenant Benson and Sergeant Clark of A Company to take twenty men and drive them out. They were to force the Indians back up the hill and to the other side, then maintain their position at the crest. Benson and his men charged the enemy in a frontal assault, weapons blazing. The Comanches fiercely contended every foot of ground up the hill, but the superior weapons and firepower of the soldiers were not to be denied. When finally at the crest of the hill, however, Benson's troops found themselves facing a new danger. Directly in front of them were about two hundred mounted Comanche warriors, lances and shields held at the ready and prepared for a charge. Benson dismounted his men, formed them into line, and began pouring a heavy and concentrated fire on the Indians, forcing them back. At the same time, another party of warriors rode to the soldiers' flank and opened up on them with small arms, firing incessantly, though with little effect.[5]

While Lieutenant Benson's men were engaging the Indians on their left flank, Griffin had managed to get the rest of his force, including the howitzer, across the arroyo. Once beyond it he ordered Lieutenant Eldridge of B Company to take twenty men and go to the support of Benson. This was done, but even as the troopers were advancing to aid their fellows, the Indian sniping suddenly stopped, and a new body of mounted warriors appeared, apparently intent on getting to the rear of Benson's position. Griffin ordered up the remainder of the cavalry and prepared to lead it himself. As he did, however, he discovered that Indians on their right wing (the Indians' left) had been moving around behind them and were fast building up a concentration of men at their rear. These Indians were easily within canister range of the howitzer, but the weapon had no more than seven men with it, the rest of the artillerymen having joined with the others preparing to charge. Griffin brought them back, along with a portion of the cavalrymen to support and protect the howitzer. Before it could be prepared for firing, however, the Comanches' right flank (the soldiers' left) gave way, while their left fell back to their original position in the sand hills. Griffin ordered Lieutenant Eldridge, with twenty men, to follow the retiring Indians on his left flank and Lieutenant Benson, with twenty men, to advance to a point in front of the Indians' left, then halt and hold himself in readiness to support Eldridge if the latter became heavily engaged. The rest of the troops under Griffin prepared to advance against a strong party of warriors positioned behind a sand hill where the left of their center rested when the action began. But before the soldiers came within canister range of the Indian center, the Comanches began to give way, doubtless well aware of what a howitzer could do to their men and horses while still beyond range of bows and arrows. Griffin halted the howitzer, had it unlimbered, and fired a round shot among them, apparently killing two men. The Comanches began a precipitate retreat from the battlefield, and within a short time no more than two could be seen. Griffin sent out two parties of cavalry to pursue them, but none were found north of the river. From the vantage of a high point of ground, Griffin then discerned a fleeing column of Indians downriver about six or seven miles, which he estimated to include some fifteen hundred people. Obviously these were the remainder of the village's inhabitants, attempting to escape the soldiers.[6]

The fight had begun at 12:00 noon on July 9 and lasted three hours. In all probability the Comanches had made their bold stand to screen the escape of their women, children, and old people. Their village was not far away, located in a sheltering grove of cottonwoods along the river and the mouth of Snake Creek on the south side of the Cimarron. Once their families were beyond the reach of the soldiers, the warriors probably broke off the engagement rather than take unnecessary losses by facing the soldiers' howitzer and superior arms. Captain Griffin estimated that in the engagement, the Comanches must have lost not less than thirty men and perhaps many more, but it was impossible to verify most of these. In accordance with tribal practice, when warriors were hit, their comrades removed them from the area of the fight. Many tied themselves to their horses, and whether they were dead or wounded, their mounts carried them away from the battle unless they, too, were hit. Griffin believed he had seen eight or ten who were shot and must have been killed outright but who were taken from the battlefield in this manner. One, however, was killed after being struck by two balls; his horse was hit by five and also killed. His friends made a desperate effort to retrieve his body, but he had fallen within sixty yards of the soldiers' line. Although the Comanches succeeded in crossing and tying his legs, preparatory to dragging him away, the heavy fire from military sharpshooters drove them back before they could complete their task, and the warrior was left behind. When the soldiers inspected his body after the fight, they found him to be about fifty years old, with a "stern countenance and intellectual features." He was wrapped in a "rich Spanish blanket," and was assumed to be a chief.[7]

A check of the soldiers revealed that none had been killed and only two injured. Lieutenant Eldridge had been slightly wounded in the hand by an arrow, and Sergeant Gibson of A Company had suffered a minor head injury when grazed by an arrow. There were several injured horses, some struck by arrows and others by balls from Indian firearms. Because all of the men were exhausted from the intensity of the fighting during the extreme heat of day, Griffin had them make camp on the battlefield next to the river. There they rested, grazed their animals, and ate their afternoon meal while scouts checked the country around them. No other Indians were found. Darkness came, but the night passed uneventfully, and at first light of day they prepared to continue their march. Nothing was to be seen or heard of the Comanches in their vicinity, so Griffin turned his column north and west, striking out for Mulberry Creek, the nearest stream draining into the Arkansas from the south. This course took them through some very broken country to their north, and likely they followed the dry beds of intermittent streams to get themselves through the worst of this and onto the rolling plains and breaks to the northwest. Since they marched for two days without water, they must have stayed to the west of the drainage of Bluff Creek, a stream usually having a surface flow in its middle and lower reaches. The column reached the Mulberry late in the evening of June 11, apparently striking it well short of the Arkansas, probably at the bend where it turned north to join the larger stream. Men and animals alike were suffering from extreme thirst, but it took them another hour to find any water in the bed of the creek, indicating they were moving downstream toward the river. Griffin put his men into camp for the night next to the water hole, nearly all being too exhausted to continue the march. The next morning the troopers examined the Mulberry to assure themselves no Comanches were camped in the area. Finding none, the column continued northeast to the Arkansas, then followed the Santa Fe road back to Fort Mann and the cavalry camp. They reached the camp on July 12, probably sometime between mid to late afternoon, ending a successful scout.[8]

Captain Griffin wrote his report of the scout on the evening of his return. After recounting the march to the Cimarron and the engagement with the Comanches, he praised his officers and men. They had, he said, performed their duty "with as much coolness and bravery as any troops could." He noted that some were always foremost in the fight but that all did so well he could not find it in his heart to make distinctions.* He thought the Indians were from the village that was the source of the raiding parties attacking traffic along the Santa Fe Trail. This was doubtless true, but this village was surely not the only source. Griffin and his men had fought the Comanches during the afternoon of July 9, and the enemy had retired southeast along the Cimarron. Early the next morning, July 10, Captain Korponay and his men fought another large body of warriors along the Arkansas. It is probable that there were two or more Comanche war parties operating along

---

*Griffin stated his belief that the location of the fight must have been nearly due south of the mouth of Coon Creek, a remarkably close guess for someone lacking the means of accurately determining his whereabouts.

the Arkansas at this time, possibly from different bands, and that Griffin and Korponay had each stumbled on one of them.[9]

The story of Griffin's march did not end with his return to Fort Mann. Following the pattern that had become too familiar with the Indian Battalion, letters written to newspapers in St. Louis suggested that the results of the scout were greatly exaggerated. One appearing in the *St. Louis New Era* stated that Griffin's force had broken up a village of about one thousand lodges of Comanches, "though without serious fighting." An article in the *St. Louis Reveille* on August 28 cited letters from Fort Mann suggesting that only one Indian had been killed, not the thirty claimed. A correspondent for the *New Era* was reported to have censured Captain Griffin's conduct, asserting that he started firing the howitzer at the Indians from a distance of nearly two miles and that, when the men charged, Griffin remained with the piece at a respectful distance from the fight. The latter seems patently false, since a six-pounder howitzer of that day did not have an effective range anywhere close to two miles, and the soldiers probably could not have seen their enemy from that distance, much less accurately aimed a howitzer. Moreover, the Indians broke before there ever was a real charge. Colonel Gilpin, however, seemed to have no doubts about the effectiveness of Griffin's brief campaign, forwarding Griffin's report with approval along with his letter of August 1 to Adj. Gen. Roger Jones. Whatever the correct number of Indian casualties, likely the deprecating letters were a part of the continuing effort to discredit Gilpin and his operations and had probably been sent by disgruntled volunteers who hid behind the cloak of anonymity.[10]

The return of Griffin and Korponay to Fort Mann on July 12 with the news of their separate fights placed Gilpin in a quandary. The presence of very large war parties in the vicinity had been confirmed, as were their temporary defeats in the recent fights. But had they truly been driven from the Arkansas, or had they merely retired beyond the reach of pursuing soldiers, intending to return another day? To answer this question, on July 15 Gilpin ordered Capt. Thomas Jones, commander of B Company, Indian Battalion, to take a detachment of cavalry and artillery, march east along the Santa Fe Trail to the south bend of the Arkansas near the Korponay fight, and then, if no Comanches were found, move south to the Cimarron. Jones was to examine the country to learn if the Indians were still present in force and, if they were found, to engage them and administer a sound defeat. Jones prepared his men, took provisions for a twelve-day march, and left Fort Mann about noon the same day. They marched steadily east on July 15 and 16, going into camp on the evening of the sixteenth a few miles below the mouth of Mulberry Creek on the north bank of the Arkansas, perhaps at the Black Pool. Here they encountered the train of the traders Bullard and Hooke, who were heading to Santa Fe, and from them learned that no Indians had been seen on or near the trail to that point. This convinced Jones that it would be useless to march farther north and east, so he decided to move south to the Cimarron the next day.[11]

When they reached their camp on the evening of July 16, Captain Jones discharged four sick men. These men probably returned to Fort Mann with the Bullard and Hooke train. Their departure left Jones with a force of sixty-seven men from Company B under Lieutenant Eldridge, sixteen men from A Company under Lieutenant Bain, and fifteen men from C Company (artillery) commanded by the intrepid Second Lieutenant Khulow, who had distinguished himself at the Pawnee Fork and Coon Creek. Jones also took one brass six-pounder howitzer and seven civilian guides and hands, including Micheau Duvall, who had guided Captain Korponay. Jones and his troops—109 mounted men in all—crossed the Arkansas at dawn on July 17 and marched due south. At first the country they traversed was a hard rolling plain, intersected occasionally by the dry sandy beds of intermittent streams, some with pools of water. These contained many signs of recent Indian usage, but no Indians were seen. As they continued south, they crossed the upper reaches of Rattlesnake Creek (at that point no more than a dry arroyo), then entered the broken country beyond. They likely followed the bed of one of the many dry streams that, in the rainy season, carried water into Bluff Creek. They probably stayed with the latter stream all the way to its junction with the Cimarron, since it provided the easiest route of march and ensured a ready supply of water. They reached the Cimarron on the evening of the nineteenth and made camp there.[12]

At first light on July 20 Captain Jones had his men back in the saddle and under way. They marched west up the Cimarron along the north bank. Jones intended to find and follow the trail of the Comanche village that Captain Griffin and his men had attacked and dispersed on July 9. If he could find it, his orders were to attack and drive the Indians south toward the Canadian and beyond. At about 10:00 A.M., the guide Duvall galloped up, reporting that he had seen Indians upriver in the direction of some groves of timber. Jones promptly reorganized his command in preparation for a fight. First he placed thirty select horsemen under the command of Lieutenant Bain to act as cavalry. Another thirty men, mounted on horses and mules, were placed under the command of Lieutenant Eldridge, with orders to support Bain and his men. The remainder of the mounted troops were retained under the control of Captain Jones, who organized them in columns of four and placed them on either side of the howitzer, thereby concealing it from the Indians. Thus arrayed, the column resumed its march up the Cimarron. In a short time they reached the lower of two sizable groves of timber. It consisted of cottonwood, black willows, Chickasaw plum bushes, and grapevines, all clustered around and near the mouth of a small stream entering the river from the south, apparently the one now known as Willow Creek, and covering about fifty acres with thick brush. As the soldiers were observing this grove, Jones's attention was called to a single mounted Indian on one of the low sand hills paralleling the river on its north bank. The warrior was engaged in a series of sham maneuvers, obviously intended to draw the soldiers in his direction. Suspicious, Jones ordered Lieutenant Bain to cross the river and examine the grove.[13]

Bain and his thirty men splashed across the shallow waters covering the sandy bottom of the Cimarron and entered the grove. As soon as they did they were attacked without warning and hotly engaged in close combat by Indians waiting in ambush. Seeing this, Jones ordered Lieutenant Eldridge to take his troops to the opposite end of the grove and support Bain. The artillery and remaining cavalry he held in reserve, much to their chagrin, but the nature of the battlefield and the positions of both the troops and the Indians permitted no other course. Crossing the river and circling the area of scrub trees and brush, Eldridge's detachment entered from the south and worked their way north. As they did, they met the Indians retreating before the superior firepower of Bain's detachment. Both of the units made successive charges through the grove, dangerously exposing themselves as they did but quickly closing the gap and trapping the warriors between them. The fighting was hand to hand and muzzle to muzzle. The Indians fought bravely, but the superior numbers and weapons of the whites soon ended the combat, and the guns fell silent. Forty-one warriors had been counted during the affair; of these, twenty-one were found dead, and six were seen to escape apparently unharmed. The dead were all shot in the chest (some having several wounds), showing that they had fought courageously until death claimed them. The remainder of the Indians were probably dead or dying, concealed by the brush and not discovered by the searchers because of their need to move on quickly. This small body of men could have been intended to delay their progress, and a larger number might even then be moving away from them farther to the west. [14]

The fight had not been without cost to the soldiers. Lieutenant Eldridge and Pvts. Phillip Kinchlo, G. W. Vance, and James B. Hoover of B Company, and Pvt. Robert Williams of A Company, had been severely wounded by arrows that struck them from behind as they moved past concealed warriors. These injuries were treated insofar as possible, but Captain Jones felt their mission was not complete, and when the wounded had been tended to, the column moved on. After a march of about five miles they came to the grove of trees and brush extending along the Cimarron and around the mouth of Snake Creek. Here they found the remains of the village abandoned by the Comanches when Captain Griffin's men had reached the area on July 9. What they saw indicated a hasty flight, with lodgepoles, saddles, bags of salt, and provisions strewn across the ground in large quantities. Based on the number of fire pits and lodge circles, Jones estimated there had been from eight hundred to one thousand lodges and a horse herd of at least fifteen hundred to two thousand head. Griffin's approach must have been discovered only a short time before the engagement, with the warriors mounting their war horses and taking their positions to provide protection until their families could move well beyond reach of the soldiers. There was no evidence that the Comanches had returned to the site since Griffin had been there. When they completed their examination of the abandoned village, Jones allowed his men to rest a bit, then prepare their afternoon meal. Scouts returned with reports that they could find no other Indians in the area. Because he had five severely wounded men needing medical attention and rest, Captain Jones decided to return to Fort Mann as rapidly as possible. They began their return march that evening.[15]

Captain Jones did not state the route taken on the return of his column, but he likely either retraced his steps to Bluff Creek and then north or continued up the Cimarron to the mouth of Crooked Creek and followed that stream northward, the route that Captain Griffin and his men had taken south. It would have been important to have a reliable supply of water on hand for the suffering wounded, and either stream would have filled that need. His subsequent observations concerning Indian campfires to the east probably mean he went back the way he came, by way of Bluff Creek. Whatever way he selected, he completed his march and reached Fort Mann on July 23, probably about midday. He wrote his report of the operation the same day, recounting the march and the ensuing combat. He stated his opinion that the Indians he fought were from a war party of Pawnees, an unlikely conclusion for which he gave no basis. It would have been suicide for a party of only forty-one men to come south into Comanche country seeking a fight. There seems to have been no grounds for Jones's assumption, and he admitted that the Indians "refused to make themselves known." In the unlikely event they were Pawnees, they were probably there to steal horses or perhaps to obtain salt from the Grand Saline or Rock Saline rivers farther south and east. But no loss of this number of Pawnee warriors in the south was noted in 1848, surely a sufficient number of casualties for the beleaguered tribe's agent to have noted in his annual report. The Indians that Jones met were on a river heavily camped along by Comanches during the height of summer, when the embattled Pawnees would have been tending their corn crops or hunting buffalo along the Platte or Republican. It is much more likely these Indians were either Comanches, come to see if anything could be salvaged from the abandoned village, or perhaps a hunting party of Kiowas. Jones also expressed his belief that the Comanches had been effectively driven from the Arkansas and had retreated in the direction of the lower Canadian River. He noted that his expedition had observed columns of smoke on the eastern horizon both going to and coming from the Cimarron, that he believed indicated the presence or passage of Indians. He thought the smoke marked camps of retreating Comanches or possibly of Osage or Kansa buffalo hunters to the east of the Great Bend of the Arkansas. His report was forwarded to the adjutant general of the army along with Gilpin's letter of August 1.[16]

The two expeditions under Griffin and Jones seem to have marked the end of serious warfare along or near the Santa Fe Trail and the Arkansas River for the remainder of 1848. Trail traffic had been heavy, both enraging and tempting the Indians. But the heavy casualties suffered by the Comanches in their encounters with the military units under Stremmel, Royall, Korponay, Griffin, and Jones seem to have convinced those bands involved to suspend their attacks and remove their families from the proximity of military operations. This was the precise result that Gilpin had contended for when he had advocated aggressive campaigns in search of Indians as the best method of protecting the trail. With the end of the Mexican War and the slowing of military activity in the West, however, the lesson was soon to be forgotten.

14

The Final Days of Fort Mann
and the Indian Battalion

The summer of 1848 saw sharp engagements between military
units and the Comanches, resulting in the northern bands of
the tribe retiring, at least temporarily, from the Arkansas and
the Santa Fe road. But warfare with the Indians was not the
only important event affecting life on the trail. Col. John
Garland and his escort had reached Fort Mann on June 30.
Garland was under orders to investigate and recommend
punishment for the troublemakers of the Indian Battalion. He
settled himself in his accommodations, then began assem-
bling information, probably by interrogating officers and men
of the two German companies, C and D, as well as William
Gilpin and others. The national holiday interrupted his task
on July 4, and this was compounded by the loss of horses and
mules suffered that morning by Capt. Gabriel de Korponay's
detachment of recruits for Ralls's Third Regiment.[1]

On July 6 Garland was finally ready to consider the first
case, that of Capt. William Pelzer. Formal charges and
specifications, prepared by Gilpin, were furnished to both
Garland and Pelzer, and the latter was ordered to appear
before Colonel Garland at 4:00 P.M. that afternoon. Pelzer
immediately requested a delay in proceedings until the
following morning so that he might confer with counsel before
entering a plea. Garland granted the request, and Pelzer
sought advice from Orville Pratt, the lawyer who had arrived
at Fort Mann with Capt. George W. Hook and his Illinois

infantry recruits. Pratt was en route to California, then to Oregon, where he had accepted a judgeship. He had apparently assisted Gilpin in preparing formal charges and was now called on by Pelzer for advice as to a defense against them. Pratt recommended that he tender his resignation again rather than face a court-marital hearing, which would surely convict him.[2]

The morning of July 7 brought news that dramatically altered Garland's ideas for restoring discipline at Fort Mann. Captain Korponay and his detachment of recruits and artillerymen had left during the early morning in search of the missing horses and mules. Shortly after their departure, an express arrived from Fort Leavenworth bringing a copy of the order directing preparation for withdrawal of American troops from Mexico. This made it clear a peace had been made and volunteer forces would soon be disbanded. The men of the Indian Battalion had enlisted for only one year, and their enlistments were due to expire in September. With that in mind, Garland was convinced it was in the best interest of the country and the service that he accept Captain Pelzer's proffered resignation and order him out of the Indian country. This he did. Another reason for doing so was his conviction that many of Pelzer's most heinous actions (particularly the killing of the Pawnees he had invited into the post) resulted from ignorance, timidity, and accident rather than a preconceived plan or desire to commit such a murderous act. Obviously Pelzer was given the benefit of the doubt.[3]

Garland next turned to the charges against Amandus Schnabel and the others. Schnabel too had tendered his resignation the morning of July 7. As in Captain Pelzer's case, the resignation was accepted, and Schnabel was ordered to leave the Indian country at once. Three other officers — 2d Lt. William Crudington, 2d Lt. William O'Hara, and 1st Lt. John Stephens — likewise submitted their resignations. On the recommendation of Colonel Gilpin these were also accepted. The three men were, in the words of Garland, "from their insufficiency . . . an absolute drawback to the discipline of the Battalion." Charges against several enlisted men, alleged to have stolen horses and mules, were dismissed when it became apparent that suspicion (no proof) was the only thing that could be brought before a court. Last to be dealt with were Pvts. Auguste Fahlbush and William Goldbeck. After court-martial proceedings against them, the latter was dismissed from the service "with disgrace," and the former, in addition to being found guilty of the same charges as Goldbeck, was sent to St. Louis and turned over to the U.S. district attorney to be tried for the murder of a fellow soldier, Mathew Ambruster. With these matters behind them, Garland and Gilpin concluded that no further investigation was necessary "for the vindication of discipline" in the Indian Battalion, and the proceedings were closed.[4]

On arrival at Fort Mann, Colonel Garland had discovered that a wounded Pawnee, captured during the incident of the previous November, remained in captivity and was held in irons. Apparently he would have been killed on Pelzer's order except for the timely intervention of one of the battalion's officers. Shocked, Garland ordered his immediate release. Following the conclusion of Garland's investigation and the resignation of Pelzer, the Indian was taken to Fort Leavenworth with directions that he be sent on to his people at the first opportunity. He was instructed to tell his chiefs and headmen that the Great Father, the president, had heard of the "unfortunate occurrence at Fort Mann" and had sent one of his chiefs to find the truth and punish the guilty and that the captain found to be responsible had been "deprived of his commission" and sent out of the Indian country "in disgrace." Whether the injured warrior or his chiefs and headmen understood what that meant is questionable.[5]

The investigation and court-martials were completed by July 14, at which time Colonel Garland issued a departmental order to the officers and men of the Indian Battalion. In addition to recounting the reasons he was sent to Fort Mann and the results of the investigation, the order required elections to replace the resigned officers, ordered Privates Fahlbush and Goldbeck taken to Fort Leavenworth in irons, chastised both German-born and native-born troops for their jealousies and suspicions, and directed them to lay aside old feuds. Garland instructed Gilpin to require his company commanders to enter appropriate remarks on their muster rolls, which would prevent volunteers who did not serve "honestly and faithfully" from getting a discharge entitling them to their bounty lands, especially those guilty of "mutinous conduct, gross violation of orders and improper traffic in horses and mules." He observed that the desire to gain popularity at the expense of discipline was doubtless a root cause of the insubordination afflicting the battalion's efficiency and expressed the hope that all would now submit to proper discipline and serve the remainder of their enlistments honestly and faithfully. Garland closed the order by noting that those doing their proper duty would be cordially welcomed home by family and friends but that no such welcome would be accorded those guilty of the violence and insubordination that had aided in bringing discredit to a battalion that could "justly boast of having in its ranks some of the finest material in the Army."[6]

His duty fulfilled, Colonel Garland apparently left Fort Mann the next day, escorted by Captain Korponay and his recruits. Concern over the possibility of further hostile Indian activity along the Santa Fe Trail weighed heavily on his mind as he traveled east, and when he and his escort camped at Jackson's Grove, probably on the afternoon of the fifteenth, he sent written instructions back to Gilpin directing additional operations against the Indians. One column with two companies was to strike southward and drive any Comanches beyond the Canadian. A second column, also consisting of two companies, was to move northward and force any Pawnees beyond the Smoky Hill River and back to the Platte. On completion of these operations, the companies were to return to Fort Mann and ready themselves to return home for discharge. With that final directive, Garland and his men continued their march to Fort Leavenworth, then on to St. Louis by riverboat. Garland reached St. Louis on August 2 and Jefferson Barracks on August 3. Awaiting him were new orders and a promotion. Before moving on, however, Colonel

Garland performed one last task relating to the Indian Battalion and its problems. On August 3 he began writing a report of
his inquiry and the results. An attack of rheumatism in his
right arm and hand delayed its completion until August 16, at
which time he forwarded it to Adj. Gen. Roger Jones in
Washington.[7]

The express rider bearing Colonel Garland's written instructions to Lieutenant Colonel Gilpin probably reached Fort
Mann sometime during the morning of July 16. In obedience
to the instructions Gilpin immediately designated Company
D as the garrison for Fort Mann, then formed two columns
from the rest of the battalion. Companies A and C, with one
six-pounder howitzer and twenty-five days' provisions, moved
south under the command of Captain Griffin. Their orders
were to find any Comanches in the area of the Arkansas and
Cimarron rivers and drive them south beyond the Canadian.
The second column consisted of companies B and E, with one
six-pounder and like provisions, and was under the command
of Captain Jones. They were to move north in search of any
Pawnees that might have come south to raid trail traffic or
steal horses from the southern Plains tribes. If any were
found, they were to be driven north beyond the Smoky Hill to
their villages on the Platte. Whether successful in finding
their foe or not, at the end of the allotted time both columns
were to return to Fort Mann and prepare for the march home. A
third party consisting of twenty-five men, evidently skimmed
from other companies, was sent to Mora and Bent's Fort to
bring back public property left there by Gilpin the previous
spring during his expedition against the Comanches and
Plains Apaches. The nature of that "public property" is spec-
ulative, but it likely included wagons for which no draft animals had been available and perhaps winter clothing and equipment not useful on a spring campaign. The detail sent to collect
it marched first to Mora via the Cimarron Route, then north over
the Raton Mountains and northeast to Bent's Fort. Property
collected from both places was then taken to Fort Mann.[8]

The most significant of the Indian fights took place along
the Arkansas and Cimarron rivers and involved the Co-

manches. But that tribe was not the only source of Indian trouble in 1848. On May 28 a large merchant train left the Missouri border westbound for Santa Fe. Among those with the train were Preston Beck, Samuel Wethered, G. Estes, Elliott Lee, Charles Towne and his brother Smith D. Towne, Thomas O. Boggs, and H. O'Neil. They proceeded together to the Middle Crossing, at which point the train crossed the Arkansas and continued along the Santa Fe Trail through the Jornada. At the crossing Lee, Charles Towne, and perhaps one or two others left the train and proceeded upriver to Bent's Fort, joining the party of Lucien Maxwell, headed for Taos. They crossed the Raton Mountains by way of Manco Burro Pass and were attacked there on June 19 by a party of Apache Indians. Of the seventeen members of the party, four were killed: Charles Towne, Blackhawk (Pascual Rivière), José Cortez, and José Carmel. Mary and James Tharp, ages six and four, were captured. They were being taken to their grandparents at Taos after the death of their father, William Tharp. Three months later they were ransomed back by Taos merchants. Lee, Maxwell, and six others were wounded but survived. At first Lee was reported killed but subsequently was found alive by a search party.[9]

Traffic on the Santa Fe Trail greatly increased during 1848 despite the end of the Mexican War and the winding down of military activity. Many of the experienced traders, having enjoyed considerable success, were now the owners of large outfits. In mid-July Francis X. Aubry left Independence for Santa Fe with a large train of more than sixty heavy mule wagons, at least half of them his. The train reached the Middle Crossing by late July, and Aubry himself arrived in Santa Fe on August 5 in advance of the wagons. This was his second trip of the year and the beginning of perhaps his greatest adventure. At about the same time Aubry was heading westward, the express from Santa Fe, consisting of James Beckwourth, Charles McIntosh, and Henry Hamilton, was arriving in Fort Leavenworth. They claimed to have left Santa Fe on June 26 and to have made the journey in seventeen days.[10]

On August 1, while his two columns were still in the field searching for Comanches or Pawnees to chase away from the Santa Fe Trail, William Gilpin sat down at Fort Mann to compose a report of his battalion's accomplishments. The expiration of enlistment was only about a month and a half away, and it was clear that, except for any success Griffin or Jones might have on their current scouts, the last chapter in the brief history of the Indian Battalion was nearly complete. It had not been filled with glory; instead it had been a frustrating experience for Gilpin, unable to control many of his mutinous, insubordinate volunteers and unable to corner his illusive enemy. His long expedition against the Comanches and Apaches had found neither, and the Comanches were busy attacking trail traffic even as Gilpin looked for them on the Canadian. The only real fights between the Comanches and units of the Indian Battalion had been the two involving Lieutenant Stremmel and his men and the separate encounters of the two columns under Griffin and Jones. In all their engagements, the men of the Indian Battalion had killed no more than seventy-four Indians, including the Pawnees slaughtered by Captain Pelzer, and possibly only sixty. The number of wounded was unknown. Despite the battalion's obvious failure to find and engage the Comanches either decisively or frequently, Gilpin managed to put the best face on its record when he prepared his letter to the adjutant general.[11]

In his report Gilpin first summarized the organization and movements of his small battalion. He carefully noted that in the summer of 1847 an estimated forty-seven Americans had been killed by Indians along the Santa Fe road, with more than three hundred wagons destroyed and sixty-five hundred head of livestock stolen. By contrast he stated that as of the date of his writing, no less than three thousand wagons, twelve thousand persons, and fifty thousand head of stock had passed Fort Mann—relatively undisturbed. He took credit for "overawing" the Cheyennes and Arapahoes while camping at the Big Timbers and claimed to have uncovered and thwarted a plot by the Comanches and Apaches to induce the former tribes to join them in a general war against whites along the trail. The intimidated Cheyennes and Arapahoes allegedly dropped all plans to join the Comanches and Apaches and even induced the Kiowas to abandon their alliance with the Comanches and move to the Arkansas to camp with them in peaceful relations with whites. Gilpin did not explain how two volunteer cavalry companies with less than two hundred men, lacking adequate food supplies and equipment and whose horses soon died from cold and starvation, could have this dramatic effect on two of the most powerful and warlike tribes of Plains Indians, especially since only one or two bands from those tribes were wintering anywhere close to the soldiers. Gilpin also gave no explanation about how those bands of Cheyennes and Arapahoes encamped at the Big Timbers could so easily persuade the Kiowas to join them and end their traditional alliance with the Comanches. Neither did he mention Thomas Fitzpatrick's part in these accomplishments nor how Fitzpatrick had evaluated the effectiveness of the Indian Battalion.[12]

Gilpin not only took credit for neutralizing the Cheyennes, Arapahoes, and Kiowas but also claimed that his fruitless campaign along the Canadian was a success, alleging that the Plains Apaches were frightened into fleeing to the safety of the White Mountains in the Mexican state of Chihuahua while the Comanches fled to west Texas. Such a claim conveniently ignored the Comanche raids taking place along the Santa Fe Trail even as Gilpin searched the Canadian. He did concede a need for patrols along the trail and mentioned the results of the fights involving Lieutenant Stremmel and Captains Griffin and Jones. Gilpin even took credit for the accomplishments of Lieutenant Royall and his Santa Fe Battalion recruits, including them with the detachments he dispatched to screen the Santa Fe road. With these actions, he asserted, he had successfully "held in check or effectually defeated" all of the most dangerous Indian tribes menacing the Santa Fe Trail, especially those inhabiting the country drained by the Upper Arkansas. Gilpin was a capable soldier, and he probably believed what he wrote to be true, at least in principal. But he was candid enough to admit that whatever success he and his troops had enjoyed, the effect would be temporary at best, and that much more would be required before the peaceful passage of traffic to Santa Fe could be ensured.[13]

Though Gilpin gave an unduly glowing report of the accomplishments of the Indian Battalion, his keen insight and common sense gave a more critical analysis of what would be required to maintain peace and safety along the trail in the future. A moving column of troops alone, he asserted, could not provide permanent security. He believed that military depots were required at convenient points along the road to support and supply the mounted troops. He recommended five of these for the road to Santa Fe: the first at the Pawnee Fork, a second at the Middle Crossing of the Arkansas, the third at Pretty Encampment (which he called "Beautiful Encampment"), the fourth at the crossing of the Canadian, and the fifth at Los Juntas.* This would have meant altering the existing course of the trail, which would then bypass the Middle Crossing and the Jornada and continue along the north bank of the Arkansas to Pretty Encampment, at which point the trail would cross the river and pass south to the headwaters of the Cimarron, apparently rejoining the original trail either there or at the crossing of the Canadian.† Gilpin also recommended, for the protection of the Bent's Fort Trail, the purchase of the adobe trading post owned by Bent, St. Vrain,

---

*"Los Juntas," or more properly "La Junta de los Rios," referred to the junction of the Mora and Sapello rivers and to the community that developed there before the Mexican War. It was the point at which eastbound traders and travelers traditionally formed themselves into large trains or caravans for protection before entering the country of the Plains Indians. Alexander Barclay, who had heard of the probability of forts being built along the trail from Thomas Fitzpatrick, built his own fort on the Mora near the junction of the two rivers for the primary purpose of selling it to the government at a profit. His hopes were thwarted when Lt. Col. E. V. Sumner ordered him off the land and built Fort Union nearby. Janet Lecompte, *Pueblo, Hardscrabble, Greenhorn*, 204, 205, 210–12. The town of La Junta was renamed Watrous shortly before the Civil War.

†This route would roughly approximate the "Aubry Route" later recommended by the "Skimmer of the Plains," Francis X. Aubry.

and Co. All the new forts were to consist of adobe buildings and corrals to protect the livestock, probably much in the form of Bent's Fort itself. To garrison the new establishments, Gilpin recommended one thousand mounted troops. In addition to new forts and more cavalry, he also advocated treaties between the United States and the Cheyenne, Arapaho, and Kiowa tribes. The Comanches and Plains Apaches, he asserted, must be conquered by invading their country. Much of what Gilpin suggested was both insightful and prophetic but was ignored at the time, or at least not implemented. The army eventually did, however, build a string of forts located at or close to many of the suggested sites.[14]

Before he closed, Gilpin could not resist taking one more swipe at the late Lt. Col. Clifton Wharton. Perhaps conscious of the extensive criticism directed at his command by Thomas Fitzpatrick, a few of the regular army officers, and the news media, he once more charged that Wharton had displayed the "most unrelenting malice" toward him and his men and had failed to furnish them with adequate supplies and equipment. His men, he said, had cheerfully borne sufferings, privations, and hardships greater than those of any other battalion in public service. Their "continually crippled condition and destitution of supplies" he alleged to have been caused by "the ignorance, the laziness and the vicious character of the officers in the frontier depots," and he claimed that this flaw had "fatally retarded the pacification of the Indian country, and heaped up unmeasurable trouble for the national government." Finally, Gilpin recommended immediate action to place the Plains Indians "under the guard of treaties, troops and fortified stations" as the only means to avoid all-out Indian war and great loss of life and property.[15]

When he finished his report to the adjutant general, Gilpin prepared for departure to Fort Leavenworth. His health had deteriorated again, and he was suffering greatly from the effects of his malaria. Within a day or so he left Fort Mann for the last time with the express from Santa Fe, which consisted of a man named Estes and one companion. These two had left Santa Fe on July 21 and, including their stop at

Fort Mann, made the trip in twenty-five days, reaching Fort
Leavenworth on August 14. They crossed the Missouri River
to Weston, Missouri, on August 16, and from there Gilpin
went downriver to Independence, Missouri, arriving on August 18. He took rooms at the Noland House and then set
about composing a letter to Colonel Garland at Jefferson
Barracks, unaware that Garland had left for Fort Crawford,
Wisconsin, the previous day. He reported that no hostile
Indians had appeared on the trail since Garland's departure
from Fort Mann and related the disposition of the battalion's
troops, made in compliance with the colonel's instructions
forwarded from Jackson's Grove. Gilpin also acknowledged
receipt of "General Order No. 35," ordering dissolution of the
Indian Battalion, which was apparently forwarded to him at
Independence from Fort Leavenworth. In response he sent a
dispatch to his companies by an express rider, directing them
to conclude their current operations and march to Independence to be mustered and discharged. He expected them to
arrive on about September 20. Because there was a great deal
of public property at Fort Mann that the marching units would
be unable to bring with them, he also ordered 2d Lt. Ashley
G. Gulley, the quartermaster, to receipt for it and to remain at
Fort Mann until October 1 or until he was relieved. He
instructed Gulley to retain the civilian employees of the post
and enough volunteers to make a total of fifty men in garrison.
The balance of his letter Gilpin devoted to expressing his
deep concern that the government take appropriate action to
protect the traffic to New Mexico, along the Santa Fe Trail. It
was his opinion that failure to take firm action would inevitably bring full-scale war to the long stretch of road through the
country of the Plains Indians.[16]

Despite the impending abandonment of Fort Mann and
dissolution of the Indian Battalion, traffic to and from Santa
Fe continued to grow. New traders, men whose names would
someday become synonymous with the economic growth of the
West, began to travel the road. On August 10 a train of twenty-
five wagons left Independence bound for Santa Fe with a large
cargo of trade goods. Included were six ox-drawn wagons

belonging to Alexander Majors of Jackson County, Missouri, making his first trip west in the freighting business. He enjoyed remarkable success, not only disposing of his goods profitably but also traveling the route in a relatively short time. In 1848 it was very dangerous to begin a trip over the trail so late in the season, unless one intended to winter in New Mexico. But Majors traveled to Santa Fe and back to Independence in only ninety-two days, the fastest round trip on record for ox-drawn wagons. Moreover, when he returned, his oxen were in such fine condition that they looked as though they had not made the trip. This feat brought Majors considerable renown among the other freighters and merchants and launched him on his well-known career in the freighting business.[17]

As Majors and his companions began their long trip to Santa Fe, another large eastbound caravan was approaching from the west, nearing the end of the return journey. It consisted of three separate trains with more than one hundred wagons and about five hundred head of loose cattle. With the caravan were 100 teamsters (mostly young Missourians), "sundry traders, travelers, and Mexican herdsmen," for a total of about 130 men. One of the travelers was 2d Lt. George D. Brewerton, First U.S. Infantry, returning east to report to his regiment in Mississippi. In early July they left their camp at the junction of the Mora and Sapello rivers in New Mexico, a place where traders regularly met to form caravans before heading east, and moved slowly across the plains to the Cimarron, which they followed to its north bend. From there they struck off to the north and east across the arid desolation of the Jornada and reached the Arkansas at the Middle Crossing in early August. Here they met the westbound train of Francis X. Aubry with more than sixty wagons. After a brief visit each train moved on toward its intended destination.

The day after their encounter with Aubry, the caravan camped near Fort Mann. Gilpin had left for Fort Leavenworth, and most of the troops of the Indian Battalion were in the field for one last attempt at finding Comanches or Pawnees. Lieutenant Brewerton described the remaining garrison as "a handful of volunteers, who drank corn whiskey, consumed Uncle Sam's bacon and hardtack, drew their pay with unde-viating regularity, and otherwise wore out their lives in the service of their country." According to Brewerton they re-lieved their boredom "by chasing buffalo, sallying forth to scout up and down, with a general understanding that they were to quarrel with the Comanches if they could catch them — a combination of circumstances which, as it requires two parties to make a bargain, occurred but seldom."

Beyond Fort Mann, apparently at a point between the Pawnee Fork and Walnut Creek, Lieutenant Brewerton fool-ishly left the afternoon camp to do a little buffalo hunting, alone and afoot, on the opposite side of the Arkansas. Two miles beyond the river and the sand hills that paralleled it, he was stalking an old bull when he was approached from downwind by three seemingly wild mustangs. He knew this was highly unusual and immediately became apprehensive. Suddenly three Comanches raised themselves to the backs of their horses and charged Brewerton. A wild chase through sand and grass followed, and Brewerton escaped only by concealing himself in the waters of the Arkansas and the tall valley grasses nearby. Fortunately the rest of the trip was less eventful, and the caravan finally reached Independence in the latter part of August, probably on August 21 when the traders Joseph H. Reynolds, John Hurd, and others from Indepen-dence were reported to have returned home.[18]

The express rider that Colonel Gilpin dispatched to Fort Mann on August 18, bearing orders to terminate operations and march for Independence, must have reached the post shortly before the end of the month. Riders probably carried the orders to the two columns in the field, which then ended their search and returned to the fort. Likely they were all back at Fort Mann during the first week of September, packing their gear and preparing wagons and livestock for the trip to Independence. Late in August a traveler named Jesse B. Thompson, from Buchanan County, Missouri, passed the fort and reported that all was quiet, indicating that most of the troops were still in the field. By mid-September, however, the situation along the trail changed dramatically. Now the road was filled with volunteer troops returning from New Mexico for discharge. Unfortunately, in this season rain returns to the plains once again, putting water into normally dry beds and lifting streams that do flow far above their usual depth. On September 14 and 15, the eastbound Aubry passed Maj. William W. Reynolds and three companies of Ralls's Third Regiment, Maj. Robert Walker and his Santa Fe Battalion, 1st Lt. John Love and twenty-five men from the First Dragoons, the train of traders Findlay, Allen, and Cary & McCarty, all waterbound at the usually bone-dry North Fork of the Cimarron River. Col. John Ralls, his staff, and others from his regiment were similarly stalled near Battle Ground. Later Aubry passed Brig. Gen. Sterling Price and his staff, Maj. Israel B. Donalson and several companies of Newby's First Regiment of Illinois Infantry Volunteers, and 2d Lt. William Khulow with part of Company C, Indian Battalion, all of whom were held up by the flooded Pawnee Fork. Within a day or so the sun returned, and the streams dropped rapidly, allowing the men to continue their journey. The trail remained crowded through the rest of September and October as the various regiments returned from New Mexico, bringing a belated end to the war with Mexico.[19]

On August 5 the "Skimmer of the Plains," twenty-three-year-old Francis X. Aubry, reached Santa Fe on his second trading trip of the year. His train arrived some days later, but he had again disposed of his goods before its arrival. By early September he was ready to return to Independence and prepare for his third trading caravan of 1848. He left Santa Fe alone on the morning of September 12, intending to break his own record for speed, and began one of the most incredible rides in history. Rain and high water forced Aubry and his horse to swim nearly every stream he crossed, and at one point he rode in rain for twenty-four hours consecutively. He traveled through mud for 600 of the 780 miles he covered. He was delayed by business at Fort Mann and with the various bodies of traders (including his own) and the troops he met, but he nevertheless averaged about 141.8 miles of travel for each twenty-four-hour period (he claimed 190 miles per twenty-four-hours). He slept two and a half hours en route, ate only six meals, broke down six horses, and had to walk twenty miles. At last he reached Independence on the evening of September 17, five days and sixteen hours after leaving Santa Fe. His horse was foaming as it half ran, half staggered into town. Aubry himself had to be helped from the horse, and it was reported by several newspapers that his own blood had caked him to the saddle. He slept six hours, then left for St. Louis by riverboat. Ten days after his departure from Santa Fe, he stepped ashore in St. Louis. Aubry never tried for a record again, and his was never broken.[20]

Despite all the civilian traffic on the Santa Fe Trail, by far the greatest number of travelers were volunteer soldiers returning east for muster and discharge. Between September 20 and October 1, the entire First Regiment of Illinois Infantry Volunteers — including Col. Edward W. B. Newby, Lt. Col. Henderson P. Boyakin, and Maj. Israel B. Donalson — reached Fort Leavenworth. Except for Donalson's companies, halted briefly at the rain-swollen Pawnee Fork in mid-September, they experienced no significant difficulties. The troops were loaded aboard Missouri River steamboats and carried downriver to St. Louis, then north on the Mississippi to Alton, Illinois, where they arrived between September 22 and October 10. They were paid and mustered out of service there. The only mishap occurred when one of the riverboats, the *Plough Boy*, snagged a sandbar and sank above Portland, Missouri. Aboard were Companies I and K, whose men were plucked from the river and carried on to Alton aboard the *Amelia*.[21]

Unlike the Illinois volunteers, the returning troops from Missouri continued on the Santa Fe Trail, bypassing Fort Leavenworth and marching directly to Independence for discharge in their home state. On September 29 Brig. Gen. Sterling Price and his staff, escorted by 1st Lt. William B. Royall and his Santa Fe Battalion recruits, reached Independence and camped at the edge of town. Royall's men had arrived in Santa Fe just in time to join in the return march and had never been assigned to companies. Lt. Col. Alton R. Easton and his entire battalion arrived in Independence on October 3 and also camped outside of town, and on October 6 Ralls's Third Regiment of Missouri Mounted Volunteers joined them. Finally, on October 7 the Santa Fe Battalion, commanded by Maj. Robert Walker, marched past Independence and established themselves outside of Wayne City on the Missouri River, about three miles away. For reasons unknown, some of these troops were not mustered out of service until well into November. They had to be paid first by the army paymaster, Maj. Thomas S. Bryant, then mustered out by Col. Ethan A. Hitchcock. Perhaps there was insufficient money on hand to pay them all, and the remainder were held until additional funds arrived. Whatever the cause for delay, as they were mustered out of service they were taken aboard riverboats at Wayne City and transported to St. Louis. The last to arrive there were about one hundred men from Ralls's Third Regiment, who reached the city aboard the *Alexander Hamilton* on November 7. Thus did the last of the volunteer forces raised to seize and occupy New Mexico and California pass into history.[22]

As the troops from New Mexico marched by Fort Mann, it too was in the process of abandonment. The companies in the field returned to the post immediately on receiving their summons, then joined the march eastward. Like the others, they experienced no difficulties as they moved up the trail. Apparently they did not march as a battalion but rather as companies. Companies A and B (cavalry), commanded by Captains Griffin and Jones, arrived first and were paid and mustered out of service on September 28. E Company (infantry) was next, being honorably discharged on September 30, followed by Captain Holtzscheiter's D Company (infantry) on October 1. The last of the five companies to be mustered out of service was Company C, the artillery, which was paid and discharged on October 2. Finally, on October 3 Lieutenant Colonel Gilpin and his field and staff officers were honorably discharged, writing the last lines of the final chapter for the Indian Battalion.[23]

Gilpin's final order to the troops at Fort Mann had instructed the quartermaster, Lieutenant Gulley, to remain there with civilian personnel and enough of the volunteers to provide a total of fifty men with which to protect the government property. Gulley was to stay until October 1 or until relieved. There is no known record of when that relief arrived. However, Gilpin likely saw to it that an empty train of government wagons started west at the earliest possible time to collect the supplies and other property remaining at the fort. Or perhaps orders were dispatched directing one of the empty supply trains returning east from New Mexico to stop at the post and pick up the property. Whatever the solution, the supplies were probably being loaded by mid to late September. Personnel were still at the fort at the beginning of October, likely attending to the final removal of property and to housekeeping chores preparatory to abandonment. Maj. William W. Reynolds of Ralls's Third Regiment, who had been waterbound with his troops at the Cimarron's north fork in mid-September, reached Fort Mann a few days later. Burning with fever, he was too sick to continue, and his troops left him there to recover rather than be exposed to the rigors of the trail during the rest of the march to Missouri. Unfortunately Reynolds did not recover but died at the nearly empty post during the first days of October. This is the last event known to have occurred at the fort. Probably within a few days of Reynolds's death, the last of the remaining wagons formed a small train and, taking his body with them, began their slow trek back to Fort Leavenworth. Fort Mann, which had lived two lives filled with danger, excitement, adventure, mutiny, seething discontent, and death, now began the long process of returning to the dust from which it had sprung.[24]

On October 6, while the train returning from Fort Mann was still along the Arkansas, Indian Agent Thomas Fitzpatrick wrote his annual report to the superintendent of Indian affairs, Thomas H. Harvey. He said much the same as William Gilpin had concerning the need to protect the trails from Indian attack and the manner in which that should be done. But about the Indian Battalion and the effectiveness of its service, he had few kind things to say. He believed that the battalion had "acted altogether on the defensive, and did not even succeed in that, as the Indians took by force many of their horses." Fitzpatrick further stated that such a force, properly armed and equipped and "under the command of an officer who knows his duty, and willing to do it, would soon put that country in such a state of safety that one man, with his wife and child, could pass to New Mexico, or the Rocky Mountains, unmolested." He noted that many letters and reports from New Mexico and the Indian country suggested that the Indians had partially ceased their attacks on the traffic of the Santa Fe Trail, "inasmuch as fewer attacks have been reported, and comparatively but little loss sustained the past season." This he attributed not to the actions of the Indian Battalion but rather to the fact that the Indians had in 1846 and 1847 "secured so much booty by their daring outrages upon travelers" that they were then, and had been the past summer, "luxuriating in and enjoying the spoils." Fitzpatrick also stated his firm belief that the tribes involved would ultimately desist only when it was perfectly clear to them that the government had the ability and willingness to chastise them "not only for what they have already done, but also what they may attempt in the future." He asserted that nothing short of an "efficient military force stationed in the country" could keep the tribes quiet, obviously implying that this solution had not yet been tried. Failure to act promptly, he said, would result in open hostility by the Indians, "who acknowledge no superior in war," and it would cost much "blood and treasure" to subdue them. In a later day, such words make it hard for many people to believe that Fitzpatrick was the most highly regarded of all the agents who served the tribes of the southern plains. But despite his views about the use of force, he was honest and fair, did not cheat his charges, and stood up for them against those who would do otherwise. The Indians always knew where he stood and for what he could be counted on. His assessment of the needs to protect the trail accorded with Gilpin's, even though he gave both Gilpin and the battalion low marks as an effective military unit.[25]

Though Fitzpatrick had little regard for the services of the Indian Battalion and its commander, opinion on this subject varied. The July 14, 1848, issue of the *Weekly Tribune* of Liberty, Missouri, included a short article reporting that orders had been forwarded from Washington directing the immediate disbandment of the battalion. Noting that the troops had been raised to "keep in check the Indians who had been committing frequent depredations on the Government trains and robbing the traders" along the Santa Fe Trail, the article asserted that the War Department was "greatly dissatisfied with the manner in which the duty assigned to this corps" had been discharged and was "satisfied of its incompetency," leading to the order to disband. But on December 1, 1848, in his annual report to the president, Secretary of War Marcy stated that the battalion, under Gilpin's command, had had several encounters with the Comanches near Fort Mann during July, "which resulted in a manner credible to our troops" and in which the Indians "were defeated and dispersed." Subsequently the Missouri State Senate delivered its unanimous thanks on behalf of the people of the state to William Gilpin, his officers, and his men "for their brave and energetic conduct" against the "wild and restless" Pawnees and Comanches. The truth probably lies somewhere between the two extremes.

The Indian Battalion accomplished very little indeed until June and July of 1848. But it was not for lack of effort. As Fitzpatrick had accurately observed, not a man in the battalion, from its commander on down, knew the least thing about the Plains Indians or could even identify the tribes. They were provided with inadequate supplies and equipment and had no experience in fighting Indians. So it is small wonder that Gilpin's brave attempt at intimidating the Indians during his spring expedition met with so little success. When the season of travel returned to the trail, however, he fared much better with small scouts and brief campaigns. The Comanches were bloodied in clashes along the Cimarron and the Arkansas, both by Gilpin's men and by the troops under Lieutenant Royall and Captain Korponay. No one can say with certainty, but it seems probable that the intensive raids that had started in the area from Walnut Creek to the Coon Creeks were abruptly ended when the Comanches decided that too high a price would be paid as long as the troops were around. Seen from the perspective of the government and its aims, then, Gilpin's Indian Battalion had been a limited success. Just as Gilpin feared, however, it would be some years before his farsighted plan to protect the trail would be implemented, and even longer before the policy of aggressive pursuit of hostile war parties would be adopted to deal with raiding along the length of the trail through Indian country.[26]

The season of travel along the Santa Fe road was winding down when Fort Mann was abandoned, but noteworthy events were still ahead. On October 2 Kit Carson left Missouri westbound for New Mexico. He probably passed the newly abandoned Fort Mann in about the middle of the month. By November 1 he was at Santa Fe. In the meantime, stories of the rich gold strikes in California began to appear in the Missouri newspapers. One of these claimed, "An immense bed of gold, 100 miles in extent, has been discovered in California." Such articles stirred the imagination, and greed, of a great many young, middle-aged, and even old men, all of whom dreamed of finding a fortune and spending the rest of their days surrounded by the trappings of wealth. As history reveals, "many were called, but few were chosen." From the perspective of the Santa Fe Trail, however, these news articles laid the groundwork for the next great wave of travelers to rush across it, stunning the Indian population with their numbers, slaughtering the bison and other game, and trampling Indian rights into Indian land as they went. Some went to Santa Fe, then on to California by way of the Gila or other trails; others continued along the Arkansas to the mountains, then moved north and west along the old Trappers Trail (Taos Trail) to a junction with the Oregon-California Trail, which they followed to the gold country. This enormous movement of whites astonished the natives, causing a restless fear that would someday grow into the tragic period of the Indian wars. Now, even the usually peaceful Cheyennes became apprehensive, foretelling their imminent change from friend to foe.[27]

Never one to submit to the travel restrictions placed on most people by nature and the seasons of the calendar, Francis X. Aubry left Independence on October 8, heading for Santa Fe on his third trading trip of the year. He was no longer interested in speed records, only in profitable commerce. Most of his goods finally did arrive in Santa Fe and were sold at a profit, but the trip proved to be disastrous financially, for he lost 150 mules in the process, half to severe weather and the rest stolen by Plains Apaches. Leaving Independence in mid-October was Indian Agent Thomas Fitzpatrick, traveling in the company of Ceran St. Vrain and a party bound for Bent's Fort. Fitzpatrick left the others at the Big Timbers, where he had summoned chiefs of the Comanches, Plains Apaches, Kiowas, and Arapahoes to council. Spread along the Arkansas in the shelter of the trees were six hundred lodges belonging to the bands in attendance. Fitzpatrick hoped to engineer peace treaties with the Plains tribes—treaties that were intended to restore harmony along the trails and end intertribal warfare. While he was engaged in this council, the explorer John C. Frémont and his party arrived (on November 11 or 12), remaining in camp for three days. Frémont and his men were in the early stages of their ill-fated fourth expedition, which would ultimately lead them to disaster amid the winter snows of the Rocky Mountains. On October 22 David Waldo, who would gain fame by carrying the mail to Santa Fe, arrived in Independence after traveling from Santa Fe in about eleven days. As if to close out the year on a note of finality, emphasizing that the period of the Mexican War was at an end, Brig. Gen. Stephen Watts Kearny died at the home of Meriwether Lewis Clark in St. Louis on October 31. The death of this famous general, who played such a large part in the history and growth of the United States, marked the end both of an era and of the important events affecting the Santa Fe Trail during 1848.[28]

The war was over, the troops were gone, and as the year waned, winter descended across the trail, ending travel to or from New Mexico for all but the most daring or most foolhardy. Far out in the remote desolation of the plains, the forlorn silhouette of the abandoned Fort Mann stared out across the trail from near the banks of the Arkansas. Already a few travelers were beginning to dismantle the wood framework of the cabins and the gate for use as firewood. The adobe bricks encasing the buildings, no longer being inspected and re-placed, slowly began to crumble before the onslaught of wind and weather. Soon, like a melting snowbank, the structure would be little more than mounds of earth, a reference in old reports filed in forgotten boxes in some distant army post in the East, and a fading memory for those who had served there or passed by the fort as they moved along the trail. Death comes to all things, and so it came to Capt. Daniel Mann's fortress on the plains. Yet the long road to Santa Fe, which it had been built to guard, had not finished its three score years of life. Much more was yet to come. But that is another story.

Epilogue

Like a great river endlessly carrying its burden to the sea, oblivious of the dramas lived out upon or along its waters, the tide of travel on the Santa Fe Trail scarcely faltered with the end of the Mexican War. To be sure, military traffic waned for a time after the return of the volunteers. But it was quickly replaced and surpassed by trade caravans traveling to and from the newly acquired territories and especially by the rush to the goldfields of California. In time, a small but significant flow of immigrants also began to use this largely commercial road. There was, in addition, a continuing movement of government supply trains servicing the regular army troops posted at several new forts intended to protect the roads and towns of New Mexico and California. The great westward migration of Europeans had begun and would soon create a unified nation, spanning the continent from ocean to ocean. Yet for those who inhabited the country these travelers crossed, this unending traffic foretold the end of their world and their way of life. It was another step in the clash of cultures that would erupt into the Indian wars.

The vast increase in traffic along the Santa Fe Trail and other roads west brought additional tragedy for the Plains Indians. Asiatic cholera and smallpox, diseases for which Indians had no natural immunity, were introduced to all the tribes inhabiting the country through which the western trails passed. The effect was devastating, with some tribes losing

well over half their population. The sickness brought by
European whites, together with the demise of the buffalo
herds, ultimately did more to defeat the proud warriors of the
plains than did the numerous military operations against
them. As the Indians began to comprehend the threat to their
people, their culture, and their traditional way of life, mounting fear, desperation, and frustration drove them to ever more
violent attacks on those traveling through their country. As
the end of their world loomed before them, they could see no
place for themselves in the new one being created by alien
intruders. To the Indian peoples, in their deeply religious
view of the world and the natural order they believed had been
established by the Creator, what should be was. They wanted
nothing different and could neither understand nor accept the
lowly place envisioned for them by these pale-faced strangers
who crossed the great waters in unimaginable numbers,
coming to seize the Indian land. They watched as their sacred
places were desecrated and mocked by whites and as the
game they depended on was driven away, used wastefully, or
slaughtered for sport or for hide. They saw their culture
demeaned, their religion belittled, their land stolen. The
Plains Indians were great horsemen and warriors, and as their
country and way of life narrowed, they began to fight the war
that most knew could never be won.

The conquest of the country of the Plains Indians would be
an odd war. There were no battle lines, no Indian armies. The
war against these Indians was rather a long, drawn-out
struggle, typified by sudden hit-and-run attacks on small
trains, military units, isolated settlements, lone riders, and
sleeping camps, much as had occurred along the Santa Fe
Trail during the Mexican War. Seldom was there any coordi-
nated effort between tribes or any grand strategy. Their
struggle was more like the defensive battle of a wounded
buffalo, here charging its antagonists, there running to escape its tormentors, gradually tiring, and with the inevitable
end always in sight. Often attacks were made as much to
obtain goods and food with which to survive as to defeat the
enemy. For the Plains Indians, as for the hunted buffalo, it

would be a matter of little time before freedom ended, before their country was taken and their way of life only a memory. The U.S. Army was ordered to bring them to bay and force them onto reservations. It was to be a grim and tragic end.

The convulsive death struggle of the Indian world was felt and seen nowhere more dramatically than along the great western trails. The close of 1848 found the entire length of the Santa Fe Trail through the Indian country once again nearly devoid of military protection, except that afforded by Fort Leavenworth near the Missouri border and Fort Marcy at Santa Fe. The army was much too small to provide regular patrols of sufficient size to deal with the powerful horse Indians, and the distance between the two posts was too great for effective patrols had the personnel been available. The admonitions of Thomas Fitzpatrick and William Gilpin were proving true; but without money and manpower, the military could do little. Finally, the need became too great for even a parsimonious Congress to ignore. In July 1850 Lt. Col. E. V. Sumner led mounted troops of the First Dragoons and Sixth Infantry to the Middle Crossing of the Arkansas. There they established a temporary camp, dubbed Camp Mackey, while they looked for a suitable site for a permanent post. From this encampment they scouted the surrounding country, eventually selecting a location about three-quarters of a mile west of the abandoned Fort Mann. The site was above the junction of the Wet and Dry routes and below the important river crossings, thus ensuring that nearly all through trail traffic would pass the new post. Here they erected a fort of eight or nine adobe buildings surrounded by a high sod wall. First named Fort Mackey, then called Fort Sumner for its builder, and finally officially named Fort Atkinson by the army, it was eventually garrisoned by one company of the Sixth Infantry and, for the term of the summer travel season, by one company of the First Dragoons. The latter used the post as a base for patrolling the trail west to the Cimarron and east to Walnut Creek, the zone of greatest danger. They also patrolled the road along the Arkansas west to the ruins of Bent's Fort, which had been abandoned and partially destroyed the previous year. During the brief period of its existence, Fort Atkinson provided the only effective protection for trail traffic through the Indian country between Fort Leavenworth and Santa Fe.

In 1851 Lieutenant Colonel Sumner, by then commander in New Mexico, moved most of his troops away from Santa Fe to a new site near the junction of the Cimarron Route and the road from Bent's Fort, within a dozen years to become known as the Mountain Branch of the Santa Fe Trail. Here they built Fort Union, a log post that in time would grow into the largest fort and principal supply depot for all of the military installations in the desert Southwest. Located one hundred miles north and east of Santa Fe, it provided, when it could, mounted troops to patrol the trail across the plains to the Cimarron and beyond to the Arkansas. In the early summer of 1853 construction was started on another new post located at the point where the Republican and Smoky Hill rivers joined to form the Kansas River. On June 27, 1853, it was named Fort Riley in honor of Maj. Gen. Bennet Riley, who had led the first military escort for trade caravans westbound to Santa Fe. From its location, patrols were sent out on both the Santa Fe and the Oregon-California trails. In September 1853 Fort Atkinson was abandoned. It was too distant from points of supply, its garrison was too small to do much more than defend themselves, and it was almost constantly surrounded by very large encampments of hostile Indians. Nevertheless, it had its day in the sun when Thomas Fitzpatrick used it to meet with the tribes of the southern plains on June 19, 1851, attempting to persuade them to attend the Grand Council to be held at Fort Laramie. The southern bands of Cheyennes and Arapahoes accepted, but the others declined. On September 17 those present entered into a peace treaty with the United States at the mouth of Horse Creek. Finally Fitzpatrick persuaded the Kiowas, Plains Apaches, and northern bands of Comanches to do the same, and on June 26, 1853, they signed the Treaty of Fort Atkinson, the final moment of glory for the post. It was formally abandoned on September 22, 1853.

The absence of a significant military presence along the Arkansas did not go unnoticed long, and the terror for

travelers returned. By the mid-1850s the situation was so bad
that the U.S. Army undertook a number of punitive actions.
Many of these were the ideas of staff officers in the East who
neither knew nor had ever fought Indians. Their solution was
to attack and punish them, and it made little difference to
these officers whether a tribe or a band was guilty of the
grievances they proposed to redress. The result too frequently
was unprovoked attacks on innocent friendly Indians, causing
them to make war to avenge their losses. In this manner the
Cheyennes ceased to be friends and became bitter enemies of
the white intruders. A major expedition was launched against
them in 1857, causing few actual casualties but having a
serious economic impact on the tribe for the next several
years. In 1859 a similar expedition was sent against the
northern bands of Comanches, resulting in two sharp fights
that inflicted significant casualties on them. Unfortunately,
in the long run these operations further alienated most tribal
members.

Recognizing the dangerous situation along the Santa Fe
Trail, in June 1859 the army sent three companies of the First
Cavalry from Fort Riley to establish a summer camp at the
ruins of Fort Atkinson. From there they were to patrol the trail
and pursue any war parties they might encounter. Later they
were joined by a fourth company. During late summer one of
these companies was sent to the Pawnee Fork to protect the
mail station being constructed by Hall and Company, a
station the Kiowas and Comanches had promised to destroy.
By October this encampment was moved to a different location
and established as a military post. It first was known as
"Camp on Pawnee Creek," then was called "Camp Alert,"
and finally was officially named Fort Larned on May 29,
1860. It served as both military post and depot for the
southwestern plains and also as the Indian agency for the
tribes of the upper Arkansas. Helpful as it was, more was
needed. In 1860 Fort Wise was built next to Bent's New Fort
near present Lamar, Colorado, then renamed Fort Lyon when
the Civil War began. Later it was moved to a new site near
present Las Animas, Colorado.

Following the great outbreak of the southern Plains tribes during the spring of 1864 (the year of the Sand Creek Massacre), more new forts were established to protect the vital lifeline from Missouri to Santa Fe and beyond. In 1864 Fort Dodge was built near the western junction of the Wet Route and the Dry Route, a few miles east of the sites of Fort Mann and Fort Atkinson. Also in 1864, the army built a small one-company post near the mouth of Walnut Creek and named it Fort Zarah. Farther west, at a point near where the Aubry Route struck off to the southwest from the Arkansas, another one-company fort was constructed in 1865, not surprisingly named Fort Aubry. During the summer of 1865, a time of great unrest among the tribes, a temporary military camp was established at the crossing of the Little Arkansas and another (Camp Nichols) near Cedar Spring in the present-day Oklahoma Panhandle. The smaller posts and camps were abandoned after only brief lives, but Fort Larned, Fort Dodge, and Fort Lyon each lasted until well after the threat of Indian warfare had subsided along the Santa Fe Trail and indeed outlasted the trail itself.

When the Civil War finally ended in the East, the westward movement of people and commerce began once again, this time with greatly increased volume. Gold had been found in the Colorado mountains, and immigrants hungry for both land and mineral wealth flooded the trails. This was the period of the final conquest of the Indian country, when regiments, not companies, took to the field to find and fight the elusive warriors of the plains. By the mid-1870s the struggle was all but over in the south and along the Santa Fe Trail, and by the close of the decade the wars were substantially at an end across the plains, though there would be sporadic uprisings and clashes. But even as the final chapters were being written, another momentous event both ensured the end of freedom for the Plains Indians and brought to a close the great historic saga of the Santa Fe Trail: the arrival in the West of the railroad.

Railroads were already relatively well established east of the Mississippi, but until the conquest of New Mexico and

California, the acquisition of Oregon, and the annexation of Texas, there had been no great need for a rail line crossing the middle of the continent and ending in a foreign country. With the rise of the concept of Manifest Destiny, however, came the idea of a railroad that would span North America from coast to coast, binding the states and territories of the United States together with sinews of steel and making the whole into one unified country. At first the expense of such an undertaking was so enormous that no one thought there would ever be more than one transcontinental railroad and not even that without substantial governmental assistance. In part, the concept of a railroad was fueled by the promise of trade with the countries of Asia and of avoiding the long trips by sea around Cape Horn, the portage across the malaria-infested Isthmus of Panama, or the slow, dangerous trip across the semiarid plains by wagon train. Each region of the country, each state, and each city clamored to be the beginning point of such a line, paralyzing a Congress whose members had to support their own constituency. Finally, after years of partisan and sectional wrangling, the Civil War brought the opportunity as well as the need.

On July 1, 1862, Abraham Lincoln signed the Pacific Railroad Act, a law that sought to induce private investors to provide capital by authorizing substantial assistance with the grant of government lands and the use of government bonds. The act also chartered a new corporation, to be known as the Union Pacific Railroad Company, and provided for assistance to the Central Pacific Railroad Company chartered under California law the previous year. The former was to build west from the Missouri River while the latter would build east until the two met. Because of more difficult terrain, it was assumed that the Central Pacific would probably get no farther than the California state line before meeting the westbound Union Pacific. The act specified no beginning point, but Omaha was finally selected by the president to appease interests in Chicago. To assuage St. Louis interests, the act had also authorized the Leavenworth, Pawnee and Western Railroad Company to construct a railroad from the Missouri River at the mouth of the Kansas River northwest to the one-hundredth meridian, where it was to connect with the Union Pacific Railroad building west from Omaha.

Construction of all three lines began in 1863, but it was not until the end of the Civil War in 1865 that work began in earnest. The Union Pacific reached the one-hundredth meridian in the fall of 1866, and the Kansas road, by now renamed the Union Pacific Railway (Eastern Division) and given a new destination (Denver), reached Fort Riley the same year. By June 1867 the latter road reached Fort Harker and the following year (under the new name Kansas Pacific Railway) was near Fort Wallace. On May 10, 1869, the golden spike was driven at Promontory Summit, Utah Territory, finally joining the country by rail from one coast to the other. One year later the Kansas Pacific reached Denver. As these two lines moved west they displaced the existing trails, and end-of-the-line military posts and communities quickly became the point from which supplies were received for transshipment across the plains in wagons. Fort Riley, Fort Harker, and Fort Hays thus successively became the beginning point for traffic on the Santa Fe Trail as the Kansas Pacific reached them. Then in 1868 the Atchison, Topeka and Santa Fe Railroad began building west from Topeka, placing its rails either on or close to the ruts of the Santa Fe Trail for much of its route. It followed the Mountain Branch of the trail to ensure reliable water supplies and to traverse country with established communities and commercial activity that could generate business. The new road reached the Colorado border in 1873, purchased Richens Lacy "Uncle Dick" Wootton's toll road over Raton Pass in 1878, and by 1880 brought its first trains to Lamy, near Santa Fe, ending the need for a long-distance wagon road to the New Mexican capital. Though stretches of the old trail were doubtless used for local traffic between small communities, ranches, and farms for a few years more, the coming of the automobile and paved roads soon ended even that. And so the great winding road that had played such a key role in the expansion of the country and the growth of the commerce that united it now quietly faded into memory without fanfare. Though much of its trace was subsequently covered by railroads, highways, and construction, or was plowed under, its history, legends, and lore live on in the consciousness and literature of the nation it helped to create.

The story of the Santa Fe road during the Mexican War spanned a brief period of no more than three years. But these were critical years in the development of the United States, and by their close the country was a young giant, sitting athwart the North American continent from the Atlantic to the Pacific oceans. The ethnic and cultural composition of the country was dramatically altered by the absorption of the vast Hispanic territories formerly constituting northern Mexico. And this sudden growth of the nation sounded the death knell for the free, independent, nomadic existence of the Plains Indians. Gone was the old concept of a Permanent Indian Frontier and an Indian Territory in which the indigenous natives would be free to live their lives as they chose within their own lands, free of white encroachment or exploitation. Soon Indian lands were opened for settlement by white immigrants from the East and from Europe. The Santa Fe Trail played its part in this drama as well, and many more years of struggle and adventure were ahead for those who trod its dusty ruts before the wheels of the last wagon to cross its length made their final turn. Today many of the surviving ruts, long covered by the tough shortgrasses of the plains, are being preserved as a part of the Santa Fe National Historic Trail. Along with the remaining trail landmarks and historic buildings, they evoke a dream of times and events long gone and people long dead. If they could speak, what stories might they tell of the growth of a nation.

Notes

List of Abbreviations Used

AGO   Adjutant General's Office
CIA   Commissioner of Indian Affairs
KHC   *Kansas Historical Collections*
KHQ   *Kansas Historical Quarterly*
MHSC *Missouri Historical Society Collections*
NA   National Archives
OIA   Office of Indian Affairs

Chapter 1. The Army of the West

1. K. Jack Bauer, *The Mexican War, 1846–1848,* 48; George Rutledge Gibson, *Journal of a Soldier under Kearny and Doniphan,* 21–23; Abraham Robinson Johnston, Marcellus Ball Edwards, and Philip Gooch Ferguson, *Marching with the Army of the West,* 13; David Nevin, *The Mexican War,* 28; James Knox Polk, *Polk: The Diary of a President, 1845–1849,* 90; Raymond W. Settle and Mary Lund Settle, *War Drums and Wagon Wheels,* 17.

2. Louise Barry, *The Beginning of the West,* 586; Bauer, 127–28; Gibson, *Journal of Soldier,* 23–24; John T. Hughes, *Doniphan's Expedition,* 21–25; Johnston, Edwards, and Ferguson, 23–25; Nevin, 31, 109; Leo E. Oliva, *Soldiers on the Santa Fe Trail,* 55; Settle and Settle, 17–18.

3. Barry, 586, 592–95; Bauer, 130; James M. Cutts, *The Conquest of California and New Mexico, 1846–1848,* 33; Gibson, *Journal of a Soldier,* 32, 34–37; Hughes, 25–27; Johnston, Edwards, and Ferguson, 23–26; Peter J. Michel, "No Mere Holiday Affair," *Gateway Heritage* 9, no. 4 (Spring 1989): 18–19; Nevin, 109; Oliva, *Soldiers on the Santa Fe Trail,* 61–63; Settle and Settle, 17–18.

4. Hughes, 29–30; Michel, 19; Oliva, *Soldiers on the Santa Fe Trail*, 60–61; Walker D. Wyman, "The Military Phase of Santa Fe Freighting, 1846–1865," *KHQ* 1, no. 5 (1932): 415–16; Settle and Settle, 18–20.

5. Gibson, *Journal of a Soldier*, 41; Hughes, 34.

6. Barry, 590, 591, 596, 626; Hughes, 29; Oliva, *Soldiers on the Santa Fe Trail*, 63; Jacob S. Robinson, *A Journal of the Santa Fe Expedition under Colonel Doniphan*, 13.

7. Barry, 617, 621, 623; Hughes, 30–34.

8. Wyman, 418.

9. Wyman, 418.

10. Settle and Settle, 20; Wyman, 416.

11. Barry, 618; Hughes, 43–44; Settle and Settle, 20, 21.

12. Barry, 558, 598–99; Bauer, 130–31; Johnston, Edwards, and Ferguson, *Marching with the Army of the West*, 118–22; Stanley B. Kimbell, "Rediscovering the Fort Leavenworth Military Branch of the Santa Fe Trail," in *The Mexican Road*, ed. Mark L. Gardner, 59–68.

13. Barry, 617–22; Hughes, 47; Henry Smith Turner, *The Original Journal of Henry Smith Turner*, ed. Dwight L. Clarke, 59–60.

14. 2d Lt. J. W. Abert, "Notes of Lieutenant J. W. Abert," House Ex. Doc. No. 41, 30th Cong., 1st sess., vol. 4 (Serial 517), 391, 401; Barry, 618; Gibson, *Journal of a Soldier*, 147, 149; Hughes, 44, 48; Frank S. Edwards, *A Campaign in New Mexico with Colonel Doniphan*, 30; Turner, 61.

15. Barry, 621, 623; Gibson, *Journal of a Soldier*, 153; Hughes, 49; Settle and Settle, 21.

16. Abert, "Notes" 401–3; Barry, 621; Gibson, *Journal of a Soldier*, 158; Edwards, 33–34; Turner, 63–64.

17. Edwards, 34; Turner, 64.

18. Edwards, 36–37; Hughes, 58–59; Turner, 65–66.

19. Gibson, *Journal of a Soldier*, 51–53; Hughes, 56; Johnston, Edwards, and Ferguson, 91; Edwards, 37; Oliva, *Soldiers on the Santa Fe Trail*, 71–72; Turner, 66–67.

20. Sen. Ex. Doc. No. 23, 30th Cong., 1st sess., vol. 4 (Serial 506), 4; Edwards, 36–37; Settle and Settle, 22; Wyman, 416–17.

21. Gibson, *Journal of a Soldier*, 57–60, 165–74; Hughes, 60–61; Johnston, Edwards, and Ferguson, 91–93, 140–43; Edwards, 38–39; Oliva, *Soldiers on the Santa Fe Trail*, 71–73; Settle and Settle, 22; Turner, 67–68; Ralph Emerson Twitchell, *The Story of the Conquest of Santa Fe*, 14–15; Otis E. Young, *The West of Philip St. George Cooke, 1809–1895*, 176–78.

22. Bauer, 131–34; Gibson, *Journal of a Soldier*, 53–55, 75–84; Hughes, 65–66, 77–81; Janet Lecompte, "Manuel Armijo and the Americans," *Journal of the West* 29, no. 3 (1980): 60; Janet Lecompte, "When Santa Fe Was a Mexican Town," in *Santa Fe: History of an Ancient City*, ed. David Grant Noble, 95; Michel, 20–24; Oliva, *Soldiers on the Santa Fe*

Trail, 75–76; Turner, 68–72; Twitchell, 19–23, 28–30; John P. Wilson, "The American Occupation of Santa Fe," in *Santa Fe: History of an Ancient City*, ed. David Grant Noble, 104.

23. Johnston, Edwards, and Ferguson, 26–56; Michel, 24; Oliva, *Soldiers on the Santa Fe Trail*, 55; Twitchell, 39–40.

Chapter 2. Soldiers and Traders: The Trail in 1846

1. George E. Hyde, *The Pawnee Indians*, 8–12, 22, 177, 179.

2. Hyde, 177, 179, 189, 217, 223.

3. Mildred P. Mayhall, *The Kiowas*, 71–72; James Mooney, *Calendar History of the Kiowa Indians*, 86; Kenneth Franklin Neighbours, *Robert Simpson Neighbors and the Texas Frontier, 1836–1859*, 29–30; Rupert Norval Richardson, *The Comanche Barrier to South Plains Settlement*, 83–85, 141–42; Robert M. Utley, *Frontiersmen in Blue*, 76; Ernest Wallace and E. Adamson Hoebel, *The Comanches: Lords of the South Plains*, 296–97; Donald E. Worcester, *Forked Tongues and Broken Treaties*, 179–81.

4. *Daily Missouri Republican*, Feb. 16, March 26, 1846; *New York Weekly Tribune*, Feb. 7, April 14, 1846; Barry, 570–71.

5. *Daily Missouri Republican*, March 26, May 15, 21, 1846; *New York Weekly Tribune*, April 14, 1846; *Niles' National Register*, vol. 70 (June 6 and July 4, 1846), 213, 281; *Weekly Tribune*, May 9, 1846; Barry, 572–73, 574, 580.

6. *Daily Missouri Republican*, May 21, June 25, July 17, 1846; *New York Weekly Tribune*, June 13, 1846; *St. Louis Daily Union*, Aug. 24, 1846; Barry, 580–81; James Josiah Webb, *Adventures in the Santa Fe Trade, 1844–1847*, 179–82.

7. *Daily Missouri Republican*, June 1, 1846; Barry, 587–88, 589; Lewis H. Garrard, *Wah-to-Yah and the Taos Trail*, 28; Gibson, *Journal of a Soldier*, 41–42; Frederick A. Wislizenus, "Memoirs of a Tour to Northern Mexico in 1846 and 1847 Connected with Colonel Doniphan's Expedition," 8.

8. *Daily Missouri Republican*, Aug. 3, 1846; *New York Weekly Tribune*, Aug. 15, 1846; *Niles' National Register*, vol. 70 (July 11, 1846), 304; Barry, 590–91; Gibson, *Journal of a Soldier*, 28–29, 41–43; Oliva, *Soldiers on the Santa Fe Trail*, 64–65; Johnston, Edwards, and Ferguson, 114; Webb, 181 n. 204.

9. Barry, 580–81; Gibson, *Journal of a Soldier*, 41 n. 81; Webb, 180–81.

10. *Daily Missouri Republican*, June 25, 1846; *St. Louis Weekly Reveille*, August 17, 1846; House Ex. Doc. No. 458, 30th Cong., 1st

sess., vol. 2 (Serial 525), 1–2; Barry, 588, 590; Ralph P. Bieber, ed., "Letters of James and Robert Aull," *MHSC* 5 (June 1928): 291–93; William E. Connelley, *Doniphan's Expedition and the Conquest of New Mexico and California*, 477, 646–47; Susan Shelby Magoffin, *Down the Santa Fe Trail and into Mexico*, ed. Stella M. Drumm, 50 n. 14.

11. *Daily Missouri Republican*, June 25, 1846; *Missouri Reporter*, May 20, 1846; *St. Louis Reveille* (daily), Aug. 11, 1846; Barry, 596, 600, 617, 626; Bieber, 291–93; Magoffin, 10, 20–21, 40, 45; Johnston, Edwards, and Ferguson, 73.

12. Abert, "Notes," 398; Barry, 623, 624, 626–27; Connelley, *Doniphan's Expedition*, 190; Gibson, *Journal of a Soldier*, 199, 200, 243, 244; Johnston, Edwards, and Ferguson, 99.

13. Barry, 628–29; Garrard, 14.

14. Barry, 630–31; Oliva, *Soldiers on the Santa Fe Trail*, 76–77; Settle and Settle, 23–24.

15. *Gazette*, Sept. 11, 1846; *New York Weekly Tribune*, Aug. 29, Sept. 12, 1846; Barry, 631, 635–36; Connelley, *Doniphan's Expedition*, 74–76, 256–61; Oliva, *Soldiers on the Santa Fe Trail*, 77; Settle and Settle, 24.

16. Barry, 635–36; Connelley, *Doniphan's Expedition*, 74–76, 256–61; Oliva, *Soldiers on the Santa Fe Trail*, 77; Settle and Settle, 24.

17. Barry, 596–97, 632; Bernard DeVoto, *Year of Decision: 1846*, 240–47; Oliva, *Soldiers on the Santa Fe Trail*, 77–78.

18. Barry, 632–33; Oliva, *Soldiers on the Santa Fe Trail*, 78.

19. Barry, 633.

20. Barry, 634; Gibson, *Journal of a Soldier*, 88, 89, 91; Johnston, Edwards, and Ferguson, 27; Young, 183–223.

21. *Daily Missouri Republican*, Sept. 2, 1846; *Gazette*, Sept. 11, 1846; Lieutenant James W. Abert, "Report of His Examination of New Mexico in the Years 1846–1847," House Ex. Doc. No. 41, 30th Cong., 1st sess., vol. 4 (Serial 517), 420; Barry, 634, 637; Magoffin, 21 n. 10.

22. *Daily Missouri Republican*, Sept. 2, 1846; *Gazette*, Sept. 11, 1846; *St. Louis Daily Union*, Sept. 3, 1846; Abert, "Report," 426; Barry, 634, 637, 638, 639, 642; Settle and Settle, 24.

23. *Daily Missouri Republican*, Sept. 2, 1846; *Gazette*, Sept. 11, 18, 1846; *New York Weekly Tribune*, Sept. 12, 1846; Abert, "Report," 426; Barry, 637, 638, 640.

24. Barry, 645; Garrard, 8–14.

25. Barry, 581–82, 645, 646; Garrard, 14–42; Francis Parkman, *The Oregon Trail*, 306–411, 702–3 n. 16.

26. *Gazette*, July 20, 1849; *New York Weekly Tribune*, Oct. 24, Nov. 21, 1846, July 14, 1849; *St. Louis Daily Union*, Oct. 8, 1846, April 17, 19, May 3, 6, 7, 11, 1847; *St. Louis Daily New Era*, Sept. 15, 1849; *St. Louis Reveille* (daily), April 10, 18, 1847; *Weekly Tribune*, May 15, 1847, Aug. 31, 1849; *Annual Report, C.I.A.* (1849), 157; Barry, 647–48, 668.

27. *Daily Missouri Republican*, Oct. 9, 13, 1846; *New York Weekly*

Tribune, Oct. 24, 31, 1846; *St. Louis Daily Union*, Oct. 9, 12, 1846; Barry, 649, 650.

28. *Gazette*, Nov. 20, 1846; *New York Weekly Tribune*, Nov. 28, Dec. 12, 1846; *St. Louis Daily Union*, Nov. 23, 1846; *St. Louis Daily New Era*, Nov. 9, 1846; Barry, 651, 652; Garrard, 30–31.

29. *New York Weekly Tribune*, Jan. 6, 1847; *St. Louis Daily Union*, Dec. 28, 1846; *Weekly Tribune*, Dec. 5, 1846; Barry, 652–53; Connelley, *Doniphan's Expedition*, 522, 523; Garrard, 43–44.

30. *Daily Missouri Republican*, Nov. 16, 1846; *Gazette*, Nov. 27, 1846; *New York Weekly Tribune*, Nov. 28, 1846; *St. Louis Daily Union*, Nov. 16, 1846; Barry, 656; Gibson, *Journal of a Soldier*, 251, 251 n. 385; LeRoy R. Hafen, *Broken Hand*, 242–44; Leroy R. Hafen, "Thomas Fitzpatrick and the First Indian Agency of the Upper Platte and Arkansas," *Mississippi Valley Historical Review* 15, no. 3 (Dec. 1928): 375.

31. *New York Weekly Tribune*, Feb. 6, 27, 1847; *St. Louis Daily Union*, Jan. 18, 1847; Barry, 659.

32. *New York Weekly Tribune*, April 24, 1847; *St. Louis Daily Union*, Jan. 18, April 28, 1847; *St. Louis Reveille* (daily), March 4, 1847; *St. Louis Weekly Reveille*, April 10, 1847; Abert, "Report," 530; Barry, 662.

33. *Daily Missouri Republican*, Feb. 19, 1847; *Gazette*, Feb. 26, 1847; *New York Weekly Tribune*, March 6, 1847; *Niles' National Register*, vol. 72 (March 6, 1847), 7; Barry, 663.

34. *Daily Missouri Republican*, Feb. 26, March 11, 1847; *New York Weekly Tribune*, March 6, 13, April 3, 1847; *Niles' National Register*, vol. 72 (March 6, April 3, 1847), 7, 73; *St. Louis Daily Union*, Feb. 20, 25, March 2, 9, 11, 1847; *St. Louis Reveille* (daily), Feb. 26, March 9, 11, 1847; *Weekly Tribune*, Feb. 20, 1847; Abert, "Report," 507–46; Barry, 663, 664, 665, 666.

35. *Daily Missouri Republican*, April 28, 1847; *Jefferson Inquirer*, March 6, 1847; *New York Weekly Tribune*, March 27, April 3, May 15, 1847; *St. Louis Daily Union*, March 30, 31, April 1, 28, 1847; *St. Louis Reveille* (daily), March 9, 30, 31, April 10, 24, 28, 1847; *Weekly Tribune*, March 6, 27, 1847; Abert, "Report," 540–46; Barry, 665, 668, 673.

Chapter 3. Fort Mann: Its Genesis and First Abandonment

1. *Daily Missouri Republican*, July 31, 1847; *Democratic Standard*, Aug. 10, 17, 1883; *St. Louis Reveille* (daily), April 23, 24, 1847; Barry, 671–72; Johnston, Edwards, and Ferguson, 299–300; Oliva, *Soldiers on the Santa Fe Trail*, 80; George Frederick Ruxton, *Ruxton of the Rockies*, ed. LeRoy R. Hafen, 287–88.

2. William Gilpin to Roger Jones, Aug. 1, 1848, House Ex. Doc. No. 1, 30 Cong., 2d sess., vol. 1 (Serial 537), 139–40; Thomas Fitzpatrick to Thomas H. Harvey, Oct. 6, 1848, House Ex. Doc. No. 8, 30th Cong., 1st

sess., vol. 2 (Serial 515), appendix 473; Hafen, *Broken Hand*, 242–45; Oliva, *Soldiers on the Santa Fe Trail*, 92.

3. Barry, 369–670; Garrard, 255; Oliva, *Soldiers on the Santa Fe Trail*, 80–81.

4. Barry, 652–53; Oliva, *Soldiers on the Santa Fe Trail*, 80.

5. Barry, 669–71; Garrard, 255, 259; Oliva, *Soldiers on the Santa Fe Trail*, 81.

6. *Daily Missouri Republican*, May 17, 18, 1847; *New York Weekly Tribune*, May 29, June 5, 1847; *St. Louis Daily Union*, May 18, 20, 22, 1847; *St. Louis Reveille* (daily), May 18, 28, 1847; Barry, 670, 682–83.

7. Barry, 670; Garrard, 255–56.

8. Barry, 687–88; Garrard, 249–51; George Bird Grinnell, "Bent's Old Fort and Its Builders," *KHC* 15 (1919–22): 91; Ruxton, 272–74.

9. Barry, 670, 688; Garrard, 251–56; Ruxton, 274–79.

10. Barry, 670; Garrard, 257–62.

11. Barry, 670, 686; Garrard, 262–63.

12. Barry, 670; Garrard, 264–67.

13. Garrard, 267.

14. Barry, 670; Garrard, 269–71.

15. Barry, 670–71, 674; Garrard, 271–74; George P. Hammond, *Alexander Barclay, Mountain Man*, 148.

16. Barry, 671, 690; Garrard, 274; Hammond, 148.

17. Barry, 671; Garrard, 274–77.

18. Barry, 671, 693–94; Garrard, 278–89.

19. Barry, 671.

Chapter 4. The Death of Red Sleeve

1. Barry, 685; Mooney, 284, 286; Stanley Vestal, *The Old Santa Fe Trail*, 126.

2. *Daily Missouri Republican*, May 29, 1847; *St. Louis Daily Union*, May 29, 1847; Barry, 685; Vestal, 126–27.

3. Barry, 685; Mooney, 286; Vestal, 126–27.

4. Mooney, 169–70, 286; Vestal, 126–27.

5. Mooney, 286; Vestal, 127.

6. Barry, 685; Mooney, 286; Vestal, 127.

7. Mooney, 286; Vestal, 127.

8. Barry, 685; Mooney, 286; Vestal, 127–28.

9. Vestal, 128.

10. *Daily Missouri Republican*, May 29, 1847; *St. Louis Daily Union*, May 29, 1847; Barry, 685; Johnston, Edwards, and Ferguson, 306.

11. Barry, 692–93; Garrard, 290.

12. Mooney, 286–87.

Chapter 5. A Hazardous Trip

1. Barry, 671; Garrard, 277–81.
2. Garrard, 278, 279, 281.
3. Abert, "Notes," 403; Barry, 1090; Garrard, 282; Young, 109–25.
4. Garrard, 282.
5. Garrard, 282–83.
6. Garrard, 283.
7. Garrard, 283–84.
8. Garrard, 284.
9. Garrard, 284–85.
10. Garrard, 285.
11. Garrard, 285–86.
12. Garrard, 286–87.
13. Garrard, 287–88.
14. Garrard, 288.
15. Garrard, 288–89.
16. Barry, 693; Garrard, 289–90.

Chapter 6. Lieutenant Love's Defeat

1. *New York Weekly Tribune*, July 24, 1847; *St. Louis Daily Union*, July 7, 1847; *St. Louis Reveille* (daily), July 13, 1847; *Weekly Tribune*, July 10, 1847; Barry, 693–94; Cutts, 240–42; Garrard, 292–93.
2. *New York Weekly Tribune*, Aug. 7, 1847; *St. Louis Reveille* (daily), May 16, 1847; Fitzpatrick to Harvey, Sept. 18, 1847, *Annual Report, CIA* (1847), appendix, also in Sen. Ex. Doc. No. 1, 30th Cong., 1st sess., vol. 1 (Serial 503), appendix, 238; Barry, 689, 690; Cutts, 242; Ruxton, 289.
3. *Daily Missouri Republican*, June 14, 1847; *Democratic Standard*, Aug. 10, 1883; *New York Weekly Tribune*, June 26, 1847; *St. Louis Daily Union*, June 21, 1847; *St. Louis Weekly Reveille*, June 14, 21, 1847; Barry, 686, 688; Hammond, 148–49.
4. *New York Weekly Tribune*, July 24, 31, 1847; *Niles' National Register*, vol. 72 (July 17, 1847), 320; *St. Louis Daily Union*, May 29, July 7, Aug. 1, 1847; *St. Louis Reveille* (daily), July 13, 1847; *Weekly Tribune*, July 10, 1847; Barry, 692–93; Cutts, 240–42; Garrard, 276–89; Webb, 291, 293.
5. *New York Weekly Tribune*, July 31, 1847; *Niles' National Register*, vol. 72 (July 17, 1847), 320; *St. Louis Daily Union*, May 29, 1847; Barry, 693; Cutts, 240–42; Garrard, 290–91.
6. *New York Weekly Tribune*, July 31, 1847; *Niles' National Register*, vol. 72 (July 17, 1847), 320; *St. Louis Daily Union*, May 29, 1847; Barry, 693; Garrard, 290–93.
7. *New York Weekly Tribune*, July 24, 1847; *St. Louis Daily Union*,

July 7, 1847; *St. Louis Reveille* (daily), July 13, 1847; *Weekly Tribune*, July 10, 1847; Barry, 693; Cutts, 240–42; Garrard, 291–92.

8. *New York Weekly Tribune*, July 24, 1847; *St. Louis Daily Union*, July 7, 1847; *St. Louis Reveille* (daily), July 13, 1847; *Weekly Tribune*, July 10, 1847; Fitzpatrick to Harvey, Sept. 18, 1847, Sen. Ex. Doc. No. 1, 30th Cong., 1st sess., vol. 1 (Serial 503), appendix, 238; Barry, 693–94; Cutts, 241; Garrard, 292.

9. *New York Weekly Tribune*, July 24, Aug. 7, 1847; *Niles' National Register*, vol. 72 (July 17, 1847), 320; *St. Louis Daily Union*, July 7, 1847; *St. Louis Reveille* (daily), July 13, 1847; *Weekly Tribune*, July 10, 1847; Fitzpatrick to Harvey, Sept. 18, 1847, Sen. Ex. Doc. No. 1, 30th Cong., 1st sess., vol. 1 (Serial 503), appendix, 238; Barry, 693; Cutts, 241; Garrard, 292–93.

10. *New York Weekly Tribune*, July 31, Aug. 7, 1847; *Niles' National Register*, vol. 72 (July 17, August 14, 1847), 343, 375; *St. Louis Daily Union*, July 7, 1847; *St. Louis Reveille* (daily), July 13, 1847; *Weekly Tribune*, July 10, 1847; Fitzpatrick to Harvey, Sept. 18, 1847, Sen. Ex. Doc. No. 1, 30th Cong., 1st sess., vol. 1 (Serial 503), appendix, 238–39; Barry, 694; Cutts, 241.

11. *New York Weekly Tribune*, July 31, Aug. 7, 1847; *Niles' National Register*, vol. 72 (July 31, August 14, 1847), 343, 375; *St. Louis Daily Union*, July 10, 29, Sept. 7, 1847; *Weekly Tribune*, July 10, 1847; Fitzpatrick to Harvey, Sept. 18, 1847, Sen. Ex. Doc. No. 1, 30th Cong., 1st sess., vol. 1 (Serial 503), appendix, 239; Barry, 694; Cutts, 241.

12. *New York Weekly Tribune*, July 31, Aug. 7, 1847; *Niles' National Register*, vol. 72 (July 31, 1847), 343; *St. Louis Daily Union*, July 10, 29, Sept. 7, 1847; *Weekly Tribune*, July 10, 1847; Fitzpatrick to Harvey, Sept. 18, 1847, Sen. Ex. Doc. No. 1, 30th Cong., 1st sess., vol. 1 (Serial 503), appendix, 239; Barry, 694; Cutts, 241; Webb, 290–92.

13. *New York Weekly Tribune*, July 31, Aug. 7, 1847; *Niles' National Register*, vol. 72 (July 31, 1847), 343; *St. Louis Daily Union*, July 10, 29, Sept. 7, 1847; *Weekly Tribune*, July 10, 1847; Fitzpatrick to Harvey, Sept. 18, 1847, Sen. Ex. Doc. No. 1, 30th Cong., 1st sess., vol. 1 (Serial 503), appendix, 239; Barry, 694; Cutts, 241; Webb, 291.

14. *New York Weekly Tribune*, July 31, Aug. 7, 1847; *Niles' National Register*, vol. 72 (July 31, 1847), 343; *St. Louis Daily Union*, July 10, 29, Sept. 7, 1847; *Weekly Tribune*, July 10, 1847; Fitzpatrick to Harvey, Sept. 18, 1847, Sen. Ex. Doc. No. 1, 30th Cong., 1st sess., vol. 1 (Serial 503), appendix, 239–40; Barry, 694; Cutts, 241; Webb, 291.

15. *Daily Missouri Republican*, July 17, 1847; *New York Weekly Tribune*, July 31, Aug. 7, 1847; *Niles' National Register*, vol. 72 (July 31, 1847), 343; *St. Louis Daily Union*, July 10, 29, Sept. 7, 1847; *Weekly Tribune*, July 10, 1847; Fitzpatrick to Harvey, Sept. 18, 1847, Sen. Ex. Doc. No. 1, 30th Cong., 1st sess., vol. 1 (Serial 503), appendix, 240; Barry, 694; Cutts, 241.

16. *Daily Missouri Republican*, July 17, 1847; *New York Weekly Tribune*, July 31, Aug. 7, 1847; *Niles' National Register*, vol. 72 (July 31, 1847), 343; *St. Louis Daily Union*, July 10, 29, Sept. 7, 1847; *Weekly Tribune*, July 10, 1847; Fitzpatrick to Harvey, Sept. 18, 1847, Sen. Ex. Doc. No. 1, 30th Cong., 1st sess., vol. 1 (Serial 503), appendix, 240; Barry, 694; Cutts, 241–42.

17. *Daily Missouri Republican*, July 17, 1847; *New York Weekly Tribune*, July 31, Aug. 7, 1847; *Niles' National Register*, vol. 72 (July 31, 1847), 343; *St. Louis Daily Union*, July 10, 29, Sept. 7, 1847; *Weekly Tribune*, July 10, 1847; Fitzpatrick to Harvey, Sept. 18, 1847, Sen. Ex. Doc. No. 1, 30th Cong., 1st sess., vol. 1 (Serial 503), appendix, 240; Barry, 694; Cutts, 242; Webb, 292.

18. *Daily Missouri Republican*, July 17, 1847; *New York Weekly Tribune*, July 31, Aug. 7, 1847; *Niles' National Register*, vol. 72 (July 31, 1847), 343; *St. Louis Daily Union*, July 10, 29, Sept. 7, 1847; *Weekly Tribune*, July 10, 1847; Fitzpatrick to Harvey, Sept. 18, 1847, Sen. Ex. Doc. No. 1, 30th Cong., 1st sess., vol. 1 (Serial 503), appendix, 240; Barry, 694.

19. *Daily Missouri Republican*, July 19, 1847; *New York Weekly Tribune*, July 31, 1847; *Niles' National Register*, vol. 72 (July 31, 1847), 343; *St. Louis Reveille* (daily), July 18, 20, 1847; *Weekly Tribune*, July 17, 1847; Barry, 699–700; Webb, 290–92.

20. *New York Weekly Tribune*, July 31, Aug. 7, 1847; *Niles' National Register*, vol. 72 (July 31, 1847), 343; *St. Louis Daily Union*, July 8, 10, 29, Sept. 7, 1847; *Weekly Tribune*, July 10, 1847; Fitzpatrick to Harvey, Sept. 18, 1847, Sen. Ex. Doc. No. 1, 30th Cong., 1st sess., vol. 1 (Serial 503), appendix, 240; Barry, 695, 702, 703, 705.

21. *New York Weekly Tribune*, July 31, Aug. 7, 1847; *Niles' National Register*, vol. 72 (July 31, 1847), 343; *St. Louis Daily Union*, July 10, 29, Sept. 7, 1847; *Weekly Tribune*, July 10, 1847; Fitzpatrick to Harvey, Sept. 18, 1847, Sen. Ex. Doc. No. 1, 30th Cong., 1st sess., vol. 1 (Serial 503), appendix, 239–40; Barry, 694.

Chapter 7. More Soldiers for Santa Fe

1. *Alton Telegraph and Democratic Review*, May 7, 1847; *Daily Missouri Republican*, April 20, May 3, 1847; Johnston, Edwards, and Ferguson, 56–57.

2. *Alton Telegraph and Democratic Review*, May 7, 21, 28, June 4, 11, 18, 25, Oct. 1, 1847; *Daily Missouri Republican*, April 20, May 1, 3, 4, 15, 17, 25, June 7, 19, 22, 23, 25, 29, July 7, 12, 19, 1847; *Democratic Standard*, Aug. 10, 1883; *Gazette*, July 23, 1847; *New York Weekly Tribune*, July 17, 31, 1847; *Missouri Statesman*, June 25, 1847; *St. Louis Daily New Era*, May 4, 8, 15, 22, 25, 29, 1847; *St. Louis Daily Union*,

April 26, May 10, 11, 13, 15, 17, 29, 31, June 1, 3, 8, 9, 15, 21, July 5, 8, 10, 19, 1847; *St. Louis Reveille* (daily), May 29, 1847; *St. Louis Weekly Reveille*, May 24, 31, 1847; Barry, 684–85, 691–92; Johnston, Edwards, and Ferguson, 57–60.

3. *Daily Missouri Republican*, July 7, 1847; *Democratic Standard*, Aug. 10, 17, 1883; *New York Weekly Tribune*, July 10, 24, 27, 31, Aug. 28, Oct. 9, 1847; *Niles' National Register*, vol. 72 (July 17, 1847), 320; *St. Louis Daily Union*, June 25, 26, July 10, 14, 19, Aug. 2, 12, 16, 19, Sept. 7, 1847; *St. Louis Reveille* (daily), June 27, July 10, 13, 18, Aug. 5, 12, 15, 1847; Barry, 690–91, 696.

4. *Democratic Standard*, Aug. 10, 17, 1883; *New York Weekly Tribune*, July 10, 24, 27, 31, Aug. 28, Oct. 9, 1847; *Niles' National Register*, vol. 72 (July 17, 1847), 320; *St. Louis Daily Union*, June 25, 26, July 10, 14, 19, Aug. 2, 12, 16, 19, Sept. 7, 1847; *St. Louis Reveille* (daily), June 27, July 10, 13, 18, Aug. 5, 12, 15, 1847; Barry, 690–91.

5. *Daily Missouri Republican*, July 7, 1847; *Democratic Standard*, Aug. 10, 17, 1883; *New York Weekly Tribune*, July 10, 24, 27, 31, Aug. 28, Oct. 9, 1847; *Niles' National Register*, vol. 72 (July 17, 1847), 320; *St. Louis Daily Union*, June 25, 26, July 10, 14, 19, Aug. 2, 12, 16, 19, Sept. 7, 1847; *St. Louis Reveille* (daily), June 27, July 10, 13, 18, Aug. 5, 12, 15, 1847; Barry, 691, 696.

6. *Democratic Standard*, Aug. 10, 17, 1883; *New York Weekly Tribune*, July 10, 24, 27, 31, Aug. 28, Oct. 9, 1847; *Niles' National Register*, vol. 72 (July 17, 1847), 320; *St. Louis Daily Union*, June 25, 26, July 10, 14, 19, Aug. 2, 12, 16, 19, Sept. 7, Dec. 21, 1847; *St. Louis Reveille* (daily), June 27, July 10, 13, 18, Aug. 5, 12, 15, 1847; *St. Louis Weekly Reveille*, Aug. 9, 1847; Barry, 691, 705–6.

7. *Democratic Standard*, Aug. 10, 17, 1883; *New York Weekly Tribune*, July 10, 24, 27, 31, Aug. 28, Oct. 9, 1847; *Niles' National Register*, vol. 72 (July 17, 1847), 320; *St. Louis Daily Union*, June 25, 26, July 10, 14, 19, Aug. 2, 12, 16, 19, Sept. 7, Dec. 21, 1847; *St. Louis Reveille* (daily), June 27, July 10, 13, 18, Aug. 5, 12, 15, 1847; *St. Louis Weekly Reveille*, Aug. 15, 1847; Barry, 705–6.

8. *Daily Missouri Republican*, Aug. 12, 16, 1847; *Democratic Standard*, Aug. 10, 17, 1883; *New York Weekly Tribune*, July 10, 24, 27, 31, Aug. 28, Oct. 9, 1847; *Niles' National Register*, vol. 72 (July 17, 1847), 320; *St. Louis Daily Union*, June 25, 26, July 10, 14, 19, Aug. 2, 12, 16, 19, Sept. 7, Dec. 21, 1847; *St. Louis Reveille* (daily), June 27, July 10, 13, 18, Aug. 5, 12, 15, 1847; *St. Louis Weekly Reveille*, Aug. 15, Dec. 21, 1847; Barry, 705–6.

9. *Daily Missouri Republican*, Aug. 12, 16, 1847; *Democratic Standard*, Aug. 10, 17, 1883; *New York Weekly Tribune*, July 10, 24, 27, 31, Aug. 28, Oct. 9, 1847; *Niles' National Register*, vol. 72 (July 17, 1847), 320; *St. Louis Daily Union*, June 25, 26, July 10, 14, 19, Aug. 2, 12, 16, 19, Sept. 7, Dec. 21, 1847; *St. Louis Reveille* (daily), June 27, July 10, 13,

18, Aug. 5, 12, 15, 1847; *St. Louis Weekly Reveille*, Aug. 15, Dec. 21, 1847; Barry, 705–6.

10. *Daily Missouri Republican*, July 7, 1847; *Democratic Standard*, Aug. 10, 1883; *New York Weekly Tribune*, July 24, 1847; *Niles' National Register*, vol. 72 (July 17, 1847), 320; *St. Louis Daily Union*, Sept. 7, Dec. 21, 1847; *St. Louis Reveille* (daily), July 13, 1847; Barry, 696, 705–6.

11. *Daily Missouri Republican*, June 29, July 19, Aug. 2, Sept. 20, 22, 1847; *Democratic Standard*, Aug. 17, 1847; *Gazette*, July 23, 1847; *Jefferson Inquirer*, Sept. 17, 1847; *New York Weekly Tribune*, July 17, 31, Aug. 14, Oct. 2, 9, 1847; *St. Louis Daily Union*, June 3, 23, July 8, August 2, 9, Sept. 1, 7, 20, 23, Oct. 4, Dec. 22, 1847; *St. Louis Reveille* (daily), May 29, July 18, Sept. 17, 22, Nov. 2, 1847; *Weekly Tribune*, Oct. 1, 1847; Barry, 691–92, 696–98.

12. *New York Weekly Tribune*, July 31, Aug. 7, 1847; *Niles' National Register*, vol. 72 (July 31, 1847), 343; *St. Louis Daily Union*, May 29, June 8, 21, July 8, Sept. 7, 1847; *St. Louis Reveille* (daily), July 18, 1847; *Weekly Tribune*, July 10, 1847; Barry, 695, 702; Cutts, 240–42; Johnston, Edwards, and Ferguson, 283–361; Webb, 290–93.

13. *St. Louis Daily Union*, July 29, 1847; *St. Louis Reveille* (daily), June 23, 26, July 18, 1847; House Ex. Doc. No. 17, 31st Cong., 1st sess., vol. 5 (Serial 573), 247; Barry, 697–98, 704; Kit Carson, *Kit Carson's Autobiography*, ed. Milo Milton Quaife, 120; Johnston, Edwards, and Ferguson, 319.

14. *Daily Missouri Republican*, Aug. 16, 1847; *St. Louis Daily Union*, July 29, 1847; *St. Louis Reveille* (daily), June 23, 26, July 18, 1847; House Ex. Doc. No. 17, 31st Cong., 1st sess., vol. 5 (Serial 573), 247; Barry, 704; Carson, 121; Johnston, Edwards, and Ferguson, 319.

15. *Daily Missouri Republican*, July 19, Aug. 2, Sept. 20, 22, 1847; *Democratic Standard*, Aug. 17, 1883; *Jefferson Inquirer*, Sept. 17, 1847; *New York Weekly Tribune*, July 31, Aug. 14, Oct. 2, 9, 1847; *St. Louis Daily Union*, June 3, 23, Aug. 2, 9, Sept. 1, 7, 20, 23, Oct. 4, Dec. 22, 1847; *St. Louis Reveille* (daily), July 18, Sept. 17, 22, Nov. 2, 1847; *Weekly Tribune*, Oct. 1, 1847; Barry, 697–98.

16. *Daily Missouri Republican*, Sept. 22, 1847; *New York Weekly Tribune*, Oct. 9, 1847; *St. Louis Daily Union*, June 10, July 14, Aug. 2, 26, Sept. 7, 21, 30, 1847; *St. Louis Reveille* (daily), Nov. 2, 1847; Barry, 700–701.

17. *Daily Missouri Republican*, Sept. 22, 1847; *New York Weekly Tribune*, Oct. 9, 1847; *St. Louis Daily Union*, June 10, July 14, Aug. 2, 26, Sept. 7, 21, 30, 1847; *St. Louis Reveille* (daily), Nov. 2, 1847; Barry, 701.

18. *Daily Missouri Republican*, Sept. 22, 1847; *New York Weekly Tribune*, Oct. 9, 1847; *St. Louis Daily Union*, June 10, July 14, Aug. 2, 22, Sept. 7, 21, 30, 1847; *St. Louis Reveille* (daily), Nov. 2, 1847; Barry,

701; Charles Henry Buercklin, "Autobiography of Charles Henry Buercklin, 1821–1909," 28–30.

19. Buercklin, 31, 33.

20. Buercklin, 30–31.

21. Buercklin, 31.

22. Buercklin, 31–32.

23. Buercklin, 32.

24. *Daily Missouri Republican*, Sept. 22, 1847; *New York Weekly Tribune*, Oct. 9, 1847; *St. Louis Daily Union*, June 10, July 14, Aug. 2, 26, Sept. 7, 21, 30, 1847; *St. Louis Reveille* (daily), Nov. 2, 1847; Barry, 479, 701.

Chapter 8. 1847: A Time of Trouble

1. *Daily Missouri Republican*, May 18, 1847; *New York Weekly Tribune*, June 5, 1847; *St. Louis Daily Union*, May 22, June 1, 1847; *St. Louis Reveille* (daily), May 28, 1847; Barry, 673–74.

2. *Daily Missouri Republican*, Sept. 7, 1847; *New York Weekly Tribune*, Sept. 18, 1847; *St. Louis Daily Union*, May 8, 11, 29, June 2, 26, Sept. 7, 1847; *Weekly Tribune*, July 17, 1847; Barry, 674–75; Hammond, 148, 202.

3. *Daily Missouri Republican*, Sept. 7, 1847; *New York Weekly Tribune*, Sept. 18, 1847; *St. Louis Daily Union*, May 8, 11, 29, June 2, 26, Sept. 7, 1847; *Weekly Tribune*, July 17, 1847; Barry, 674–75; Hammond, 148, 202.

4. *St. Louis Reveille* (daily), April 23, 24, 1847; OIA, Letters Received from Fort Leavenworth Agency (M234–R302); Barry, 569–70, 671–72, 689–90.

5. Barry, 675; Donald Chaput, *Francois X. Aubry*, 40–41.

6. *New York Weekly Tribune*, July 31, 1847; *St. Louis Daily Union*, July 19, 1847; *St. Louis Reveille* (daily), May 28, 1847; *Weekly Tribune*, July 17, 1847; Barry, 683–84.

7. *Daily Missouri Republican*, June 14, 1847; *New York Weekly Tribune*, June 26, 1847; *St. Louis Weekly Reveille*, June 14, 21, 1847, April 3, 1848; Barry, 686; Garrard, 295; Hammond, 149.

8. Sen. Ex. Doc. No. 1, 30th Cong., 1st sess., vol. 1 (Serial 503), appendix, 241–42; Donald J. Berthrong, *The Southern Cheyennes*, 107–8; Hammond, 148.

9. *Democratic Standard*, Aug. 10, 1883; *St. Louis Daily Union*, June 21, 1847; Barry, 670–71, 675, 688; Garrard, 271–74, 294–95; Hammond, 148–49.

10. *St. Louis Weekly Reveille*, June 28, 1847; Settle and Settle, 26; Wyman, 421.

11. *Daily Missouri Republican*, Aug. 2, 1847; *Democratic Standard*,

Aug. 10, 1883; *New York Weekly Tribune*, Aug. 11, 1847; *St. Louis Daily Union*, Aug. 5, 1847; *St. Louis Reveille* (daily), July 18, Aug. 5, 1847; Barry, 703; Connelley, *Doniphan's Expedition*, 566.

12. *Daily Missouri Republican*, Sept. 7, 1847; *New York Weekly Tribune*, Sept. 18, 1847; *St. Louis Daily Union*, Sept. 7, 1847; *St. Louis Reveille* (daily), Sept. 7, 21, 1847; Barry, 713–14; Chaput, 45–46.

13. *Daily Missouri Republican*, Sept. 20, 22, 1847; *New York Weekly Tribune*, Oct. 2, 9, 1847; *St. Louis Daily Union*, Sept. 20, 25, Oct. 4, 1847; *St. Louis Reveille* (daily), Sept. 19, 23, 28, 1847; *Weekly Tribune*, Oct. 1, 1847; Barry, 716–18; Connelley, *Doniphan's Expedition*, 517, 523, 524.

14. *New York Weekly Tribune*, Nov. 20, 1847; *St. Louis Daily Union*, Nov. 11, 1847; *St. Louis Reveille* (daily), Nov. 2, 1847; *Weekly Tribune*, Nov. 19, 1847; Barry, 724.

15. *New York Weekly Tribune*, Jan. 29, 1848; *St. Louis Daily Union*, Oct. 1, 1847, Jan. 12, 1848; *St. Louis Reveille* (daily), Nov. 2, 1847, Jan. 12, 1848; *Weekly Tribune*, Jan. 28, 1848; Barry, 719, 730–31; Chaput, 49–52.

16. House Ex. Doc. No. 1, 30th Cong., 2d sess., vol. 1 (Serial 537), 136; Barry, 722.

Chapter 9. Fort Mann and the Indian Battalion

1. *Annual Report, Secretary of War, 1847*, House Ex. Doc. No. 8, 30th Cong., 1st sess., vol. 2 (Serial 515), 545; Thomas L. Karnes, "Gilpin's Volunteers on the Santa Fe Trail," *KHQ* 30, no. 1 (1964): 1–2; Thomas L. Karnes, *William Gilpin: Western Nationalist*, 190–92; Leo E. Oliva, "Missouri Volunteers on the Santa Fe Trail," *The Trail Guide*, part 1, vol. 15, no. 2 (June 1970): 1–5; Oliva, *Soldiers on the Santa Fe Trail*, 84.

2. *Jefferson Inquirer*, Sept. 25, 1847; *Weekly Tribune*, Oct. 15, 1847; Gilpin to Roger Jones, Aug. 1, 1848, AGO, Letters Received, 449 G 1848, RG 94, NA, also in House Ex. Doc. No. 1, 30th Cong., 2d sess., vol. 1 (Serial 537), 136; Karnes, "Gilpin's Volunteers," 1–2; Karnes, *William Gilpin*, 191; Oliva, "Missouri Volunteers," part 1, 2–5; Oliva, *Soldiers on the Santa Fe Trail*, 84.

3. *Jefferson Inquirer*, Sept. 25, 1847; *Weekly Tribune*, Oct. 15, 1847; Hubert Howe Bancroft, *The History and Life of William Gilpin*, 36–37; Karnes, "Gilpin's Volunteers," 2–3; Oliva, "Missouri Volunteers," part 1, 5.

4. *St. Louis Weekly Reveille*, Aug. 30, 1847.

5. *Daily Missouri Republican*, Sept. 4, 8, 1847; *Jefferson Inquirer*, Sept. 1, 1847; *St. Louis Daily Union*, Aug. 6, Sept. 13, 14, Oct. 2, 10, Dec. 14, 1847; *St. Louis Reveille* (daily), Sept. 3, 9, 11, 12, 22, Oct. 31, Nov. 2, Dec. 12, 15, 16, 19, 31, 1847; *Weekly Tribune*, Sept. 24, Oct. 16,

Nov. 19, Dec. 31, 1847; *Annual Report, Secretary of War, 1847*, House Ex. Doc. No. 1, 30th Cong., 2d sess., vol. 1 (Serial 537), 136, 223; Barry, 714–15; Connelley, *Doniphan's Expedition*, 147–49; William E. Connelley, "Mr. Gilpin's Santa Fe Trace Battalion," *KHC* 10 (1907–8): 114; Karnes, "Gilpin's Volunteers," 3; Karnes, *William Gilpin*, 191; Oliva, "Missouri Volunteers," part 1, 5.

6. Gilpin to Marcy, Jan. 8, 1848, AGO, Letters Received, 62 G 1848, RG 94, NA; Karnes, "Gilpin's Volunteers," 3–4; Karnes, *William Gilpin*, 192–93; Oliva, "Missouri Volunteers," part 1, 6–8.

7. Karnes, "Gilpin's Volunteers," 3; Karnes, *William Gilpin*, 192; Oliva, "Missouri Volunteers," part 1, 9.

8. Karnes, "Gilpin's Volunteers," 3; Karnes, *William Gilpin*, 192; Oliva, "Missouri Volunteers," part 1, 5, 9–10.

9. Gilpin to Marcy, Jan. 8, 1848, AGO, Letters Received, 62 G 1848, RG 94, NA; Karnes, "Gilpin's Volunteers," 4; Karnes, *William Gilpin*, 193; Oliva, "Missouri Volunteers," part 1, 6–8.

10. General Order, No. 63, Headquarters, Fort Leavenworth, Sept. 20, 1847, printed in *Daily Missouri Republican*, Nov. 1, 1847; Oliva, "Missouri Volunteers," part 1, 6–7.

11. *Daily Missouri Republican*, Oct. 11, 1847; Oliva, "Missouri Volunteers," part 1, 7.

12. Gilpin to Garland, August 18, 1848, AGO, Letters Received, 398 G 1848, RG 94, NA; Karnes, *William Gilpin*, 210; Oliva, "Missouri Volunteers," part 1, 9.

13. *St. Louis Daily Union*, Oct. 10, 1847; *St. Louis Reveille* (daily), Oct. 31, 1847; *Weekly Tribune*, Nov. 19, 1847; Gilpin to Jones, Aug. 1, 1848, House Ex. Doc. No. 1, 30th Cong., 2d sess., vol. 1 (Serial 537), 136; Barry, 720–21; Karnes, "Gilpin's Volunteers," 4; Karnes, *William Gilpin*, 193–94; Oliva, "Missouri Volunteers," part 1, 7, 9 n. 32; Oliva, *Soldiers on the Santa Fe Trail*, 84.

14. Court Martial Records of Amandus V. Schnabel and William Pelzer, enclosed with Garland to Roger Jones, Aug. 16, 1848, AGO, Letters Received, 368 G 1848, RG 94, NA (M567–R377); Karnes, "Gilpin's Volunteers," 3; Karnes, *William Gilpin*, 192; Oliva, "Missouri Volunteers," part 1, 9–10.

15. *St. Louis Daily Union*, Oct. 10, Dec. 14, 1847; *St. Louis Reveille* (daily), Oct. 31, Nov. 2, Dec. 13, 1847; *Weekly Tribune*, Nov. 19, Dec. 31, 1847; Gilpin to Roger Jones, Aug. 1, 1848, House Ex. Doc. No. 1, 30th Cong., 1st sess., vol. 1 (Serial 537), 136–37; Barry, 720; Berthrong, 108–9; George E. Hyde, *The Pawnee Indians*, 226–29; Karnes, "Gilpin's Volunteers," 4; Karnes, *William Gilpin*, 194; Oliva, "Missouri Volunteers," part 1, 10–11; Oliva, *Soldiers on the Santa Fe Trail*, 84–85; Virginia Cole Trenholm, *The Arapaho: Our People*, 127.

16. *St. Louis Daily Union*, Oct. 10, Dec. 14, 1847; *St. Louis Reveille* (daily), Oct. 31, Nov. 2, Dec. 15, 1847; *Weekly Tribune*, Nov. 19, Dec. 31,

1847; Gilpin to Jones, Aug. 1, 1848, House Ex. Doc. No. 1, 30th Cong., 1st sess., vol. 1 (Serial 537), 136–37; Barry, 720–21; Hafen, *Broken Hand*, 251, 254; Karnes, "Gilpin's Volunteers," 4; Karnes, *William Gilpin*, 194; Oliva, "Missouri Volunteers," part 1, 11; Oliva, *Soldiers on the Santa Fe Trail*, 85.

17. *St. Louis Daily Union*, Oct. 10, Dec. 14, 1847; *St. Louis Reveille* (daily), Oct. 31, Nov. 2, Dec. 6, 12, 15, 1847; *Weekly Tribune*, Nov. 19, Dec. 31, 1847; Gilpin to Jones, Aug. 1, 1848, House Ex. Doc. No. 1, 30th Cong., 1st sess., vol. 1 (Serial 537), 136–37; Barry, 720–21, 728; Karnes, "Gilpin's Volunteers," 4; Karnes, *William Gilpin*, 194; Oliva, "Missouri Volunteers," part 1, 11; Oliva, *Soldiers on the Santa Fe Trail*, 85.

18. Hafen, *Broken Hand*, 256, 258–60; Karnes, "Gilpin's Volunteers," 6–7; Karnes, *William Gilpin*, 194, 198–200; Oliva, "Missouri Volunteers," part 1, 11–13; Oliva, *Soldiers on the Santa Fe Trail*, 85.

19. Oliva, "Missouri Volunteers," part 1, 13–14.

20. *St. Louis Daily Union*, Jan. 1, Feb. 8, 9, 1848; *St. Louis Reveille* (daily), Dec. 15, 16, 19, 31, 1847; *Weekly Tribune*, Dec. 31, 1847; Pelzer to Gilpin, Nov. 19, 1847, enclosed with Garland to Roger Jones, Aug. 16, 1848, AGO, Letters Received, 368 G 1848, RG 94, NA (M567–R377); Barry, 727; Karnes, "Gilpin's Volunteers," 4–5; Karnes, *William Gilpin*, 195; Oliva, "Missouri Volunteers," part 1, 14.

21. *St. Louis Daily Union*, Jan. 1, Feb. 8, 9, 1848; *St. Louis Reveille* (daily), Dec. 15, 16, 19, 31, 1847; *Weekly Tribune*, Dec. 31, 1847; Pelzer to Gilpin, Nov. 19, 1847, enclosed with Garland to Roger Jones, Aug. 16, 1848, AGO, Letters Received, 368 G 1848, RG 94, NA (M567–R377); Barry, 727; Karnes, "Gilpin's Volunteers," 4–5; Karnes, *William Gilpin*, 195; Oliva, "Missouri Volunteers," part 1, 14–15.

22. *St. Louis Daily Union*, Jan. 1, Feb. 8, 9, 1848; *St. Louis Reveille* (daily), Dec. 15, 16, 19, 31, 1847; *Weekly Tribune*, Dec. 31, 1847; Pelzer to Gilpin, Nov. 19, 1847, enclosed with Garland to Roger Jones, Aug. 16, 1848, AGO, Letters Received, 368 G 1848, RG 94, NA (M567–R377); Barry, 727; Hafen, *Broken Hand*, 258; Karnes, "Gilpin's Volunteers," 4–5; Karnes, *William Gilpin*, 195; Oliva, "Missouri Volunteers," part 1, 15.

23. Pelzer to Gilpin, Nov. 19, 1847, enclosed with Garland to Roger Jones, Aug. 16, 1848, AGO, Letters Received, 368 G 1848, RG 94, NA (M567–R377); Oliva, "Missouri Volunteers," part 1, 15.

24. *St. Louis Daily Union*, Dec. 14, 1847; *St. Louis Reveille* (daily), Dec. 31, 1847; Court Martial Records of Schnabel, included with Garland to Roger Jones, August 16, 1848, AGO, Letters Received, 368 G 1848, RG 94, NA (M567–R377); Barry, 728; Karnes, "Gilpin's Volunteers," 5; Karnes, *William Gilpin*, 196; Oliva, "Missouri Volunteers," part 2, 4.

25. *St. Louis Daily Union*, Dec. 14, 1847; *St. Louis Reveille* (daily), Dec. 31, 1847; *St. Louis Weekly Reveille*, July 3, 1848; Barry, 728; George Rutledge Gibson, *Over the Chihuahua and Santa Fe Trails, 1847–1848:*

George Rutledge Gibson's Journal, ed. Robert W. Frazer, 83; Karnes, "Gilpin's Volunteers," 5; Karnes, *William Gilpin*, 196–97; Oliva, "Missouri Volunteers," part 2, 4.

26. Charge 2, Specification 3, Court Martial Records of Pelzer, included with Garland to Roger Jones, Aug. 16, 1848, AGO, Letters Received, 368 G 1848, RG 94, NA (M567–R377); Karnes, "Gilpin's Volunteers," 10–11; Karnes, *William Gilpin*, 197; Oliva, "Missouri Volunteers," part 2, 4–5.

27. Garland to Roger Jones, Aug. 16, 1848, AGO, Letters Received, 368 G 1848, RG 94, NA (M567–R377), and Court Martial Records of Fahlbush and Goldbeck enclosed; Gilpin to Marcy, Jan. 8, 1848, AGO, Letters Received, 32 G 1848, RG 94, NA; Karnes, "Gilpin's Volunteers," 10–11; Karnes, *William Gilpin*, 197; Oliva, "Missouri Volunteers," part 2, 4–5.

Chapter 10. The Spring of 1848: War, Peace, and Frustration

1. *Daily Missouri Republican*, Feb. 7, 1848; *New York Weekly Tribune*, Feb. 26, 1848; *St. Louis Daily Union*, Feb. 8, 1848; Gilpin to Roger Jones, Aug. 1, 1848, House Ex. Doc. No. 1, 30th Cong., 2d sess., vol. 1 (Serial 537), 137; Barry, 731; Oliva, "Missouri Volunteers," part 2, 12–13.

2. *Daily Missouri Republican*, Feb. 7, June 3, 1848; *New York Weekly Tribune*, Feb. 26, June 17, 1848; *St. Louis Daily Union*, Feb. 8, April 11, May 23, June 9, 1848; *St. Louis Reveille* (daily), Feb. 8, April 12, 1848; *Weekly Tribune*, March 17, May 26, June 2, 1848; Fitzpatrick to Harvey, Sept. 18, 1847, House Ex. Doc. No. 8, 30th Cong., 1st sess., vol. 2 (Serial 515), 238–49; Gilpin to Marcy, Jan. 8, 1848, AGO, Letters Received, 32 G 1848, RG 94, NA; Barry, 732–34; Karnes, *William Gilpin*, 200.

3. *Daily Missouri Republican*, Feb. 7, April 11, 1848; *New York Weekly Tribune*, Feb. 26, 1848; *St. Louis Daily Union*, Feb. 8, April 11, 1848; *St. Louis Reveille* (daily), Feb. 8, April 12, 13, 1848; *Weekly Tribune*, March 17, 1848; Barry, 732–33; Karnes, "Gilpin's Volunteers," 7; Oliva, "Missouri Volunteers," part 2, 6.

4. House Ex. Doc. No. 1, 30th Cong., 2d sess., vol. 1 (Serial 537), 45, 173, 174; Barry, 733, 755; Bauer, 382–88; Nevin, 222.

5. Holtzscheiter, Colston, and Albert Schnabel to Gilpin, Feb. 20, 1848, Petition of Companies C and D to Gilpin, Feb. 22, 1848, and Stremmel to Gilpin, March 9, 1848, all enclosed with Gilpin to Marcy, March 10, 1848, AGO, Letters Received, 62 G 1848, RG 94, NA; Karnes, "Gilpin's Volunteers," 7; Karnes, *William Gilpin*, 201; Oliva, "Missouri Volunteers," part 2, 6.

6. *Weekly Tribune*, April 7, 1848; Gilpin to Marcy, March 10, 1848, AGO, Letters Received, 62 G 1848, RG 94, NA, and Roger Jones

endorsement of same, dated April 29, 1848; Oliva, "Missouri Volunteers," part 2, 6–7.

7. *New York Weekly Tribune*, March 10, 1849; *Annual Report, CIA, 1848*, and report of Agent Thomas Fitzpatrick therein, also in House Ex. Doc. No. 1, 30th Cong., 2d sess., vol. 1 (Serial 537), 470–73; Gilpin to Roger Jones, Aug. 1, 1848, House Ex. Doc. No. 1, 30th Cong., 2d sess., vol. 1 (Serial 537), 137; Barry, 737; Hafen, *Broken Hand*, 260.

8. *Gazette*, June 2, 1848; *St. Louis Daily Union*, March 10, 1848; *St. Louis Reveille* (daily), March 9, 19, April 11, 1848; *Weekly Tribune*, June 9, 1848; Barry, 738–39, 740.

9. Gilpin to Roger Jones, Aug. 1, 1848, House Ex. Doc. No. 1, 30th Cong., 2d sess., vol. 1 (Serial 537), 137; Hammond, 79, 86, 87, 88 nn. 16 and 17, 155, 206 n. 118; Karnes, "Gilpin's Volunteers," 7–8; Oliva, "Missouri Volunteers," part 2, 7.

10. Gilpin to Roger Jones, Aug. 1, 1848, House Ex. Doc. No. 1, 30th Cong., 2d sess., vol. 1 (Serial 537), 137; Barry, 753; Hammond, 155; Oliva, "Missouri Volunteers," part 2, 7; Oliva, *Soldiers on the Santa Fe Trail*, 85–86.

11. *St. Louis Reveille* (daily), May 31, 1848; Gilpin to Roger Jones, Aug. 1, 1848, House Ex. Doc. No. 1, 30th Cong., 2d sess., vol. 1 (Serial 537), 137; Barry, 753; Karnes, "Gilpin's Volunteers," 7–8; Karnes, *William Gilpin*, 201; Oliva, "Missouri Volunteers," part 2, 7; Oliva, *Soldiers on the Santa Fe Trail*, 85–86.

12. Gilpin to Roger Jones, Aug. 1, 1848, House Ex. Doc. No. 1, 30th Cong., 2d sess., vol. 1 (Serial 537), 137; Avarem Bender, *The March of Empire*, 130–31; Richardson, 144–58; Utley, 75–76; Wallace and Hoebel, 297–98.

13. *Gazette*, May 5, 1848; *Expositor*, April 29, 1848; *New York Weekly Tribune*, May 13, 1848; *St. Louis Daily New Era*, April 26, 1848; *St. Louis Daily Union*, Feb. 8, April 14, 26, 27, May 9, 1848; *St. Louis Reveille* (daily), April 13, 14, 1848; *Weekly Tribune*, April 21, 1848; Barry, 743, 744.

14. *Daily Missouri Republican*, June 3, 1848; *New York Weekly Tribune*, June 17, 1848; *St. Louis Daily Union*, May 26, 1848; Royall to Roger Jones, June 21, 1848, House Ex. Doc. No. 1, 30th Cong., 2d sess., vol. 1 (Serial 537), 141; Barry, 750–51.

15. *Daily Missouri Republican*, June 3, 1848; *Expositor*, May 29, 1848; *Gazette*, June 2, 1848; *New York Weekly Tribune*, June 17, 1848; *St. Louis Daily Union*, June 5, 1848; *St. Louis Reveille* (daily), June 3, 1848; Barry, 753–54.

16. *Daily Missouri Republican*, June 3, 1848; *New York Weekly Tribune*, June 17, 1848; *St. Louis Reveille* (daily), June 1, 10, 1848; *Weekly Tribune*, June 9, 1848; Barry, 750; Gibson, *Over the Chihuahua*, 58–73.

17. Gibson, *Over the Chihuahua*, 72–81.

18. *Daily Missouri Republican*, June 3, 9, 1848; *New York Weekly Tribune*, June 17, 1848; *St. Louis Reveille* (daily), June 1, 10, 1848; *Weekly*

Tribune, June 9, 1848; Barry, 750; Gibson, *Over the Chihuahua*, 80–81; Oliva, "Missouri Volunteers," part 2, 8.

19. *Daily Missouri Republican*, June 3, 1848; *New York Weekly Tribune*, June 17, 1848; *St. Louis Reveille* (daily), June 1, 10, 1848; *Weekly Tribune*, June 9, 1848; Barry, 750; Gibson, *Over the Chihuahua*, 81–82; Oliva, "Missouri Volunteers," part 2, 8–9.

20. *New York Weekly Tribune*, July 29, 1848; *St. Louis Reveille* (daily), July 2, 1848; Gilpin to Roger Jones, Aug. 1, 1848, House Ex. Doc. No. 1, 30th Cong., 2d sess., vol. 1 (Serial 537), 138; Barry, 755.

21. *St. Louis Reveille* (daily), July 2, 1848; Gilpin to Roger Jones, Aug. 1, 1848, House Ex. Doc. No. 1, 30th Cong., 2d sess., vol. 1 (Serial 537), 138; Barry, 755; Oliva, "Missouri Volunteers," part 2, 9.

22. *St. Louis Reveille* (daily), July 2, 1848; Gilpin to Marcy, July 10, 1848, AGO, Letters Received, 270 G 1848, RG 94, NA; Barry, 755; Oliva, "Missouri Volunteers," part 2, 14.

Chapter 11. The Battle of Coon Creek

1. Royall to Robert Jones, June 21, 1848, House Ex. Doc. No. 1, 30th Cong., 2d sess., vol. 1 (Serial 537), 141–44; Barry, 751, 757; George F. Price, *Across the Continent with the Fifth Cavalry*, 292–93; Joseph B. Thoburn, "Indian Fight in Ford County in 1859," *KHC* 12(1911–12):320 n. 8.

2. *New York Weekly Tribune*, July 29, Aug. 19, 1848; *St. Louis Daily Union*, July 20, Aug. 23, 1848; *Weekly Tribune*, July 28, Aug. 11, 1848; Royall to Roger Jones, June 21, 1848, House Ex. Doc. No. 1, 30th Cong., 2d sess., vol. 1 (Serial 537), 141; Barry, 757; James H. Birch, "The Battle of Coon Creek," *KHC* 10(1907–8):409–10.

3. *New York Weekly Tribune*, July 29, 1848; Stremmel to Gilpin, June 23, 1848, House Ex. Doc. No. 1, 30th Cong., 2d sess., vol. 1 (Serial 537), 144–45; Barry, 759.

4. *New York Weekly Tribune*, July 29, 1848; Stremmel to Gilpin, June 23, 1848, House Ex. Doc. No. 1, 30th Cong., 2d sess., vol. 1 (Serial 537), 144–45; Barry, 759.

5. *New York Weekly Tribune*, July 29, 1848; Stremmel to Gilpin, June 23, 1848, House Ex. Doc. No. 1, 30th Cong., 2d sess., vol. 1 (Serial 537), 144–45; Barry, 759.

6. *New York Weekly Tribune*, July 29, 1848; Stremmel to Gilpin, June 23, 1848, House Ex. Doc. No. 1, 30th Cong., 2d sess., vol. 1 (Serial 537), 144–45; Barry, 759.

7. *New York Weekly Tribune*, July 29, 1848; Stremmel to Gilpin, June 23, 1848, House Ex. Doc. No. 1, 30th Cong., 2d sess., vol. 1 (Serial 537), 144–45; Barry, 759.

8. *New York Weekly Tribune*, July 29, Aug. 19, 1848; *St. Louis Daily Union*, July 20, Aug. 23, 1848; *Weekly Tribune*, July 28, Aug. 11, 1848;

Royall to Roger Jones, June 21, 1848, House Ex. Doc. No. 1, 30th Cong., 2d sess., vol. 1 (Serial 537), 141; Barry, 757, 759.

9. Royall to Roger Jones, June 21, 1848, House Ex. Doc. No. 1, 30th Cong., 2d sess., vol. 1 (Serial 537), 141; Birch, 410.

10. Royall to Roger Jones, June 21, 1848, House Ex. Doc. No. 1, 30th Cong., 2d sess., vol. 1 (Serial 537), 141; Birch, 410.

11. Royall to Roger Jones, June 21, 1848, House Ex. Doc. No. 1, 30th Cong., 2d sess., vol .1 (Serial 537), 141; Birch, 410–11.

12. Royall to Roger Jones, June 21, 1848, House Ex. Doc. No. 1, 30th Cong., 2d sess., vol. 1 (Serial 537), 141; Birch, 410–11.

13. Royall to Roger Jones, June 21, 1848, House Ex. Doc. No. 1, 30th Cong., 2d sess., vol. 1 (Serial 537), 141; Birch, 410–11.

14. *New York Weekly Tribune*, July 29, Aug. 19, 1848; *St. Louis Daily Union*, July 20, Aug. 23, 1848; *Weekly Tribune*, July 28, Aug. 11, 1848; Royall to Roger Jones, June 21, 1848, House Ex. Doc. No. 1, 30th Cong., 2d sess., vol. 1 (Serial 537), 141; Stremmel to Gilpin, June 23, 1848, House Ex. Doc. No. 1, 30th Cong., 2d sess., vol. 1 (Serial 537), 145; Barry, 758; Birch, 411.

15. *New York Weekly Tribune*, July 29, Aug. 19, 1848; *St. Louis Daily Union*, July 20, Aug. 23, 1848; *Weekly Tribune*, July 28, Aug. 11, 1848; Royall to Roger Jones, June 21, 1848, House Ex. Doc. No. 1, 30th Cong., 2d sess., vol. 1 (Serial 537), 141–42; Stremmel to Gilpin, June 23, 1848, House Ex. Doc. No. 1, 30th Cong., 2d sess., vol. 1 (Serial 537), 145–46; Barry, 758; Birch, 411.

16. Birch, 409–10.

17. *New York Weekly Tribune*, July 29, Aug. 19, 1848; *St. Louis Daily Union*, July 20, Aug. 23, 1848; *Weekly Tribune*, July 28, Aug. 11, 1848; Royall to Roger Jones, June 21, 1848, House Ex. Doc. No. 1, 30th Cong., 2d sess., vol. 1 (Serial 537), 142; Barry, 758; Birch, 411–12.

18. *New York Weekly Tribune*, July 29, Aug. 19, 1848; *St. Louis Daily Union*, July 20, Aug. 23, 1848; *Weekly Tribune*, July 28, Aug. 11, 1848; Royall to Roger Jones, June 21, 1848, House Ex. Doc. No. 1, 30th Cong., 2d sess., vol. 1 (Serial 537), 142; Barry, 758.

19. *New York Weekly Tribune*, July 29, Aug. 19, 1848; *St. Louis Daily Union*, July 20, Aug. 23, 1848; *Weekly Tribune*, July 28, Aug. 11, 1848; Royall to Roger Jones, June 21, 1848, House Ex. Doc. No. 1, 30th Cong., 2d sess., vol. 1 (Serial 537), 142; Stremmel to Gilpin, June 23, 1848, House Ex. Doc. No. 1, 30th Cong., 2d sess., vol. 1 (Serial 537), 146; Barry, 758.

20. *New York Weekly Tribune*, July 29, Aug. 19, 1848; *St. Louis Daily Union*, July 20, Aug. 23, 1848; *Weekly Tribune*, July 28, Aug. 11, 1848; Royall to Roger Jones, June 21, 1848, House Ex. Doc. No. 1, 30th Cong., 2d sess., vol. 1 (Serial 537), 142–43; Stremmel to Gilpin, June 23, 1848, House Ex. Doc. No. 1, 30th Cong., 2d sess., vol. 1 (Serial 537), 146; Barry, 758.

21. *New York Weekly Tribune*, July 29, Aug. 19, 1848; *St. Louis Daily Union*, July 20, Aug. 23, 1848; *Weekly Tribune*, July 28, Aug. 11, 1848; Royall to Roger Jones, June 21, 1848, House Ex. Doc. No. 1, 30th Cong., 2d sess., vol. 1 (Serial 537), 142; Stremmel to Gilpin, June 23, 1848, House Ex. Doc. No. 1, 30th Cong., 2d sess., vol. 1 (Serial 537), 146; Barry, 758.

22. *New York Weekly Tribune*, July 29, Aug. 19, 1848; *St. Louis Daily Union*, July 20, Aug. 23, 1848; *Weekly Tribune*, July 28, Aug. 11, 1848; Royall to Roger Jones, June 21, 1848, House Ex. Doc. No. 1, 30th Cong., 2d sess., vol. 1 (Serial 537), 142–43; Barry, 758; Birch, 412.

23. Royall to Roger Jones, June 21, 1848, House Ex. Doc. No. 1, 30th Cong., 2d sess., vol. 1 (Serial 537), 143; Birch, 412.

24. Royall to Roger Jones, June 21, 1848, House Ex. Doc. No. 1, 30th Cong., 2d sess., vol. 1 (Serial 537), 143; Birch, 412.

25. Royall to Roger Jones, June 21, 1848, House Ex. Doc. No. 1, 30th Cong., 2d sess., vol. 1 (Serial 537), 143; Birch, 412.

26. Royall to Roger Jones, June 21, 1848, House Ex. Doc. No. 1, 30th Cong., 2d sess., vol. 1 (Serial 537), 143; Barry, 758.

27. Royall to Roger Jones, June 21, 1848, House Ex. Doc. No. 1, 30th Cong., 2d sess., vol. 1 (Serial 537), 143–44; Barry, 758; Birch, 412.

28. Royall to Roger Jones, June 21, 1848, House Ex. Doc. No. 1, 30th Cong., 2d sess., vol. 1 (Serial 537), 143–44; Barry, 758; Birch, 413.

29. Birch, 413.

30. *New York Weekly Tribune*, July 29, Aug. 19, 1848; *St. Louis Daily Union*, July 20, Aug. 23, 1848; *Weekly Tribune*, July 28, Aug. 11, 1848; Royall to Roger Jones, June 21, 1848, House Ex. Doc. No. 1, 30th Cong., 2d sess., vol. 1 (Serial 537), 144; Barry, 758; Birch, 413.

31. *Santa Fe Republican*, July 18, 1848; Royall to Roger Jones, June 21, 1848, House Ex. Doc. No. 1, 30th Cong., 2d sess., vol. 1 (Serial 537), 141–44; Barry, 758.

Chapter 12. Gabriel's Barbecue

1. *St. Louis Daily Union*, Aug. 3, 5, 1848; *St. Louis Reveille* (daily), June 10, 30, 1848; *Weekly Tribune*, Aug. 11, 1848; Roger Jones to Garland, May 9, 1848, AGO, Letters Sent, 1848, RG 94, NA (M567–R377); Sen. Ex. Doc. No. 26, 31st Cong., 1st sess., vol. 6 (Serial 554), 10; Barry, 759–60; Orville C. Pratt, "Diary of Orville C. Pratt," William Robertson Coe Collection, Yale University Library, June 9–16, 1847.

2. *St. Louis Daily Union*, Aug. 3, 5, 1848; *St. Louis Reveille* (daily), June 10, 30, 1848; *Weekly Tribune*, Aug. 11, 1848; Roger Jones to Garland, Aug. 9, 1848, AGO, Letters Sent, 1848, RG 94, NA (M567–R377); Garland to Roger Jones, Aug. 3, 1848, enclosed with Garland to Roger Jones, Aug. 16, 1848, AGO, Letters Received, 368 G 1848, RG 94,

NA (M567–R377); Sen. Ex. Doc. No. 26, 31st Cong., 1st sess., vol. 6 (Serial 554), 10; Barry, 759–60.

3. *St. Louis Daily Union*, Aug. 3, 5, 1848; *St. Louis Reveille* (daily), June 10, 30, 1848; *Weekly Tribune*, Aug. 11, 1848; Garland to Roger Jones, June 20, 1848, AGO, Letters Received, 1848, RG 94, NA (M567–R377); Garland to Roger Jones, July 2, 1848, AGO, Letters Received, 1848, RG 94, NA (M567–R377); Barry, 751, 759–60; Pratt, June 16–30, 1848.

4. *St. Louis Daily Union*, Aug. 3, 5, 1848; *St. Louis Reveille* (daily), June 10, 30, 1848; *Weekly Tribune*, Aug. 11, 1848; Garland to Roger Jones, July 2, 1848, and Korponay to Garland, July 12, 1848, enclosed with Garland to Roger Jones, Aug. 2, 1848, AGO, Letters Received, 340 G 1848, RG 94, NA (M567–R377); Korponay to Roger Jones, July 12, 1848, enclosed with Garland to Roger Jones, Aug. 2, 1848, AGO, Letters Received, 340 G 1848, RG 94, NA (M567–R377); Barry, 759–60; Pratt, July 1–7, 1847.

5. Korponay to Garland, July 12, 1848; Korponay to Roger Jones, July 12, 1858; Garland to Roger Jones, Aug. 3, 1848; Griffin to Gilpin, July 12, 1858, House Ex. Doc. No. 1, 30th Cong., 2d sess., vol. 1 (Serial 537), 146–49.

6. Korponay to Garland, July 12, 1848, and Korponay to Roger Jones, July 12, 1858.

7. Korponay to Garland, July 12, 1848, and Korponay to Roger Jones, July 12, 1858.

8. Korponay to Garland, July 12, 1848, and Korponay to Roger Jones, July 12, 1858.

9. Korponay to Garland, July 12, 1848, and Korponay to Roger Jones, July 12, 1858.

10. Korponay to Garland, July 12, 1848, and Korponay to Roger Jones, July 12, 1858.

11. Korponay to Garland, July 12, 1848, and Korponay to Roger Jones, July 12, 1858.

12. *St. Louis Daily Union*, Aug. 5, 1848; *St. Louis Reveille*, Aug. 3, 1848; John Garland, Departmental Order, July 14, 1848, enclosed with Garland to Roger Jones, Aug. 16, 1848, AGO, Letters Received, 368 G 1848, RG 94, NA (M567–R377); Barry, 760.

Chapter 13. The Last Campaigns

1. Griffin to Gilpin, July 12, 1848, House Ex. Doc. No. 1, 30th Cong., 2d sess., vol. 1 (Serial 537), 146–49.

2. Griffin to Gilpin, July 12, 1848, House Ex. Doc. No. 1, 30th Cong., 2d sess., vol. 1 (Serial 537), 146.

3. Griffin to Gilpin, July 12, 1848, House Ex. Doc. No. 1, 30th
Cong., 2d sess., vol. 1 (Serial 537), 146–47.

4. Griffin to Gilpin, July 12, 1848, House Ex. Doc. No. 1, 30th
Cong., 2d sess., vol. 1 (Serial 537), 147.

5. Griffin to Gilpin, July 12, 1848, House Ex. Doc. No. 1, 30th
Cong., 2d sess., vol. 1 (Serial 537), 147.

6. Griffin to Gilpin, July 12, 1848, House Ex. Doc. No. 1, 30th
Cong., 2d sess., vol. 1 (Serial 537), 147–48.

7. Griffin to Gilpin, July 12, 1848, House Ex. Doc. No. 1, 30th
Cong., 2d sess., vol. 1 (Serial 537), 148; Thomas Jones to Gilpin, House
Ex. Doc. No. 1, 30th Cong., 2d sess., vol. 1 (Serial 537), 150.

8. Griffin to Gilpin, July 12, 1848, House Ex. Doc. No. 1, 30th
Cong., 2d sess., vol. 1 (Serial 537), 148–49.

9. Griffin to Gilpin, July 12, 1848, House Ex. Doc. No. 1, 30th
Cong., 2d sess., vol. 1 (Serial 537), 146–49.

10. *New York Weekly Tribune*, Sept. 9, 1848; *St. Louis Reveille* (daily),
Aug. 28, 1848; Barry, 764.

11. Thomas Jones to Gilpin, House Ex. Doc. No. 1, 30th Cong., 2d
sess., vol. 1 (Serial 537), 149–51; Barry, 766.

12. Thomas Jones to Gilpin, House Ex. Doc. No. 1, 30th Cong., 2d
sess., vol. 1 (Serial 537), 149.

13. Thomas Jones to Gilpin, House Ex. Doc. No. 1, 30th Cong., 2d
sess., vol. 1 (Serial 537), 149–50.

14. Thomas Jones to Gilpin, House Ex. Doc. No. 1, 30th Cong., 2d
sess., vol. 1 (Serial 537), 150.

15. Thomas Jones to Gilpin, House Ex. Doc. No. 1, 30th Cong., 2d
sess., vol. 1 (Serial 537), 150.

16. Thomas Jones to Gilpin, House Ex. Doc. No. 1, 30th Cong., 2d
sess., vol. 1 (Serial 537), 150–51.

Chapter 14. The Final Days of Fort Mann
and the Indian Battalion

1. Garland to Roger Jones, Aug. 3, 1848, enclosed with Garland to
Roger Jones, Aug. 16, 1848, AGO, Letters Received, 368 G 1848, RG 94,
NA (M567–R377).

2. Garland to Roger Jones, Aug. 3, 1848, enclosed with Garland to
Jones, Aug. 16, 1848, AGO, Letters Received, 368 G 1848, RG 94, NA
(M567–R377); Karnes, *William Gilpin*, 203; Pratt, July 1, 5, 7, 1848.

3. Garland to Roger Jones, Aug. 3, 1848, enclosed with Garland to
Jones, Aug. 16, 1848, AGO, Letters Received, 368 G 1848, RG 94, NA
(M567–R377).

4. Garland to Roger Jones, Aug. 3, 1848, enclosed with Garland to

Jones, Aug. 16, 1848, AGO, Letters Received, 368 G 1848, RG 94, NA (M567–R377).

5. Garland to Roger Jones, Aug. 3, 1848, enclosed with Garland to Jones, Aug. 16, 1848, AGO, Letters Received, 368 G 1848, RG 94, NA (M567–R377).

6. Garland to Roger Jones, Aug. 3, 1848, and John Garland, Departmental Order, July 14, 1848, enclosed with Garland to Roger Jones, Aug. 16, 1848, AGO, Letters Received, 368 G 1848, RG 94, NA (M567–R377).

7. *St. Louis Daily Union*, Aug. 5, 1848; *St. Louis Reveille* (daily), Aug. 3, 5, 1848; Garland to Roger Jones, Aug. 2, 1848, and Garland to Roger Jones, Aug. 3, 1848, enclosed with Garland to Roger Jones, Aug. 16, 1848, AGO, Letters Received, 368 G 1848, RG 94, NA (M567–R377); Gilpin to Garland, Aug. 18, 1848, AGO, Letters Received, 398 G 1848, RG 94, NA (M567–R377); Barry, 760.

8. Gilpin to Garland, Aug. 18, 1848, AGO, Letters Received, 398 G 1848, RG 94, NA (M567–R377).

9. *Daily Missouri Republican*, July 26, 1848; *New York Weekly Tribune*, Aug. 12, 1848; *St. Louis Daily Union*, July 26, Oct. 16, 1848; *St. Louis Reveille* (daily), Aug. 8, 1848; Barry, 756–57; Janet Lecompte, "The Manco Burro Pass Massacre," *New Mexico Historical Review* 41 (1966): 305–18; Janet Lecompte, *Pueblo, Hardscrabble, Greenhorn*, 199, 209.

10. Barry, 764–65.

11. Gilpin to Roger Jones, Aug. 1, 1848, AGO, Letters Received, 1848, RG 94, NA (M567–R377), also in House Ex. Doc. No. 1, 30th Cong., 2d sess., vol. 1 (Serial 537), 136–40).

12. Gilpin to Roger Jones, Aug. 1, 1848, AGO, Letters Received, 1848, RG 94, NA (M567–R377).

13. Gilpin to Roger Jones, Aug. 1, 1848, AGO, Letters Received, 1848, RG 94, NA (M567–R377).

14. Gilpin to Roger Jones, Aug. 1, 1848, AGO, Letters Received, 1848, RG 94, NA (M567–R377).

15. Gilpin to Roger Jones, Aug. 1, 1848, AGO, Letters Received, 1848, RG 94, NA (M567–R377).

16. *New York Weekly Tribune*, Sept. 16, 1848; *St. Louis Daily Union*, Aug. 29, 1848; *Weekly Tribune*, Aug. 25, 1848; Garland to Roger Jones, Aug. 16, 1848, AGO, Letters Received, 368 G 1848, RG 94, NA (M567–R377); Gilpin to Garland, Aug. 18, 1848, AGO, Letters Received, 398 G 1848, RG 94, NA (M567–R377); Barry, 771.

17. Alexander Majors, *Seventy Years on the Frontier*, 74–75.

18. *St. Louis Daily Union*, Sept. 6, 1848; *Weekly Tribune*, Aug. 25, 1848; George D. Brewerton, *In the Buffalo Country*, 21, 25–26, 38, 44, 46, 50, 60–64.

19. *New York Weekly Tribune*, Oct. 7, 1848; *Weekly Tribune*, Sept. 1, 29, 1848; Barry, 773.

20. *Daily Missouri Republican*, Sept. 11, 23, 1848; *New York Weekly Tribune*, Oct. 7, 1848; *St. Louis Reveille* (daily), Sept. 24, 1848; *Weekly Tribune*, Sept. 29, 1848; Barry, 775–76; Philip St. George Cooke, William Henry Chase Whiting, and Francois Xavier Aubry, *Exploring Southwestern Trails, 1846–1854*, 47–49; Chaput, 62–67.

21. *New York Weekly Tribune*, Sept. 30, Oct. 7, 1848; *St. Louis Daily Union*, Sept. 25, 26, 30, Oct. 4, 6, 10, 1848; *St. Louis Reveille* (daily), Sept. 29, Oct. 10, 1848; Sen. Ex. Doc. No. 26, 31st Cong., 1st sess., vol. 6 (Serial 554), 21; Barry, 777–78.

22. *New York Weekly Tribune*, Oct. 7, 1848; *St. Louis Daily Union*, Sept. 18, 22, 25, Oct. 9, 10, 17, 24, 1848; *St. Louis Reveille* (daily), Oct. 6, 10, 11, 17, Nov. 1, 8, 1848; *Weekly Tribune*, Sept. 29, 1848; Barry, 778.

23. Barry, 778; Connelley, "Mr. Gilpin's Santa Fe Trace Battalion," 114–15; Connelley, *Doniphan's Expedition*, 148–51.

24. *Expositor*, Oct. 28, 1848; *St. Louis Reveille* (daily), Oct. 11, Nov. 9, 1848; Barry, 778–79.

25. Fitzpatrick to Harvey, Oct. 6, 1848, *Annual Report, CIA, 1848*, House Ex. Doc. No. 1, 30th Cong., 2d sess., vol. 1 (Serial 537), 470–73.

26. *Weekly Tribune*, July 14, 1848, Feb. 23, 1849; *Annual Report, Secretary of War, 1848*, House Ex. Doc. No. 1, 30th Cong., 2d sess., vol. 1 (Serial 537), 77; Karnes, *William Gilpin*, 209–10.

27. *Daily Missouri Republican*, Nov. 23, 1848, Feb. 13, 1849; *Gazette*, Oct. 27, Nov. 24, Dec. 1, 1848; *St. Louis Reveille* (daily), Oct. 10, 1848; *Weekly Tribune*, Oct. 6, 13, 1848; Barry, 779–80.

28. *Daily Missouri Republican*, Nov. 23, 1848; *Gazette*, Dec. 1, 1848; *New York Weekly Tribune*, Oct. 28, Dec. 2, 1848, March 10, April 14, 1849; *St. Louis Reveille* (daily), Oct. 17, Nov. 1, 1848; *Weekly Tribune*, Nov. 10, 24, 1848; Barry, 780–85; Chaput, 70–74.

Bibliography

I. U.S. Government Documents

A. Executive Departments
   1. Interior Department
      Office of Indian Affairs
         Annual Report of the Commissioner of Indian Affairs, 1847, 1848.
            In U.S. Serials as:
               1847: Senate Ex. Doc. No. 1, 30th Cong., 1st sess., vol. 1
                  (Serial 503)
               1848: House Ex. Doc. No. 1, 30th Cong., 2d sess., vol. 1
                  (Serial 537)
               1849: House Ex. Doc. No. 5, 31st Cong., 1st sess., vol. 3
                  (Serial 569)
            Letters Received. Office of Indian Affairs.
   2. War Department
         Annual Report of the Secretary of War, 1847, 1848. In U.S.
            Serials as:
               1847: House Ex. Doc. No. 8, 30th Cong., 1st sess., vol. 2
                  (Serial 515)
               1848: House Ex. Doc. No. 1, 30th Cong., 1st sess., vol. 1
                  (Serial 537)
            Office of the Adjutant General.
               Letters Sent, U.S. Army Commands
               Letters Received, U.S. Army Commands
               Returns of the Battalion of Missouri Volunteers "For the
                  Plains"
               Muster Rolls of the Battalion of Missouri Volunteers "For the
                  Plains"

B. Congress
    1. Senate
        Sen. Ex. Doc. No. 23, 30th Cong., 1st sess., vol. 4 (Serial 506)
        Wislizenus, Frederick, A. "Memoirs of a Tour to Northern
            Mexico in 1846 and 1847 Connected with Colonel Doniphan's
            Expedition." Sen. Misc. Doc. 26, 30th Cong., 1st sess.
            (Serial 511).
        Sen. Ex. Doc. No. 26, 31st Cong., 1st sess., vol. 6 (Serial 554)
    2. House of Representatives
        2d Lt. J. W. Abert, "Notes of Lieutenant J. W. Abert," House
            Ex. Doc. No. 41, 30th Cong., 1st sess., vol. 4 (Serial 517)
        Lieutenant J. W. Abert, "Report of His Examination of New
            Mexico in the Years 1846–1847" House Ex. Doc. No. 41,
            30th Cong., 1st sess., vol. 4 (Serial 517)
        House Ex. Doc. No. 458, 30th Cong., 1st sess., vol. 2 (Serial
            525)
        House Ex. Doc. No. 17, 31st Cong., 1st sess., vol. 5 (Serial 573)

II. Newspapers and Periodicals

Alton Telegraph and Democratic Review (Alton, Ill.), May 7, 21, 28, June
    4, 11, 18, 25, Oct. 1, 1847.
Daily Missouri Republican (St. Louis, Mo.), Feb. 16, March 26, May 15,
    21, June 1, 25, July 17, Aug. 3, Sept. 2, Oct. 9, 13, Nov. 16, 1846; Feb.
    19, 26, March 11, April 20, 28, May 1, 3, 4, 15, 17, 18, 25, 29, June 7,
    14, 19, 22, 23, 25, 29, July 8, 12, 17, 19, 31, Aug. 2, 12, 16, Sept. 4,
    7, 8, 20, 22, Oct. 11, Nov. 1, 1847; Feb. 7, April 11, June 3, 9, July 26,
    Sept. 11, 23, Nov. 23, 1848; Feb. 13, 1849.
Democratic Standard (Leavenworth, Kans.), Aug. 10, 17, 1883.
Expositor (Independence, Mo.), April 29, May 29, Oct. 28, 1848.
Gazette (St. Joseph, Mo.), Sept. 11, 18, Nov. 20, 27, 1846; Feb. 26, July
    23, 1847; May 5, June 2, Oct. 27, Nov. 24, Dec. 1, 1848; July 20,
    1849.
Jefferson Inquirer (Jefferson City, Mo.), March 6, Sept. 1, 17, 25, 1847.
Missouri Reporter (St. Louis, Mo.), May 20, 1846.
Missouri Statesman (Columbia, Mo.), June 25, 1847.
New York Weekly Tribune (New York, N.Y.), Feb. 7, April 14, June 13, Aug.
    15, 29, Sept. 12, Oct. 24, 31, Nov. 21, 28, Dec. 5, 12, 1846; Jan. 6,
    Feb. 6, 27, March 6, 13, 27, April 3, 24, May 15, 29, June 5, 26, July
    10, 17, 24, 27, 31, Aug. 7, 11, 14, 28, Sept. 18, Oct. 2, 9, Nov. 20,
    1847; Jan. 29, Feb. 26, May 13, June 17, July 29, Aug. 12, 19, Sept. 9,
    16, 30, Oct. 7, 28, Dec. 2, 1848; March 10, April 14, July 14, 1849.
Niles' National Register (Baltimore, Md.), vol. 70 (June 6, 1846), 213,
    (July 4, 1846), 281, (July 11, 1846), 304; vol. 72 (March 6, 1847), 7,

(April 3, 1847), 73, (July 17, 1847), 320, (July 31, 1847), 343, (Aug. 14, 1847), 375.

St. Louis Daily New Era (St. Louis, Mo.), Nov. 9, 1846; May 4, 8, 15, 22, 25, 29, 1847; April 26, 1848; Sept. 15, 1849.

St. Louis Daily Union (St. Louis, Mo.), Aug. 24, Sept. 3, Oct. 8, 9, 12, Nov. 16, 23, Dec. 28, 1846; Jan 18, Feb. 20, 25, March 2, 9, 11, 30, 31, April 1, 17, 19, 26, 28, May 3, 6, 7, 8, 10, 11, 13, 15, 17, 18, 20, 21, 22, 29, 31, June 1, 2, 3, 8, 9, 10, 15, 21, 23, 25, 26, July 5, 7, 8, 10, 14, 19, 29, Aug. 1, 2, 5, 6, 9, 12, 16, 19, 22, 26, Sept. 1, 7, 13, 14, 20, 21, 22, 23, 25, 30, Oct. 1, 2, 4, 10, Nov. 11, Dec. 14, 21, 22, 1847; Jan 1, 12, Feb. 8, 9, March 10, April 11, 14, 26, 27, May 9, 23, 26, June 5, 9, July 20, 26, Aug. 3, 5, 23, 29, Sept. 6, 18, 22, 25, 26, 30, Oct. 4, 6, 9, 10, 16, 17, 24, 1848.

St. Louis Reveille (daily) (St. Louis, Mo.), Aug. 11, Nov. 23, 1846; Feb. 26, March 4, 9, 11, 30, 31, April 10, 18, 23, 24, 28, May 16, 18, 28, 29, June 23, 26, 27, July 10, 13, 18, 20, Aug. 5, 12, 15, Sept. 3, 7, 9, 11, 12, 17, 19, 21, 22, 23, 28, Oct. 31, Nov. 2, Dec. 6, 12, 13, 15, 16, 19, 31, 1847; Jan. 12, Feb. 8, March 9, 19, April 11, 12, 13, 14, May 31, June 1, 3, 10, 30, July 2, Aug. 3, 5, 8, 28, Sept. 24, 29, Oct. 6, 10, 11, 17, Nov. 1, 8, 9, 1848.

St. Louis Weekly Reveille (St. Louis, Mo.), Aug. 17, 1846; April 10, May 24, 31, June 14, 21, 28, Aug. 9, 15, 30, Dec. 21, 1847; April 3, July 3, 1848.

Santa Fe Republican (Santa Fe, N.M.), July 18, 1848.

Weekly Tribune (Liberty, Mo.), May 9, Dec. 5, 1846; Feb. 20, March 6, 27, May 15, July 10, 17, Sept. 24, Oct. 1, 15, 16, Nov. 19, Dec. 31, 1847; Jan. 28, March 7, 17, April 7, 21, May 26, June 2, 9, July 14, 28, Aug. 11, 25, Sept. 1, 29, Oct. 6, 13, Nov. 10, 24, 1848; Feb. 23, Aug. 31, 1849.

III. Books

Bancroft, Hubert Howe. *The History and Life of William Gilpin: A Character Study.* San Francisco: History Company, 1889.

Barry, Louise. *The Beginning of the West.* Topeka: Kansas State Historical Society, 1972.

Bauer, K. Jack. *The Mexican War, 1846–1848.* New York: Macmillan Publishing Company, 1974.

Bender, Avaram. *The March of Empire.* Lawrence: University of Kansas Press, 1952.

Berthrong, Donald J. *The Southern Cheyennes.* Norman: University of Oklahoma Press, 1963.

Brewerton, George D. *In the Buffalo Country.* Ashland, Oreg.: Lewis

Osborne, 1970. (Reprint of article in *Harper's New Monthly Magazine* 25 (Aug. 1862): 447–66.)

Carson, Christopher (Kit). *Kit Carson's Autobiography.* Edited by Milo Milton Quaife. Chicago: Lakeside Press, 1935. Reprint. Lincoln: University of Nebraska Press, Bison Books, 1966.

Chaput, Donald. *Francois X. Aubry: Trader, Trail Maker, and Voyageur in the Southwest, 1846–1854.* Glendale, Calif.: Arthur H. Clark Company, 1975.

Connelley, William E. *Doniphan's Expedition and the Conquest of New Mexico and California.* Kansas City: Bryant and Douglas, 1907.

Cooke, Philip St. George, William Henry Chase Whiting, and Francois Xavier Aubry. *Exploring Southwestern Trails, 1846–1854.* Vol. 7 of the Southwest Historical Series, edited by Ralph P. Bieber. Glendale, Calif.: Arthur H. Clark Company, 1938. Reprint. Philadelphia: Porcupine Press, 1974.

Cutts, James M. *The Conquest of California and New Mexico, 1846–1848.* Philadelphia: Cary and Hart, 1847. Reprint. Albuquerque, N.M.: Horn and Wallace, 1965.

DeVoto, Bernard. *The Year of Decision: 1846.* Boston: Little, Brown and Company, 1943.

Edwards, Frank S. *A Campaign in New Mexico with Colonel Doniphan.* Philadelphia: Cary and Hart, 1847.

Franzwa, Gregory M. *The Santa Fe Trail Revisited.* St. Louis, Mo.: Patrice Press, 1989.

Garrard, Lewis H. *Wah-to-Yah and the Taos Trail.* Norman: University of Oklahoma Press, 1979.

Gibson, George Rutledge. *Journal of a Soldier under Kearny and Doniphan, 1846–1847.* Vol. 3 of the Southwest Historical Series, edited by Ralph P. Bieber. Glendale, Calif.: Arthur H. Clark Company, 1935. Reprint. Philadelphia: Porcupine Press, 1974.

———. *Over the Chihuahua and Santa Fe Trails, 1847–1848: George Rutlege Gibson's Journal.* Edited by Robert W. Frazer. Albuquerque: University of New Mexico Press, 1981.

Hafen, LeRoy R. *Broken Hand.* Denver: Old West Publishing Company, 1931. Reprint. Lincoln: University of Nebraska Press, Bison Books, 1981.

Hammond, George P. *Alexander Barclay, Mountain Man.* Denver: Old West Publishing Company, 1976.

Hughes, John T. *Doniphan's Expedition.* Cincinnati: J. A. and U. P. James, 1848. Reprint. Chicago: Rio Grande Press, 1972.

Hyde, George E. *Life of George Bent.* Norman: University of Oklahoma Press, 1968.

———. *The Pawnee Indians.* Norman: University of Oklahoma Press, 1951.

Johnston, Abraham Robinson, Marcellus Ball Edwards, and Philip

Gooch Ferguson. *Marching with the Army of the West*. Vol. 4 of the Southwest Historical Series, edited by Ralph P. Bieber. Glendale, Calif.: Arthur H. Clark Company, 1936. Reprint. Philadelphia: Porcupine Press, 1974.

Karnes, Thomas L. *William Gilpin: Western Nationalist*. Austin: University of Texas Press, 1970.

Lecompte, Janet. *Pueblo, Hardscrabble, Greenhorn*. Norman: University of Oklahoma Press, 1978.

Magoffin, Susan Shelby. *Down the Santa Fe Trail and into Mexico*. Edited by Stella M. Drumm. New Haven: Yale University Press, 1926.

Majors, Alexander. *Seventy Years on the Frontier*. Chicago: Rand, McNally and Company, 1893. Reprint. Lincoln: University of Nebraska Press, Bison Books, 1989.

Mayhall, Mildred P. *The Kiowas*. Norman: University of Oklahoma Press, 1962.

Mooney, James. *Calendar History of the Kiowa Indians*. 1898. Reprint. Washington, D.C.: Smithsonian Institution Press, 1979.

Neighbours, Kenneth Franklin. *Robert Simpson Neighbors and the Texas Frontier, 1836–1859*. Waco: Texian Press, 1975.

Nevin, David. *The Mexican War*. Old West Series. Alexandria, Va.: Time-Life Books, 1978.

Oliva, Leo E. *Soldiers on the Santa Fe Trail*. Norman: University of Oklahoma Press, 1967.

Parkman, Francis. *The Oregon Trail*. Edited by E. N. Fellskog. Madison: University of Wisconsin Press, 1969.

Polk, James Knox. *Polk: The Diary of a President, 1845–1849*. Edited by Allan Nevins. New York: Longmans, Green and Company, 1929.

Price, George F. *Across the Continent with the Fifth Cavalry*. New York: Van Nostrand, 1883.

Richardson, Rupert Norval. *The Comanche Barrier to South Plains Settlement*. Glendale, Calif.: Arthur H. Clark Company, 1933.

Robinson, Jacob S. *A Journal of the Santa Fe Expedition under Colonel Doniphan*. Portsmouth, N.H.: Portsmouth Journal Press, 1848. Reprint. Princeton: Princeton University Press, 1932.

Ruxton, George Frederick. *Ruxton of the Rockies*. Edited by LeRoy R. Hafen. Norman: University of Oklahoma Press, 1950.

Settle, Raymond W., and Mary Lund Settle. *War Drums and Wagon Wheels*. Lincoln: University of Nebraska Press, 1966.

Trenholm, Virginia Cole. *The Arapaho: Our People*. Norman: University of Oklahoma Press, 1970.

Turner, Henry Smith. *The Original Journals of Henry Smith Turner: With Stephen Watts Kearny to New Mexico and California, 1846–1847*. Edited by Dwight L. Clarke. Norman: University of Oklahoma Press, 1966.

Twitchell, Ralph Emerson. *The Story of the Conquest of Santa Fe, New*

Mexico, and the Building of Old Fort Marcy, A. D. 1846. Santa Fe: Historical Society of New Mexico, Publication No. 24, 1921.

Utley, Robert M. *Frontiersmen in Blue: The United States Army and the Indians, 1848–1865.* New York: Macmillan Publishing Company, 1967.

Vestal, Stanley. *The Old Santa Fe Trail.* Boston: Houghton Mifflin Company, 1939.

Wallace, Ernest, and E. Adamson Hoebel. *The Comanches: Lords of the South Plains.* Norman: University of Oklahoma Press, 1952.

Webb, James Josiah. *Adventures in the Santa Fe Trade, 1844–1847.* Vol. 1 of the Southwest Historical Series, edited by Ralph P. Bieber. Glendale, Calif.: Arthur H. Clark Company, 1931. Reprint. Philadelphia: Porcupine Press, 1974.

Worcester, Donald E. *Forked Tongues and Broken Treaties.* Caldwell, Idaho: The Caxton Printers, 1975.

Young, Otis E. *The West of Philip St. George Cooke, 1809–1895.* Glendale, Calif.: Arthur H. Clark Company, 1955.

IV. Articles, Letters, Manuscripts

Barry, Louise, "The Ranch at Cimarron Crossing." *Kansas Historical Quarterly* 39, no. 3 (1973): 345–66.

Bieber, Ralph P., ed. "Letters of James and Robert Aull." *Missouri Historical Society Collections* 5 (June 1928): 291–93.

Birch, James H. "The Battle of Coon Creek." *Kansas Historical Collections* 10 (1907–8): 409–13.

Buercklin, Charles Henry. "Autobiography of Charles Henry Buercklin, 1821–1909." Ottenheimer Library Archives and Special Collections, University of Arkansas at Little Rock.

Connelley, William E. "Mr. Gilpin's Santa Fe Trace Battalion." *Kansas Historical Collections* 10 (1907–8): 114–15.

Grinnell, George Bird. "Bent's Old Fort and Its Builders." *Kansas Historical Collections* 15 (1919–22): 28–91.

Hafen, LeRoy R. "Thomas Fitzpatrick and the First Indian Agency of the Upper Platte and Arkansas." *Mississippi Valley Historical Review* 15, no. 3 (Dec. 1928): 374–84.

Karnes, Thomas L. "Gilpin's Volunteers on the Santa Fe Trail." *Kansas Historical Quarterly* 30, no. 1 (1964): 1–14.

Kimbell, Stanley B. "Rediscovering the Fort Leavenworth Military Branch of the Santa Fe Trail." In *The Mexican Road*, edited by Mark L. Gardner. Manhattan, Kans.: Sunflower University Press, 1989.

Lecompte, Janet. "The Manco Burro Pass Massacre." *New Mexico Historical Review* 41 (1966): 305–18.

———. "Manuel Armijo and the Americans." *Journal of the West* 29, no. 3 (1980): 51–63.

————. "When Santa Fe Was a Mexican Town." In *Santa Fe: History of an Ancient City*, edited by David Grant Noble, 79–95. Santa Fe: School of American Research Press, 1989.

Michel, Peter J. "No Mere Holiday Affair." *Gateway Heritage* 9, no. 4 (Spring 1989): 12–25.

Oliva, Leo E. "Missouri Volunteers on the Santa Fe Trail, 1847–1848." In *The Trail Guide*, published by the Kansas City Posse, The Westerners. Part 1 in vol. 15, no. 2 (June 1970): 1–20; part 2 in vol. 15, no. 3 (Sept. 1970): 1–20.

Pratt, Orville C. "Diary of Orville C. Pratt." William Robertson Coe Collection, Yale University Library, New Haven, Conn.

Taft, Robert. "The Pictorial Record of the Old West." *Kansas Historical Quarterly* 20, no. 1 (1952): 1–23.

Thoburn, Joseph B. "Indian Fight in Ford County in 1859." *Kansas Historical Collections* 12 (1911–12): 312–29.

Wilson, John P. "The American Occupation of Santa Fe." In *Santa Fe: History of an Ancient City*, edited by David Grant Noble, 97–113. Santa Fe: School of American Research Press, 1989.

Wyman, Walker D. "The Military Phase of Santa Fe Freighting, 1846–1865." *Kansas Historical Quarterly* 1, no. 5 (1932): 415–28.

V. Maps

Cooke, Philip St. George. "Map of the Santa Fe Trace from Independence to the Crossing of the Arkansas (with Part of the Military Road from Fort Leavenworth, West Missouri), 1843." RG 77, Q17, NA.

Franzwa, Gregory M. *Maps of the Santa Fe Trail*. St. Louis: Patrice Press, 1989.

Jackson, Henry. "Map of Indian Territory, with Parts of Neighboring States and Territories, Sept. 1869." RG 77, Q148, NA.

Merrill, William E. "Map of Kansas, with Parts of Neighboring States and Territories, Sept. 1869." RG 77, Q140, NA.

U.S. Geological Survey 1:250,000 Scale Maps. 39094-A1 (Kansas City), 38094-A1 (Lawrence), 38096-A1 (Hutchinson), 38098-A1 (Great Bend), 27098-A1 (Pratt), 36098-A1 (Woodward), 38100-A1 (Scott City), 37100-A1 (Dodge City), 36100-A1 (Perryton), 38102-A1 (Lamar), 37102-A1 (La Junta), 36102-A1 (Dalhart) 38104-A1 (Pueblo), 37104-A1 (Trinidad), 36104-A1 (Raton), 35104-A1 (Santa Fe).

Woodruff, I. C. "Map of the Reconnaissance from Fort Leavenworth to the Arkansas River via the Route of the Republican Fork of the Kansas River and for the Selection of a Site for a Depot Common to the Santa Fe and Oregon Road and for the Location of the Military Post on the Arkansas River." 1852. RG 77, U.S. 187, NA.

Index